S0-BFF-128

Transfigurations

Published with the assistance
of the V. Ray Cardozier Fund

Transfigurations

Collected Poems

Jay Wright

Louisiana State University Press
Baton Rouge

MM

Manufactured in the United States of America
First printing
09 08 07 06 05 04 03 02 01 00
5 4 3 2 1

Designer: Amanda McDonald Scallan
Typeface: Trump Mediaeval
Typesetter: Coghill Composition Co., Inc.
Printer and binder: Thomson-Shore, Inc.

Library of Congress Cataloging-in-Publication Data

Wright, Jay, 1934–
Transfigurations : collected poems / Jay Wright.
p. cm.
ISBN 0-8071-2629-2 (alk. paper)—ISBN 0-8071-2630-6 (pbk. : alk. paper)
I. Title.

PS3573.R5364 A17 2000
811'.54—dc21 00-040560

The poems herein were earlier published in collections titled *The Homecoming Singer* (Corinth Books, 1971), copyright © 1971 by Jay Wright; *Soothsayers and Omens* (Seven Woods, 1976), copyright © 1976 by Jay Wright; *Explications/Interpretations* (Callaloo Poetry Series, University of Kentucky, 1984), copyright © 1984 by Jay Wright; *Dimensions of History* (Kayak, 1976), copyright © 1976 by Jay Wright; *The Double Invention of Kọmọ* (University of Texas Press, 1980), copyright © 1980 by Jay Wright; *Selected Poems of Jay Wright* (Princeton University Press, 1987), copyright © 1987 by Jay Wright; *Elaine's Book* (Callaloo Poetry Series, University Press of Virginia, 1988), copyright © 1986 by Jay Wright; and *Boleros* (Princeton University Press, 1991), copyright © 1988 by Jay Wright. The author wishes to thank the editors of *St. Lawrence University Magazine* and *Callaloo,* in which some of the poems of *Transformations* first appeared.

"A Cowry Rispetto" first appeared in *A Garland for John Hollander* (Ampersand, 1989). "The Cradle Logic of Autumn" was reprinted in *The Best American Poetry, 1995* (Scribner's, 1995) and in *The Best of the Best, 1988–1997* (Scribner's, 1997). "The Healing Improvisation of Hair" first appeared in *The Vintage Book of African American Poetry* (Random House, 2000).

The paper in this book meets the guidelines for permanence and durability of the Committee on Production Guidelines for Book Longevity of the Council on Library Resources. ♾

Contents

EXPLICATIONS/INTERPRETATIONS

Polarity's Trio

Harmony's Trio

Love's Dozen

DIMENSIONS OF HISTORY

The Second Eye of the World: The Dimension of Rites and Acts

Modulations: The Aesthetic Dimension

BOLEROS

TRANSFORMATIONS

The Homecoming Singer

I

Wednesday Night Prayer Meeting

On Wednesday night,
the church still opens at seven,
and the boys and girls have to come in
from their flirting games of tag,
with the prayers they've memorized,
the hymns they have to start.
Some will even go down front,
with funky bibles,
to read verses from Luke,
where Jesus triumphs, or Revelations,
where we all come to no good end.
Outside, the pagan kids
scramble in the darkness,
kissing each other with a sly humility,
or urinating boldly against the trees.
The older people linger
in the freshly lit night,
not in a hurry to enter,
having been in the battle of voices
far too long, knowing that the night
will stretch and end only
when some new voice rises
in ecstasy, or deceit, only
when some arrogant youth
comes cringing down front,
screaming about sin, begging
the indifferent-faced women

for a hand, for a touch,
for a kiss, for help,
for forgiveness, for being young
and untouched by the grace
of pain, innocent of the insoluble
mysteries of being black
and sinned against, black
and sinning in the compliant cities.
What do the young know
about some corpulent theologian,
sitting under his lamp,
his clammy face wet,
his stomach trying to give up
the taste of a moderate wine,
kissing God away with a labored
toss of his pen?
How would these small black singers
know which Jesus is riding
there over the pulpit,
in the folds of the banner
left over from Sunday,
where the winners were the ones
who came, who dropped their nickels
into the felted platters with a flourish?
And how can they be expected
to remember the cadences
that will come again,
the same heart-rending release
of the same pain, as the clock turns
toward the certainty
of melancholic afternoons,
roast and leftover prayers,
the dampened hours that last through the night?
But Christ will come,
feeling injured, having gone
where beds were busy without him,
having seen pimps cane their number-running boys,
the televisions flicker over heaped up bodies,
having heard some disheveled man

shout down an empty street, where women
slither in plastic boots, toward light,
their eyes dilated and empty;
will come like a tired workman
and sit on a creaky bench,
in hope, in fear, wanting to be pleased again,
so anxious that his hands move,
his head tilts for any lost accent.
He seems to be home,
where he's always been.
His intense smile is fixed
to the rhythm of hands,
to the unhurried intensity
of this improvised singing.
He seems not to know
the danger of being here,
among these lonely singers,
in the middle of a war
of spirits who will not wait for him,
who cannot take his intense glare
to heart anymore, who cannot justify
the Wednesday nights given up
in these stuffy, tilted rooms,
while the work piles up for Thursday,
and the dogs mope around empty garbage pails,
and the swingers swing into the night
with a different ecstasy.
Caught in this unlovely music,
he spills to the floor.
The sisters circle him,
and their hands leap from bone to bone,
as if their touch would change him,
would make him see
the crooked lights like stars.
The bible-reading boy tags him with verses,
and he writhes like a boy
giving up stolen kisses,
the free play of his hand on his own body,
the unholy clarity of his worldly speech.

He writhes as if he would be black,
on Wednesday, under the uncompromising
need of old black men and women,
who know that pain is what
you carry in the mind,
in the solemn memory of small triumphs,
that you get, here,
as the master of your pain.
He stands up to sing,
but a young girl,
getting up from the mourner's bench,
tosses her head in a wail.
The women rise,
the men collect the banners
and the boys drop their eyes,
listening to the unearthly wind
whisper to the peeping-tom trees.
This is the end of the night,
and he has not come there yet,
has not made it into the stillness
of himself, or the flagrant uncertainty
of all these other singers.
They have taken his strangeness,
and given it back, the way a lover
will return the rings and letters
of a lover who hurts him.
They have closed their night
with what certainty they could,
unwilling to exchange their freedom for a god.

The Baptism

We had gone down to the river again,
without much hope of finding it
unmuddied.

The night before,
the rain tore the trees,

and we knew we'd
come up on the bank
and have to clear
the dying branches away,
while Brother Highshaw,
who always played the devil
in our redemption pageants,
cut a path along the soft earth
for the ones who would be baptized.

They came,
naked under white robes,
their hair pressed down in stocking caps,
hesitating,
and looking into the eyes
of women who had been familiar
a moment ago,
of men who had been laughable
as they shuffled to the church,
a little dim in the eye,
a whiff of Sen-Sen on their breaths.

Now, we were singing,
and the vowels seemed enough
to threaten those confessed sinners,
who would leave another world
and be buffeted by our voices,
who would take the terror in our eyes
to enter ours.

Straight on they came,
with a sudden burst of sun
twisting the water to silver daggers.

Along another path,
as if he would have nothing
to do with these uncleansed ones,
until the exact moment,
the minister came, detached,

seeming to be part of nothing
except the disordered day.
Stepping into the water,
he did not calm it,
but sanctioned its disordered rush.
Raising his eyes toward the light,
turning the song toward his mood,
he reached out to take the first
of the newly confessed
into the water,

that one,
now crying,
now shaking
as if he would turn
and run,
back,
where he would reconsider
his steps,
back,
where he would drop
the loose-fitting robe
and stand naked to God,
back,
where he would be judge
of those who come
on baptismal days
with a touch of lying
in their bearing.

Then, the words came,
defenseless,
almost scuttled
by the charge of the song,
almost too serene.
And

one by one,
he buried the stiffened bodies,

bringing them up,
swathed like mummies,
screaming,
as if they had found
some new harmony,
there at the pit of the river,
as if they would take charge
of the rhythm of those,
waiting at the bank,
still unsmiling, still
disengaged from this rhythm,
waiting for the hard
and distant confirmation
of their own unsteady truths.

Crispus Attucks

When we speak
of those musket-draped
and manqué Englishmen;
that cloistered country;
all those common people,
dotting the potted stoves,
hating the king,
shifting uneasily under
the sharp sails
of the unwelcome boats,
sometimes we forget you.
Who asked you
for that impulsive miracle?
I form it now,
with my own motives.
The flag dipping in your hands,
your crafted boots
hammering up the unclaimed streets,
all that was in that unformed moment.
But it wasn't the feel of those things,
nor the burden of the American character;

it was somehow the sense
of an unencumbered escape,
the breaking of a Protestant host,
the ambiguous, detached
judgment of yourself.
Now, we think of you,
when, through the sibilant streets,
another season drums
your intense, communal daring.

Billie's Blues

Moving around the way you have,
a family album would have been hard to keep.
But when you talk,
it isn't hard to see you, full-cheeked,
slick-haired, a smear of lipstick
spread like strawberry soda around your mouth,
bound up in chinchilla, bound down by debt,
Texas, your own bad temper and your man.
Your old friends say you had a way
with tonk, or three-card molly, could spend
the night, squinting over your cigarette,
knocking back the sleep with good bourbon,
cursing anyone who'd leave ahead of the game.
Out of all that you had,
you clutched your radio hardest,
refusing to give it up in pawn,
stripping down bare for money,
staying home with a corner of bourbon
and your blues. Your life was three months
of sporting, running the house wherever you turned up,
dropping a nickel or dime where luck was tough,
and three months of solitary, courtly waiting,
tired of the hustle, tired of your mama's ugly mouth,
tired of your old man's feeble claims
and princely walk, three months of blues,
waiting for the bright, green ships

to turn up under a full moon,
coming in the hands of the Geechee girl,
huddled in a boxcar down by the tracks,
coming in the hands of a baby boy
from Oklahoma, out of the desert,
tracking highways until he felt the need
of a woman who could teach a man,
could lie quietly until his touch was right,
challenging him with her silence,
not joyless, but waiting, as the radio crackled,
trying to bring the proper station home.
Now, you have this house,
an old and graying man,
who trades his car in every year.
You spin in the yard,
hanging clothes, watering the lawn,
humming along with the radio,
to the blues, and after all these years,
you still sometimes forget the words.

Feeding the Stove

The fluted stove is giving out.
It burns as red as a dog's penis,
then gives up some of its sides
as a share of the ashes.

No chance, no reason, to repair it.

It keeps us mushing through the snow,
going down, after dark, to the train's coal yard
to grub up the fine-grained coal,
or all over the city, where anyone is building,

to snatch a cracked, wet board,
or two, hiding them under our transparent coats,
walking from the limits of town to home,
like some version of the cross-carrying Christ.

This stove is insidious.
It makes life more dangerous than it is.

I remember one dark night,
the dry wind scenting the town with lilacs,
the tattonie trees whistling by the ditch,
we filed along the bobbed streets

to where I had seen a fine preserve of boards.
The gutted house was jack-o'-lantern sharp.
Its broken windows glinted in the hastening moon.
There was no sound,

except for our gruff shoes,
tamping the bricks and bottles
into the broken earth.
We entered in confidence,

sure that no one had heard,
sure even that, if he had,
he would not begrudge us
the warmth of a few, discarded boards.

But, from the shadows,
a black mackinaw moved,
lifting one ill-defined
and loaded hand toward our eyes.

The figured hood had lips that would not move,
eyes that could not change direction.
And there it stood, in the shifting moon,
the querulous wind whispering harshly around it.

It could not have been a man,
but some exiled figure,
ripped from the bowels of the house,
come to scream and guard against us,

come to send us cringing, ash cold,
toward our ash-crumbling and dry stove.

The Fisherman's Fiesta

Not having a pope,
the dingy Slavic captains
celebrate the catch in September,
with a bishop down from L.A.,
standing on the pier, corked,
holding onto his anarchic robes
while he waves his hands around the water,
and blesses the flagged boats.
Years ago, our brawny classmates
rode the skiffs out of the Gulf of Mexico,
tugging up tuna, lying on the idle decks
to splash salt water into cuts,
standing on the diminishing decks
and practicing the style they'd give us
once they were home with their
quarter shares, or half shares,
plunked for hair tint, cashmere sweaters,
argyle socks, skintight white ducks.
We never went out,
though we hinted and begged,
and slowly we gave up asking,
convinced somehow that fishing
with a net, after all, was best left
to the brawny blondes and biblical James.
So the boats came back, so full
they spooned the water,
and all summer long we rose at three
to take the flaky ferry to the Island,
standing three deep with buxom Slavic women
who smelled of dead fish, and never spoke English,
going to the canneries, to stand
in salty water up to the hip,
without boots, hauling overpowering fish

up onto the conveyor, where slight
and chattering Filipinos slit them from stem
to stern with one sweet shaving stroke.
At noon, we'd hustle hot tuna from the furnaces,
gorge two halves of hot-sauced bread,
and, forgetting dietary prohibitions,
wash it away with milk. This was our reward
all bright and smoggy summer.
That, and the wait for the Fisherman's Fiesta.
Awaking to the fog, in September,
suddenly aware that the brawny blondes were home,
we waited for the knock, the jug
of foot-pressed wine delivered in pidgin English.
Time, now, for our own pope,
the static prayers, the bilious
tottering at the beaches.
Time, now, for the dingy Slavic captains
to tot up the score, raid the stores,
and talk of stripping the ocean next season.
Time, now, for us to walk the pier,
slowly going down to the flagged boats
and a partial, anarchic blessing.

Jason's One Command

After the shipyard whistles
belch the weekend,
we head for Sonny's,
smoked fish and salads
that nip the tongue a little.
That check that got liberated
into my mother's hands at 7:45 A.M.
has been walking the city ever since.
We come to Friday evening
in San Pedro, California, parked
on a dusty, vacant baseball diamond
at the foot of these war-remaindered projects,

while the stern kids rip up the outfield,
rutting in from center, straight over the mound,
caroming off the backstop,
learning to drive, they say.
You stand there, in your sailor's cap,
bluffed and bluffing, remembering
the nickels dropped on witches' charms,
improvising surprise endings to all
the stories we know as well as you.
When the blonde fog dances up
to the salty rocks,
and runs toward the lighthouse,
you stand on the tar-covered pier,
tossing a line into the Pacific.
I see you,
one hand tucked in your back pocket,
watch the ships sail off for Sweden,
while the Norwegian church
bangs its bells over the Swedish hymn.
They slip into darkness,
seeming to curve off the very earth,
a puff of smoke contending with the wind.
How could they know
that your hands have been at their instruments,
preparing them for the ghostly trip into night?
Could they ever wonder at your motives,
as you sprint from dial to dial,
leaving your legend, calling on Ezili,
smiling at the demon needles
twitching under your touch?
Once, for a moment,
in a sudden shaft of light,
a gorged and aching American ship
stuttered past the pier,
and you on the edge,
in your captain's cap,
rode its pinnacles
to the end of my sight.

Two House Painters Take Stock of the Fog

Cold and stiff
as week-old cakes,
we stand at the curve
in December's fog.
Our pants are starched
with the dead, dropped paint.
Another fleeting day,
six dollars earned,
the bread burned
before we reached this hill.
Lovely to think
of all we might have done
with a full day's pay
and less frustration
from the surly bitch
whose house stands
half-painted, half-wet,
susceptible to the slap of the sea
and the December prompt fog.
This town is too full of men
who decorate the cornered lawns
and balk at bilging old houses,
too many Joe Johnsons—
proud to be *from* Texas—
too many fathers who scrape
a half to bet a show
in the fifth at Tanforan,
coming home disgusted
with their credit,
sitting on cluttered porch-parlors
cursing a seaman's luck.
We have here, at the curve,
a few moments to construct
and destroy this naval city,
wanting no credit,
wanting no trips home to Texas,

no hard-luck fathers to go home to,
thinking of it,
how young we are,
to tussle the house-wrecking fog.

Track Cleaning

Waking early,

perhaps at five or so,
with a false moon
sprinkled over the deep snow,

we pulled out of the quilts,
already dressed,
walked out to the empty coal box
and gathered our shovels.

We'd learned that,
when the snow was deep enough,
we could show up by the tracks,
looking ready and fit to work,
and after the other men had been counted out
and sent trudging along the tracks,
the foreman would sometimes turn to us.
He always saved us for the last,
even the giants, standing ready,
with their uncommon eyes gripping him.

We knew he could send us,
knew that he could justify it
with bread, old wives, nagging mothers,
the deadness of a desert town
lying under a heavy snow.

But he would stop,
waiting, he said,
until the boss ordered more workers,

glancing to see if any would leave,
as if he had come to the end of his courtesy,
as if he knew that we would wait
on every snow-deep morning,
watching the idle shovels glint all around us,

almost able to hear the cautious trains
squeeze down the mountains in the distance,
coming to dust us with warm and filthy air,
arrogant, serene, so cocksure
that they didn't owe us a thing.

The Hunting Trip Cook

How you stood up on those bunioned feet
I'll never know. But you didn't much.
Master chef you called yourself,
your unemployment card said simply, cook.
I lived with you and your mad wife,
waiting to get off to California.
I wanted to be released from your creaky house,
where the unstrung piano quarreled
with your arthritic fingers,
where we kept most of the lights off
so we could play the upright, four-legged radio,
where you and your old buddy, Will,
kept a steady block of Tokay bottles
piling up in the coalless coal box.
I was tired of the breakfasts of week-old
biscuits and sugared water that passed for syrup,
tired, too, of sleeping in a cold room,
where all the beds were piled up
under homemade quilts, to keep one room
open for paying tenants.
One night, drunk on the neighbor's
fresh biscuits, I threatened to stack
tumbleweeds against the house
and burn it down.

You sat rocking under your shaded lamp,
half in the wind, a melancholic smile on your face,
and, turning to your mad wife,
you announced your annual hunting trip.
I thought of having you come back,
peeking from the shield of a Model A,
a fat, black bear tied to the fender,
grimacing, his dead head taking command of the street,
or a handsomely crowned deer,
his injured eyes still thrust out.
Suddenly, become noble, you'd skin
and slice your gift, as expertly
as if you were the hunter,
trying to make us believe that you knew
how to kill, that you had gone
trapping up the bitter hills, alone,
with a shotgun to bring back our food.
But you were the cook,
waking with the others to set out
a pot of strong black coffee, eggs
and fresh biscuits, bobbing around
on your bunions to get the noon meal set,
while the tender doctors, their raw,
veined and unhappy faces set,
pulled off deep in the mountain woods,
where you would hear them firing, now and then,
and stop yourself to imagine it,
to be able to tell over and over again
how the encounter came about,
how you slit the throat and dragged
the victim miles by a rope,
coming into camp through silent
and evacuated plains, head modestly drooped,
taciturn according to the code of killers.
Only I, it seems, knew you couldn't shoot,
knew you stood in awe, as I did,
of those who could kill and mount the catch,
or give it away for biscuits, served up
by a bunioned, black and simple cook.

The End of an Ethnic Dream

Cigarettes in my mouth
to puncture blisters in my brain.
My bass a fine piece of furniture.
My fingers soft, too soft to rattle
rafters in second-rate halls.
The harmonies I could never learn
stick in Ayler's screams.
An African chant chokes us. My image shot.

If you look off over the Hudson,
the dark cooperatives spit at the dinghies
floating up the night.

A young boy pisses
on lovers rolling against each other
under a trackless el.

This could have been my town,
with light strings that could stand a tempo.

Now,
it's the end
of an ethnic dream.

I've grown intellectual,
go on accumulating furniture and books,
damning literature, writing "for myself,"
calculating the possibilities that someone
will love me, or sleep with me.
Eighteen-year-old girls come back from the Southern
leers and make me cry.

Here, there are
coffee shops, bars,
natural tonsorial parlors,
plays, streets,
pamphlets, days, sun,

heat, love, anger,
politics, days, and sun.

Here, we shoot off
every day to new horizons,
coffee shops, bars,
natural tonsorial parlors,
plays, streets,
pamphlets, days, sun,
heat, love, anger,
politics, days, and sun.

It is the end of an ethnic dream.
My bass a fine piece of furniture.
My brain blistered.

The Man from Chi

He'll get you there
the man from Chi
who walked west too fast
that day when wind was east
and snow past his hog cutters
choked his hat in the river
came out riding the hawk's back
his best shoes wasted
but he knew where to dry them
got loose came east
pulled some boss business
was into *money* but lost it
with his love when she walked out the door
a shaky babe he found a tear
and framed it
for this is the City
and love is a dangerous thing
get you there singing Stagolee
and looking for a woman who dips snuff

at night when the moon is out
he'll show it a piece of silver.

A Month in the Country

I needed to see myself again,
to get up in this air,
out of New York's fat-fried summer,
away from the clacking expertise
of all the doom sellers.
You offered me this house in New Hampshire.

Coming up,
your headlights teaching
me the leisured curves
of your private road,
the wakened trees throw on
their motley robes, line
the paths to sniff curiously
at my curious entrance;
the birds I cannot name
protest in their polyglot tongues;
the chipmunks dart for the lush
caves behind the barn and house.

The lights in the open port
look out, snarling at
the sour darkness around them.
But I am pleased.
This is just the right mile from town,
the right solitary ring on the party line.
Alone here, I can get beyond my loneliness.

Now, at night
the house chatters, while the wind
whips up those unplaced sounds
over the hills. I lie uneasily
in the drone of silence, afraid

that someone will steal the saw,
or the wood, or burn the barn,
or beat me for the riches I haven't got.
I lie, mocked by unfinished poems,
turning in Harlem's heat and closeness,
even here. Even here, twisting under
the weight of those disappointed voices.

Today, walking up the heart-wrenching hill,
I pass the poor, red shacks,
the idle saws, the still old men
rocking by the miniature flags.
I sense the dogs tensing their necks.
A little girl runs from her baked hideout.
"Hi!" she says, and her voice,
caught by my unfamiliar face,
stops just short of "nigger."
I amble in this New England reticence,
cocksure of my blackness,
unsure of just how white
and afraid my neighbors are.

A Non-Birthday Poem for My Father

Fathers never fit in poems,
and poems never please fathers.
On my father's seventieth birthday,
I tried to work him up a sonnet.
I guess I did,
and sent it off
with some kind of professional pride.
Everything seemed right.
He was seventy,
born October 25, 1896,
the numbers seemed to fit
in the proper mythological pattern.
I had my ritualistic materials,
his life, my art. Nothing could fail.

But he, with good reason,
never read my poem,
and I think he must have sat
in his small living room,
with the dying dog lying at his feet,
drowsing under the television's hum,
thinking how little I knew.
What metaphor was right
for the young boy,
fair and gray-eyed, with straight hair,
standing in the dry New Mexican evening
as his sisters offered him
the opportunity that they, black,
could never have?
Would he go off to medical school,
with Edmund Clapp shoes
and a Stetson hat,
court the high yellow princesses,
who drooled for doctors,
in a fifty-dollar overcoat
and a blue serge box-back suit,
a diamond stickpin gleaming
against his shroud-like white shirt?
Not my father.
The trains would roll by at night,
the trucks would scatter cactus thorns
in their haste, big-muscled men
would knock down rocks,
and shoot a skyscraper straight to God.
Action was the tongue licking at that desert.
So he went away,
leaving his sisters to their perpetual blackness,
to find his own, or discard it,
to find his life in lines not yet laid out.
And things went fast.
A circus gig. Life in the hyped-up
masculinity of lumber camps.
He learned to drive a tractor on a boast.
And then into the New Mexico hills,

making red-eye that the feds
wouldn't bust because it always
got them there, and was clean, and safe.
Drinking and rolling drunk in the snow
with heavy women who could be Indian,
or at least bragged that they were.
Having one son by a woman who had nine,
and leaving them both,
not really deserting them,
but not really knowing what to do
with either of them.
And waking in the hills,
in a flurry, drunk again,
the salt used for a hangover cure
running into his eyes.
He had never seen a god,
and though he prayed at night,
whispering in his dark cabin
as he lay on the monkish cot
with his last cigarette,
he wouldn't spit near a church.
But that night he wanted
a vision and a promise,
and he got them—his own.
Out of the hills, off the juice,
straight to California and the money,
singing hillbilly songs on Central Avenue,
making love to the princesses,
who missed their doctors,
down by Wrigley Field,
taking the trolley out to San Pedro by the sea,
never to go back to the dusty black society
of New Mexico,
never to apologize to his black sisters,
lost, now, in their blackness and their dreams.
What metaphor can tell enough about the man,
stuck in credit unions, doing two shifts,
coming up with a taste for Dodges and diamond rings,
saluting with his very breath

the flags that disappear
on newly turned ships
as they sink into the Pacific,
oblivious of my father's faithfulness?
And there in the war-hurried bungalows,
new friends came up out of the South,
and he took to them, their speech,
as if it were his.
He gave them his vision,
as they sat fingering old wounds.
His son would become a doctor,
grow out of this life
it took him such pain to make.
What would you say,
when all dreams lie so magnificently,
and sisters are moaning over the coffin
of some black princess,
dead a maid, dead in the dryness
of New Mexico, having caught a chill
in a flurry in the hills, looking
for that escaped prince,
who, once, as a boy, saw visions
of a life beyond their range?
The change was never in him,
but in the momentary bursts of black sisters,
pushing forward into what was everywhere
the gift of knowing the world,
as a seasoned bear will come from winter,
tapping through his unfamiliar home,
in spring, just as the light gives him eyes,
just as the small heat burns down
the way that salt will, in snow.
It is not a metaphor my father needs,
but a way of getting down
what it means to spring from the circle,
and come back again.
It is not a metaphor my father needs,
but a way of getting down
what it means to see his son run away,

in daylight,
run away into the crowded cities,
looking for that moment
in the dry and perfumed desert of New Mexico
when the father made his choice,
which the son must understand,
which the son must recreate
and see in the light of where he is,
where the father was,
and judge, not in innocence, but
standing at that point with his father,
getting down, without metaphor,
the years he cannot count,
the lives he cannot see again,
repenting the choices that sent
his black sisters, weeping,
to the grave of unwed princesses.

The Homecoming Singer

The plane tilts in to Nashville,
coming over the green lights
like a toy train skipping past
the signals on a track.
The city is livid with lights,
as if the weight of all the people
shooting down her arteries
had inflamed them.
It's Friday night,
and people are home for the homecomings.
As I come into the terminal,
a young black man, in a vested gray suit,
paces in the florid Tennessee air,
breaks into a run like a halfback
in open field, going past the delirious faces,
past the poster of Molly Bee
in her shiny chaps, her hips tilted forward
where the guns would be, her legs set,

as if she would run, as if she were
a cheerleader who doffs her guns
on Saturday afternoon and careens
down the sidelines after some broken field runner,
who carries it in, for now,
for all the state of Tennessee
with its nut-smelling trees,
its stolid little stone walls
set out under thick blankets of leaves,
its crisp lights dangling on the porches
of homes that top the graveled driveways,
where people who cannot yodel or yell
putter in the grave October afternoons,
waiting for Saturday night and the lights
that spatter on Molly Bee's silver chaps.
I don't want to think of them,
or even of the broken field runner in the terminal,
still looking for his girl, his pocket
full of dates and parties, as I come
into this Friday night of homecomings
and hobble over the highway in a taxi
that has its radio tuned to country music.
I come up to the campus,
with a large wreath jutting up
under the elegant dormitories,
where one girl sits looking down at the shrieking cars,
as the lights go out, one by one, around her
and the laughter drifts off, rising, rising,
as if it would take flight away
from the livid arteries of Nashville.
Now, in sleep, I leave my brass-headed bed,
and see her enter with tall singers,
they in African shirts, she in a robe.
She sits among them, as a golden lance
catches her, suddenly chubby, with soft lips
and unhurried eyes, quite still in the movement
around her, waiting, as the other voices fade,
as the movement stops, and starts to sing,
her voice moving up from its tart entrance

until it swings as freely
as an ecstatic dancer's foot,
rises and plays among the windows
as it would with angels and falls,
almost visible, to return to her,
and leave her shaking with the tears
I'm ashamed to release, and leave her
twisting there on that stool with my shame
for the livid arteries, the flat Saturdays,
the inhuman homecomings of Nashville.
I kneel before her. She strokes my hair,
as softly as she would a cat's head,
and goes on singing, her voice shifting
and bringing up the Carolina calls,
the waterboy, the railroad cutter, the jailed,
the condemned, all that had been forgotten
on this night of homecomings, all
that had been misplaced in those livid arteries.
She finishes, and leaves,
her shy head tilted and wrinkled,
in the green-tinged lights of the still campus.
I close my eyes and listen,
as she goes out to sing this city home.

W. E. B. Du Bois at Harvard

In Harvard Square,
the designing locks
swing to your pace.
The bells push you
toward the teasing dons.
Bright boys begin to trill
their lamentable lessons.
It is too early for you.
All night, again, all night,
you've been at your
fledgling history,
passing through the old songs,

through the old laments.
But here, in Harvard Square,
the prosody of those dark voices
is your connection.
In any square,
the evening bell
may be your release.

II

Moving to Wake at Six

I never wake at six,
though I lie,
wrapped to my scalp,
twirled like a mummy in my clothes,
with my ears awake to a bus
singing bass in the hills.
Though I am still not awake,
I turn and catch the white shadows
leaning at my door like drugstore cowboys.
I hear everything that moves,
or would move.
I seem myself to have split
and moved to every corner of the town,
watching jeweled vegetables drop
and float on the floor of the market,
standing on the moldy arch of the bridge,
watching a man uncurl from the braids
of a fat woman, and roll his mat,
and there, at the governor's gate,
where two soldiers march,
smug and tight as clam shells,
to hang the flag in a wisp of sun.
The town is changing voices,
changing faces, moving from one
life to another, and I am still
at that point of choosing to move
and wake, or fall off again,

one of those who cannot scurry
to the solemn cluck of a clock,
one who cannot give up
the frightening warmth of shroud-like clothes,
where perhaps I could wake,
under a tinted window,
to conjure up a glazed lake,
a bearded man and a boy,
and a vision that could be my own.

The Mormon Missionaries

Who knows what day
they keep as the Sabbath?
You can see them almost any day
come dusty down the middle
of the streets,
as if they were afraid
of gates and sidewalks.
In their Brutus haircuts,
clean white shirts and ties,
they seem to give the lie
to their gentle Bibles,
tucked in their stern arms.
I have seen them march so
through towns where their
Gabriel-scented tongues were strange,
clipping names to their boards,
intransigent as sirens.
They know no questions
that were not formed
in the tongues of prophets.
They know no death
that has not been redeemed
in Jesus' flesh.
They are certain as the still movement
of birds' wings caught in God's air.
Ah, if we,

searching for that undiscovered point,
could stand as steady as these witnesses,
as chosen as they,
as lost as we.

The Neighborhood House

1
So many people lie in this alley
we call it the neighborhood house.
If you lift your eyes,
the roofs are lined with young black boys,
threatening indifferently to jump.

2
It looks bombed-out here.
Bricks jut up like stubbled old men
bending over fragments of glass
as if they were gravestones.
Children run in the wired-in area,
spit in the familiar camp.
In the dark, among the rubble,
you might see a black girl, spread out,
her arms moving like butterfly wings
against the stiff caress of a boy.
Or maybe it's an old man,
impaled on a pole, cursing the wind.
When sirens rake up the streets,
widows and wives sing laments.
So familiar.

3
So like judgment.
Then through the silent house
a youth comes to indict us.
He tells us of his great-great-grandfather,
who stood under a saint and a gesture,
listening to fourteen strange letters,

his bones splitting at the roots.
He sings you a rhumba strung
with Mandingo, Bantu, Yoruba, Dahomeyan names,
dropping like pearls he recovered.
He stands in this filthy garden,
chanting up moon-fed pools
and the din of forests.
Tense drums beat in his eyes:
Yelofe, Bakongo, Banguila, Kumbá, Kongué.
"What does it matter?" he says,
and turns from you.
"I have a name,
an interminable name,
made from interminable names.
It is my name,
free and mine,
foreign and yours,
indifferent as the air,
and I live in the neighborhood house."

4
This is our neighborhood house,
drumming for echoes in an indifferent city.
A house nurturing epic poets
who may sing no more,
or sing
red songs
like savannas,
like fighting rings,
like the bed
of a woman just delivered.

Nicolás Guillén
"Casa de Vecindad"
"Deportes"
"El Apellido"

Morning, Leaving Calle Gigantes

The tart sun,
like a pink six o'clock grapefruit,

bursts over Guadalajara.
I have not slept,
have spent the night
straggling with mariachis,
in and out of joints,
the extra instrument,
trying to sell my own song.
Now, I walk through streets
filled with women humpbacked with babies,
and move, pocketing my fists,
toward the bridge that leads to the market.
As I pass the clamorous church,
the perfumed candles drift and catch my clothes.
My own wet and beer-laden,
stale and anxious smell reaches me.
I see black-veiled women grovel
up the aisles on their knees;
their hands sweep as if they would clutch
and buffet me into penitence.
I stop, and wish for a guitar,
to send six light and deadly notes
riffling up through the nave.
Drunken and content, I move,
but am caught in a circle of little girls,
flying from the church like doves.
They do not speak,
but come with their small hands
folded piously near their pink chasubles.
Frightened, I walk as they,
as if we could not speak,
or walk upon anything solid,
almost as if we were plucked
from a garden to float in clear air,
silently spinning, as if the wind
would take us dancing over the traffic bridge,
past the market, until we would learn
to whisper, to beg to be released
and dropped where we would wither in good light.
I think that they could walk so forever,
unburdened by my smell,

waiting for me to speak,
or break the circle,
waiting, perhaps, for me to tear my shirt,
and scream, fall and roll stuttering
at their innocent feet,
rise and rip their innocent chasubles,
growl and gnaw at their innocent hands,
curse and drag them down on the bridge,
caught in their calm eyes.
They would not speak.
They have no language
to contain that kind of desire.
No Jesus can teach them
to flock like doves,
where I am waiting to stay my death
with theirs.

Chapultepec Castle

This is the castle where they lived,
Maximilian and Carlota,
and here is where Carlota slept.
From the window, the city's streets
spread out like gray arrows,
lurching above the gardens in elegant
abandon. At this hour, it's true,
you can see the shiver of a forelock
off there miles in the distance.
In the winter, when the absence of leaves
mutes the summer's cellos, a shadow
stretches up to the headboard, where,
crutched in the drowsiness of dawn
and the emperor's distracted salute,
she would lie twiddling her able body,
slowly waking, listening
for any different drumming. Close your eyes.
The last echo of any movement
circles in the still room like cannons.

Not even the swing of seasons can blunt
that recognition. The subtle, historical
Mexicans, dying and hardly living,
were waiting, too. And Carlota, tossing
in a fit of ancestry and half-conscious
dreams of a diaspora, must have thought
it marvelous to feel the gardens quiver to silence.

Jalapeña Gypsies

When you come out of that
clean bus station in Jalapa,
and walk west toward the Tecajetes,
three gypsies flutter from the gardens,
and come at you
like flowers floating up
in the stiff summer wind.
The heavy one approaches first,
while her sisters stand
as if they expected nothing good from you,
as if they could see in your eyes
how afraid they make you.
She speaks, easily and surely,
"Put something in your hand
so I can tell you something
good about your life."
You look at her half-whispering breasts,
at the virgin and the pagan medals
dangling there, and you stop
in that voice, really afraid
that she does know you.

You listen/
you aren't there/for a moment/
you go back to your bus/
gray and empty in those hills/
pink and yellow buds steeped in mud/

the green shaded into green into brown
into soft orange against blue/

How can you move
in this womb,
and feel the city's sting?
How can you sit
in the droning bus,
and not sleep in innocence?

Behind you,
a little girl
playing with dolls and dishes
watches the slow movement of colors.
"Me encanta esa.
Tu crees en las cosas . . . ?
No, ya estoy sorda."
What makes her silent
is in the gypsy's fingers
going over your forehead,
in the quick step of her tongue
in your life/
in your life/
in a sculptor's eyes
as he tells you
that the night
is feminine and diabolical.

And Percy would always
make it at night,
high on speed, or gin,
or sounds,
clinched with legs
he wouldn't release,
until he would,
as if the night
and his woman
would run off together,

laughing, not ever in the act,
not satisfied.

Can you believe a gypsy?
Can you believe any woman
who would leave you,
or make you sit silent
under whispering leaves?
But what is there
in your life
that you would protect
against her?
All you can remember
is the motion
of your obscure fingers,
scurrying over other bodies,
warped by the very warmth
of your insatiable touch.
All you feel is
the radiation of your own touch.

You want to touch the gypsy,
as your hand comes up
like a magnet toward her lips
and down her neck/
your hand/like water
running over her body/
and she is not so strange/
only a traveler
inviting you behind
that clean bus station/
with lips parting
like a flower budding/
with harsh teeth in your neck/
a harsh grind in love/
she knows you have left
enchanting gardens before/
she knows you will recognize yourself
in any prophecy that she makes/

she knows you don't want to see
danger in moping trees/
or a child's silence/
or the intoxicated loving
of black men in closed
sweaty rooms/

You are the traveler
she waits for,
the one who will touch
a city in darkness,
and leave before dawn
shows you its other face.
You are always looking
for gypsies, and signs in rainy forests,
and love in rooms
that you can shuffle
like a deck of cards
and cast away.
You are always
in the beginning
of some prophecy
that you will not believe
to save your life.

You travel in cities
that travel in you,
lost in the ache
of knowing none.

Bosques de Chapultepec

Soft bubbles of the morning steam the grass.
The birds blink and shudder back to sleep.
The iron door of the Museum,
like a wrinkled old face,
yawns and invites you in.

You ride all night from Guadalajara,
awake, awed by the bus,
loping like a bright-eyed cougar
over the dead ground,
and watch the dance
of Mexicans in Ike jackets and white hats,
as they move into the lights,
into the silent fires baking the mud huts.

With an elegance learned somewhere
in the still hidden history of their flesh,
the sleepless peddlers peddle
along the scrubbed streets.
Shaved men, in tinted glasses,
grind out of the suburbs,
down the Reforma.

Go up, now, to that yawning door,
through the parks, full of innocent statues,
over the horses, and lions, and bulls,
prancing in the wet grass.
Go up, now, into the rock-heavy halls.

Alone with your silent steps in the patio,
there is time for you to touch
the forbidden stones, the glassless costumes,
the sturdy furniture;
time to wait for answers,
and be given back part of your self.
You come, black and bilingual,
to a passage of feeling,
to a hall of remembered tones,
to the acrylic colors of your own death.

Pictures of the water.
The lines strung tight from Africa
to south of where you were.
Pictures of the dancers.
The bones even and strong.

The grace of the dance
caught endlessly in your eye.
The sound, the laugh of your presentness
caught on the page.
An ambitious joy
makes the stones sing.
The carved weapons
beat *biribing* time *biribing.*
And you move, in this language,
toward the first compassionate face you see.
You move, begging forgiveness
for having been gone so long.

Reflections Before the Charity Hospital

1
I live almost within this hospital.
All day someone grumbles
through the speaker system.
Whey-faced doctors give consultations
to the poor, outside the doors.
Few are ever admitted.
Even this bush-headed wild man,
snuffing up gelatin in the street,
will never enter there.
For those who have made it in,
there is a line of ragged people
who gather hours before the visiting hour,
moving casually about, talking,
casually buying the sweets, ices and tacos
that the idle men casually sell.
Though they know the hour without clocks,
they watch each face that appears,
as if it had the secret for an early entrance,
as if it had the force to sweep them inside,
where they would take the halls
and rescue the dying, who would be
crawling down the jellied tiles,

choking and screaming, tearing their white,
stringless garments from their bodies,
hammering at each other,
trying to ravish the nurses and sick women.
But it never comes to that.
And when the fuming ambulance coughs
along the streets, with its hiccuping siren,
they stand and line the walls, and whisper
to each other, perhaps feeling some comfort
in knowing that here is another barely saved,
here is another to be bumped from the muddy cab
into the mud-blank rooms,
and they are still standing, somehow,
clutching the three-tiered lunch buckets,
waiting for the familiar face to lead them in.

2
Each day, the rain washes us out of time.
From my window,
the hills close in and disappear.
The trees become no more than shadows,
swaying under the rain's charge.
An hour or two, and the voices
of the carwash boys will be gone.
The fat churro vendor will howl out of sight.
There will be silence.
Only the sturdy water pipe,
at the top of the building,
will show any sign of life.
Inside the hospital, I imagine the wounded,
leaning and arrayed like shades,
among the crowded rooms.
Only now will I stare at the facade,
and count the windows over again,
and count, in my mind, the day's broken bodies
pushed from cabs,
and clothe the women in pink gowns,
and wait, almost insanely, for sirens,
to draw me back down from my rooms

to watch the attendants, helmeted
and mud-bespattered like combat medics,
rush through the doors with a still body,
wrapped from head to foot in a bedcover,
or an old rug.
I cannot turn from this.
I am standing too near,
trying to turn my fascinated body
away from the briefly opened doors.

3

I sit at this desk, now,
close to the hermetic patio.
There is a Dutch landscape of Brueghel's there,
with the shattered windmills dominating.
The full-bodied horses passively submit
to being bridled, or freed, you can't tell which.
Two birds, so much in motion, they hang in the sky.
Is it morning, or evening?
It is evening here,
and nothing enters the hospital.
I can hear my breath falling.
Cursing Brueghel's healthy peasants,
I feel blood coursing in my left ear.
My left arm shudders and falls to the desk.
I move, and feel secret twinges
that, fearing self-pity, I can tell no one.
I listen intently, and, now,
run to the window, throwing back the curtain,
to see if he is there. That man.
The dark, slew-footed man shuffling
among the iron benches in front of the hospital,
arguing with himself, whimpering now,
finally settling under his threaded blanket
for the night, where he will sleep,
heedless to all, at the foot of death,
waking, exactly at the sixth bell,
to stumble off in the city,

disguised as one who is whole,
until night and he comes again.
But I would move him,
or have him wait, as I do,
till midafternoon, and lend his eyes
to the search for that face with the sense of entrance
to appear.

4
All night, the silence takes me.
I will not sleep.
I do not sleep,
but lie, counting heartthrobs.
The walls reverberate and hum,
as I hear them, there, breathing,
crying out, trying to defeat
the self-pity and self-disgust
that will take them quicker
than diminished heartthrobs.
All night, we listen.
I will not rise,
and go to my window now.
I lie, stretched,
getting used to it—
never entering in there—
feeling the gentle dissolution
of all motion within me,
feeling, at last, that they
haven't needed my pity,
that I could not give it to them,
and lying, burdened with the ecstatic pang
of being gone from the window,
gone from the waiting,
gone from myself.
It is not death
that I have felt within these walls.
It is the senseless, weightless,
time-denying feeling of not being here.

An Invitation to Madison County

I ride through Queens,
out to International Airport,
on my way to Jackson, Tougaloo, Mississippi.
I take out a notebook,
write "my southern journal," and the date.
I write something,
but can't get down the apprehension,
the strangeness, the uncertainty
of zipping in over the Sunday streets,
with the bank clock flashing the weather
and time, as if it were a lighthouse
and the crablike cars mistook it
for their own destination.
The air terminal looks
like a city walled in, waiting for war.
The arrivals go down to the basement,
recruits waking at five A.M. to check out their gear,
to be introduced to the business end of the camp.
Fifteen minutes in the city,
and nothing has happened.
No one has asked me to move over
for a small parade of pale women,
or called me nigger, or asked me where I'm from.
Sure only of my destination, I wait.

Now, we move out through the quiet city,
past clean brick supermarkets,
past clean brick houses with nameplates and bushy lawns,
past the sleepy-eyed travelers,
locked tightly in their cars.
No one speaks. The accent I've been
waiting to hear is still far off,
still only part of that apprehension
I had on the highway, in Queens.

The small campus springs up
out of the brown environment,

half-green, half-brown, covered over
with scaly white wooden houses.
It seems to be fighting this atmosphere,
fighting to bring some beauty
out of the dirt roads, the tense isolation of this place.
Out to Mama T's, where farmers, young instructors
and students scream for hamburgers and beer,
rub each other in the light of the jukebox,
and talk, and talk. I am still
not in Jackson, not in Mississippi,
still not off that highway in Queens,
nor totally out of Harlem, still
have not made it into this place,
where the tables creak, and the crickets
close up Sunday, just at evening,
and people are saying good night early.
Afraid now, I wonder how I'll get into it,
how I can make my hosts forget
these impatient gestures, the matching socks and tie.
I wonder how long I'll have to listen
to make them feel I listen, wonder
what I can say that will say,
"It's all right. I don't understand . . .
a thing. Let me meet you here, in your home.
Teach me what you know,
for I think I'm coming home."

Then I meet a teenaged girl
who knows that I can read.
I ride with her to Madison County,
up back roads that stretch
with half-fulfilled crops,
half-filled houses, half-satisfied
cows, and horses, and dogs.
She does all the talking,
challenging me to name the trees,
the plants, the cities in Mississippi, her dog.
We reach her house,
a shack dominated by an old stove,

with its smoky outline going up the wall
into the Mississippi air, mattresses tossed
around the table, where a small piece of cornbread
and a steaming plate of greens wait for her.
Her mother comes out, hands folded before her
like a madonna. She speaks to me,
moving step by step back into the house,
asking me to come again,
as if I were dismissed,
as if there were nothing more
that I could want from her, from Madison County,
no secret that I could ask her to repeat,
not even ask about the baby resting there on her belly,
nor if she ever knew anyone with my name
in Madison County, in Mississippi.

Since I can't, and will not, move,
she stays, with her head coming up,
finally, in a defiant smile.
She watches me sniff the greens,
look around at the bare trees
heaving up out of the bare ground.
She watches my surprise,
as I look at her manly nine-year-old
drive a tractor through the fields.
I think of how she is preparing him
for death, how one day he'll pack
whatever clothes remain from the generations,
and go off down the road,
her champion, her soldier, her lovable boy,
her grief, into Jackson, and away,
past that lighthouse clock,
past the sleepy streets,
and come up screaming,
perhaps on the highway in Queens,
thinking that he'll find me,
the poet with matching socks and tie,
who will tell him all about the city,
who will drink with him in a bar

where lives are crackling, with the smell
of muddy-rooted bare trees, half-sick cows
and simmering greens still in his nose.

But I'm still not here,
still can't ask an easy question,
or comment on the boy, the bright girl,
the open fields, the smell of the greens;
can't even say, yes, I remember this,
or heard of it, or want to know it;
can't apologize for my clean pages,
or assert that I must change, after being here;
can't say that I'm after spirits in Mississippi,
that I've given up my apprehension
about pale and neatly dressed couples
speeding past the lighthouse clock,
silently going home to their own apprehensions;
can't say, yes, you're what I really came for,
you, your scaly hands, your proud, surreptitious
smile, your commanding glance at your son,
that's what I do not search, but discover.

I stand in Madison County,
where you buy your clothes, your bread,
your very life, from hard-line politicians,
where the inessential cotton still comes up
as if it were king, and belonged to you,
where the only escape is down that road,
with your slim baggage, into war,
into some other town that smells the same,
into a relative's crowded house
in some uncertain city, into the arms
of poets, who would be burned,
who would wake in the Mississippi rain,
listening for your apprehension,
standing at the window in different shadows,
finally able to say, "I don't understand.
But I would be taught your strength."

The father comes down the road,
among his harness bells and dust,
straight and even, slowly, as if each step
on that hard ground were precious.
He passes with a nod,
and stands at the door of his house,
making a final, brief inventory
all around and in it.
His wife goes in, comes out with a spoon,
hands it to you with a gracious little nod,
and says, "Such as . . ."

"Such as . . . ," as I heard
when my mother invited the preacher in,
or some old bum, who had fallen off
a boxcar into our small town
and come looking for bread crumbs,
a soup bowl of dishwater beans,
a glass of tap water, served up
in a murky glass.
"Such as . . . ," as I heard
when I would walk across the tracks
in Bisbee, or Tucson, or El Paso, or Santa Fé,
bleeding behind the eyes,
cursing the slim-butted waitresses
who could be so polite.
"Such as . . . ," as I could even hear
in the girded ghettos of New York.
"Such as . . . ," as I heard
when I was invited behind leaky doors,
into leaky rooms, for my loneliness,
for my hunger, for my blackness.
"Such as . . . ," as I hear
when people who have only themselves to give
offer you their meal.

III

The Invention of a Garden

I'm looking out of the window,
from the second floor,
into a half-eaten patio
where the bugs dance deliriously
and the flowers sniff at bits of life.
I touch my burned-out throat,
with an ache to thrust
my fingers to the bone,
run them through the wet
underpinnings of my skin,
in the thick blood, around
the cragged vertebrae.
I have dreamed of armored insects
taking flight through my stomach wall,
the fissured skin refusing to close,
or bleed, but gaping
like the gory lips of an oyster,
stout and inviting, clefts of flesh
rising like the taut membrane of a drum,
threatening to explode and spill
the pent-up desires I hide.
Two or three birds
invent a garden,
he said,
and I have made a bath
to warm the intrepid robins
that glitter where the sun

deserts the stones.
They come, and splash, matter-of-factly,
in the coral water, sand-driven
and lonely as sandpipers
at the crest of a wave.
Could I believe in the loneliness
of beaches, where sand crabs
duck camouflaged in holes,
and devitalized shrubs and shells
come up to capture the shore?
More, than in this garrisoned room,
where this pencil scratches
in the ruled-off lines,
making the only sound
that will contain the taut,
unopened drum that beats the dance
for bugs and garden-creating birds.

Preparing to Leave Home

Trying to come out of it,
I see you shutter the windows
and silently pack my bags.
Here, at midnight,
even the rain is hushed.

I am not ready to leave this place,
and turn toward the wall,
hoping that you will stop and whisper
that it has all been called off,
or that, strangely, I've returned
without incident,
without having you sit and shudder
for my passage.

Outside, I can see
the last café bring down its metal gate.
A man in a white hat

leads a girl over the cobblestones.
Only one light, at the taxi stand,
stands off the assault of bugs.
Only one driver leans on his numbered car.
Only he and I are awake now,
and I go with one bag,
to offer it to him,
to deliver myself of it,
to ride unburdened in scented air,
coffined in the drone of his car,
moving as if we would glide on water,
toward other lights,
where I would deliver up all tickets.

I see no other passenger.
I hear the dank sound of an empty carriage
coming toward us, on wheels
that jingle like horses' bells.
I still hold myself from that other sleep,
but cannot say, now,
what sleep I shall enter here.
My eyes still insist
that I have not left you here.
I try to come out of it,
waiting for your whisper
to send me again into sleep.
The melancholy bells repeat themselves.
I have not prepared.
I have gone too soon.

Origins

We've been here alone for days.
You hardly move.
You sit by the fire,
cradling your Bible
in the canopy of your lap.

Once, as I woke,
still a little hazy,
the play of the fire over the pages
made the letters fuse,
and I thought you held a baby,
dressed in brilliant black,
shrouded and coffined in bone white ribbons.
Your hands moved
as if they caressed it,
limb by limb, bone by bone;
you seemed to learn its rhythm.
I would have called you from it,
but could not.
It is better, I thought,
for my mother to embrace my delusions
than to have her call again
the death and loss of all her daughters.

Now, we wait here as one,
knowing my father walks the hills
east of Albuquerque,
where I have seen him speak
to Navajo runners, standing
with their feathered legs and arms.
And now perhaps he stands
like a stolid old chief,
in a thunder of drums,
with his discontent eyes staring past
the dancers, up the hills,
and has sighted a wolf,
stalking, asking to be captured
and wrenched into the ceremony.

Ah, mother,
even here alone in the room with you,
how can we lament your daughters,
born or unborn, dead or lost,
when the triplet drums
take our feet along the pearl gray ground,

where we can stalk down some other beast
with weapons we have never used,
in a strange tongue,
coming up at the top of a hill,
contemptuous of crosses,
beast-tall and naked as memory?

The Player at the Crossroads

At a crossroads, sits the
player. No drum, no umbrella, even
though it's raining. Again, and we
are somehow less miserable because
here is a hero, used to being wet.
—LeRoi Jones, "Poem for Willie Best," III

1
We know they pass this way,
bag and baggage,
their scarred legs bandaged
with old, water-soaked handkerchiefs.
Six days' traveling
across these open, treeless wastes
have turned them dark as we are.
We sometimes hear *them* crying out for rain,
cursing, trying to insult God
into bringing the season on early.
Their camels clatter with gifts,
and they walk, turning from side to side,
their catatonic eyes bursting from their heads.

2
This is our season,
when we pause,
thirsty and lascivious,
to celebrate the rain,
as if we made it.

Not many of us would miss
the dance, or the slow, intense
caress of the moon maidens,
and so we send the tongueless player
to the crossroads, alone,
with his shining gun,
to wait for the haggard travelers,
knowing that since he cannot
scream or play anymore,
he will perform his one,
necessary act, warning us
above the din of dancing,
above the crash of the rain,
sitting there, even if no one appears,
even when the rain comes
and pins him to the rock
like a lonely, detached leaf.

3
It is his pleasure to wait,
while we go on turning and turning,
mad with the necessity of having
to pretend that we are captured by a god,
angry because we have to perform the steps in time,
to sing in the same cadences,
loudly, spiritedly, without flinching
at the thought that our one, supreme
actor may be dead, or out of temper.

4
The world cannot and must not enter here.
And the tongueless player,
who has lost all arts but one,
sits at the crossroads,
the solitary link to any life but this.

5
Singing and turning,
closed off where we become

our own dead, the blood-caressing act
changes us to what we were,
and only the player,
waiting there with no drum,
no umbrella, holding his shining gun,
may find the gift of something impossible.

Death as History

1
Those, who would make you
want to live, are dying,
passing with no lament,
not even understood in their necessity.
Young poets sit in their rooms
like perverted Penelopes,
unraveling everything,
kicking the threads
into the wind,
and I stop,
woolly-eyed,
trying to record
this peculiar American game.
But they are dying,
the living ones,
and I am sapped of all resolve,
fleeced, finally, of the skill
to live among these others.

To be charged with so much living
is such an improbability,
to be improbable about living
is such a charge to hold
against oneself,
against those who are dying.

2
Dropping his history books,
a young man, lined against the horizon

like an exclamation point with nothing to assert,
stumbles into the dance.
The dancers go round and round
like drones on an unhappy flight.
They look to him for another possibility.
They hum.
They plead.
They circle him with outstretched hands.
They offer him their own salvation.
And he moves forward with a rose.
All that long search
to bring back death.
Who wants that old mystery?

3

But still there is the probable.
And even in Madrid
the golden ages settle
in their sturdy coffins.
Oh, you can say that there,
where the olive trees burst up
through the asphalt cells,
where well-endowed bulls butt
the tail end of tame Sundays,
and the coquettish river flings
its hips at the cattle-mouthed mountains.
Everything there is an imitation.
The girls always advance on the square,
repeating the vital moments,
needing no bookish priests
to redeem that dance.
And it is always the credible dance.

4

It is always like the beginning.
It is always having the egg
and seven circles,
always casting about in the wind
on that particular spot;

it is that African myth
we use to challenge death.
What we learn is that
death is not complete in itself,
only the final going from self to self.

5
And death is the reason
to begin again, without letting go.
And who can lament
such historical necessity?
If they are all dying,
the living ones,
they charge us with the improbable.

The Crucifixion of the Vine

for Mary Lewis

1
Like a slim and eastern goddess,
I think I'll always find you here,
perched on your Persian rug,
haloed in thick smoke,
lit like a gem in tilted light.
Your room leaves little to choose
but silence.
Along the edge of the rug,
a thin vine struggles toward the window,
and disappears in a green tangle
of leaves and flowers you cannot name.
You have the rhythm of this vine
at your fingertips. You sit,
repeating a single challenge
in the same unburdened manner.
"Speak to this."

2
But only you can account
for the play of its rhythm in the room.

You link the vine to Jesus,
appalled by the Gospel saint
who would have him go up
and kneel in the dark of a garden,
give himself up to the doddering breast
of one who could understand
neither his tears nor his exaltation
at having it all complete.

3
You would never keen at that cross,
would never submit to the passion
of one who could grapple
with the terminus of things,
and enter here, amazed
by the desire of a thin vine
to leap through the window,
escaping the silence of a room,
where you sit, trying to speak to a rhythm
that insults your very bones.

4
You are my slim, black goddess,
breaking the silence of your room,
with the crucifixion of a vine.
I turn my eyes,
and do not listen.

Historical Days

I go out on these days,
down to the foot of the bridge,
with the gasps of water hoses
echoing in my ear,
down past steel bars
cracking up into the fat brown fences
like darts into cork boards,
and bougaloo on old cars.

I turn down streets
picked clean as kosher hens,
watching locks indecently
dangling from shuttle thin houses.
Summer. And yet old, brandy-eyed
and flat men huddle in plucked overcoats.
I think they must remember
the negligent wind that their
silent, twisted mouths accuse me of.
The seasons, in this circle,
are so unchanging.
When I'm alone at night,
sleep is a dirty rug,
and I sit up, a jaded historian,
and announce,
It was a day
        like any other
            as they say.

Variations on a Theme by LeRoi Jones

I
KNOWLEDGE OF THE FACE

The face sings, alone
at the top
        of the body.
    —LeRoi Jones, "Poem for Willie Best," I

Step and turn,
the pirouettes that leave
no dent in the earth.
Whatever music
that rises here,
a rich harmony
surrounding the stark
melody of your body,

you preen as if it were yours,
as this withered body is,
though this body threatens
to dismember itself
sometimes in joy,
sometimes helplessly turning
away and into its own pain.
And at the top,
the face sings, alone,
caught in its own music,
a certain parade of triumphs
that the body cannot know.
This head,
where the breath is,
you guard against
the secret stalkers.
I have seen pictures
of defeated warriors,
trussed up in sand,
with only their heads thrust out,
like flowers introducing
themselves to the sun,
and there they wait,
as the victors gallop toward them,
shouting, their mean eyes narrowed,
their lances coming accurately.
The body does not move the earth,
but the eyes, riveted
on some single spot,
move everything about them.
This is enough to canker kings.
Your shriveled body
will not startle anyone, anymore,
but you catch them at your head,
where the face sings, alone,
in knowledge that will not move
to the disrupted harmonies
that take your body.

II
The Point

A cross. The gesture, symbol, line
arms held stiff, nailed stiff, with
no sign, of what gave them strength.
The point, become a line, a cross, or
the man, and his material, driven in
the ground . . .
—LeRoi Jones, "Poem for Willie Best," II, 2

They measure the American continent:
these massive limestone crosses,
or a stiff Jesus,
with his impassive beard,
driven staunchly on a mountain,
impervious as well to the babble
of tongues as to the absurd heights.
But I would not have him there,
marking some inaccessible point,
the line of his arms as right
and impossible as his biblical life.
He would have to come down,
and bend his back on the line,
chattering and singing with amazing grace,
and sit at night around the straight fires,
learning about the new deaths,
the rumor of his own,
feeling an insatiable desire
to break free and become a sign,
a living gesture, unearthed,
yet rooted in earth, in flesh.
He would have to listen on stubbled corners,
in darkness, standing flayed to the heart
with improbable memories, listening
to groomed merchants of the soul
bargain guardedly for every part of him,
letting the echo of exile change him,

turn him unholily mad, send him
screaming through the city to take it,
not as a god, but as a god would.
This point, become a line, a cross,
or the man, and his ground,
a gesture of those who would praise
none but an earth-winning hero.

III
A Simple Act

As simple an act
as opening the eyes. Merely
coming into things by degrees.
—LeRoi Jones, "Way Out West," 1–3

West of west,
north and the spinning
axis,
and every direction
colored.
The jeweled flowers
lit for the eye,
each structured leaf
complete
and turned,
in strength,
against the center,
are like diamonds
tossing the sun's light
for pleasure and preening.
Here, there is no entry
for what is brutal.
Behind the eye,
a name is given,
innocently.
As simple an act

as opening the eyes, merely
coming into things by degrees.

You will babble,
feeling something strain,
against all hope,
to enter, to turn
in its loveliness
within you.
You awake
with cankered eyes,
unable to speak
of the simple gesture
of a hand, caught
in its lonely movement
toward some other,
toward some indefinable,
secret history of yourself.
You have no mind,
only this simple act of the eyes,
coming upon an untutored harmony
by degrees.

Idiotic and Politic

Your letter reached me
in the darkness of my fever,
when all my dawns
were some corrupt play of shadows,
when I was pulsing with the banal discoveries
we come to with such idiotic exhilaration.
Your candidacy is a fear I never held,
but now I fear your timid power,
brushing against the locks of our diffidence.
I can't imagine you a ghetto Solon,
linked to a line of escape.
But there are more tyrannies than service.
Holding your last statement,

I see your flippant breast cocking its way
into the canons of a careful city,
certain now of the creed's flexibility,
taking the ordered gestures as some sign
of consent.

Remember this.
Those nights we lingered
over the boldness of a dime not spent,
it was you, passionate
in holding passion in the bridge of our lives,
slack-eyed from your peripatetic graces,
damning our people as a world of beggars.
I had no strength then,
only the sympathy to adopt your eyes
and the brash rhythm of a seer
too wise to riddle.
Now, we go our separate ways.
I, even wiser now, a seer,
living in cities I cannot love,
and you, no longer a part
of the idiocy you engendered.
How politic.
But how like you, to find your historic form so soon.

Here I sit in the stolid temper of my study,
fidgeting with the system of a myopic Frenchman,
trying to find my politic self.
But this perversion mocks the Florentine,
would have stung the Philosopher to mockery.
And you, now unphilosophical,
have made up your mind to cozen ethics.
Oh, if I could reason now,
and find some determinate responsibility
lurching in the caverns of my mind,
if I could turn toward some beatific kiss.
There is a season all men dream of,
the ague released, all meanness brought to virtue,
no solitary captains and no wars.
But I walk in a city,

where harmonies are only heroic deeds,
marvelous paradoxes to the life of man,
myths to scale your life upon.
Your letter leaves me here.
Celtic kings would have smoked the night at your death.
Trumpet-tongued Roland would forget the art of
hesitation.
You would have held assemblies enthralled,
menacing the care of wives.
And all like you have ended there
where none began, the idiotic wax
of personality shaped by a politic temper.
Let this rest, and count no vote of mine.
There is something indignant,
paradoxical, and too true,
in the static flux of a life.

My Mother Dances on the Jut of God's Good Hip

It is that time of night
when the only lights in the cabin
are the sullen ends of cigarettes.

I have you here,
in a quarter's worth of moon,
trying to win a bet with your fate.
You are facing east,
directly under the moon,
with a brand-new dime pinched
between your thumb and forefinger.
Speaking softly to yourself,
you take the dime on a trip
three times around the moon's halo
and down along its slotted curve.
You pocket the dime
and scratch your right hand,
spitting into it, rubbing it
briskly against your right hip.

You have taught me
how to make a dime dance
in moon rays, and come up
multiplied and heavy in my pockets.
Somehow, I must have lost the touch.
Perhaps I never knew how
to start its exhilarated leap,
or the proper penitent formula.
Perhaps I have simply forgotten
everything you taught me.

But I have made my mother dance
in blue silk
on the jut of God's hip,
tracing her finger along it
as she would the veined map
that we keep tacked on a hall door.
This is easy.
For I know her body,
having played with its rhythm
while I discovered my own.
I can trace even now
the cut of Virginia's loins
along her soft skin,
can feel the weight of her father's body
still struggling to leave them both,
can almost hear a sound there
like the wind playing with leaves.
And you are here, far from that,
in mountain air and the smell
of old pine and cactus,
listening to sheep dogs and wolves
cast their challenges over the distance,
coming down, from the silent stills,
to stand davening before the cabin door,
your bones like heavy seashells,
washed in your frightened blood,
hiding your black hands, now,
like priceless pearls, from the moon,

waiting to enter the dark cabin,
where you will turn toward each voice,
still feeling the strangeness of its rhythm,
still wanting to run from this clamor
of old pine and cactus and lonely men,
taking only your familiar moon,
to bring it back where my eyes hold you,
back where I stand, enchanted,
watching my gentle mother,
escaped from those weighted loins,
dance, in blue silk and solid bones,
along the jut of God's good hip.

Destination: Accomplished

Six miles between
my stop and this.
A Mexican night, a bus,
to diminish the bleakness
of New York's errant summer.

Mexicans flip like marlins.
A terrier yaps cadence
to a rhumba at the corner.
An untenanted Indian shawl
beguiles the neighborhood.

Six miles
of a Jersey turnpike
were never like this
and yet
those six vacant leagues
narrow in my memory
to a frieze
of inexpressible beauty.

But time to stop now
for this solitary room

where leftover patches
of yesterday fasten them-
selves to my melancholy,
a big and open patio to watch
a drunken fog insinuate
itself into the distance.
Back to these history books,
to my stroking of these beautiful,
discarded masks I keep.
A simple weight of all I am,
or would be.

This necessary chaos follows me.
Something to put in place,
new categories for the soul
of those I want to keep.
What I needed was to be thrown
into this toneless school,
an arrogant rhythm to release
my buried style.

This journey will end
with a double entry,
bought by poems
to all my hidden loves.

I have covered
more than six miles
to uncover
my necessary gestures.

From city to city,
from tongue to tongue,
I move in settled style,
a journey of the soul,
accomplished once,
accomplished
with what is mine.

Pastel

Cigar waving,
I swagger through
this city of hills
and spontaneous guitars.
Just at the foot of Mexiamora,
an old woman slices
and sauces oysters,
the red sauce running
over her green dress.
Mariachis in blue jackets
sing their way up into the lights,
those capricious fireflies
now flitting through the park,
where I wait for you,
where I turn, and take you,
without courtesy,
through the dark corners of the walk.

Tonight, I'll ask you for your love,
as quick as that,
not wanting it to come so easily,
but needing to have you writhe
and say you love me, as quick as that,
needing to feel you die under me,
destroying me in you,
as I do these cities.

When the gentle air titters through these hills,
and the guitarróns slide darkly through the night,
what we call love will come to face us,
and I'll swagger in your arms,
listening to this city
choke in you, in me,
in love without a cause.

IV

The Regeneration

The wind, taut as piano wire,
peels me apart.
I go down, down through the evening,
standing somewhere between light and dark.
On this hill
I hear a child's voice
grumble like a soldier's,
and feel the weight of some dead man on my back,
his fingers tightened around my throat,
his brief knees tucked at my waist.
The child, at the summit,
calls into the darkness.
"I charge you to bury him."
I go on, where the wooden monuments
fall like banderillas in the leathery ground.
No light. No bells.
The flame of a cigar coming toward me.
A black man, in dashiki and crown,
holds his mutilated fingers in my eyes.
He asks me to count.
I cannot speak.
He sends me on.
The dead man extends his arm
along the ridge. I follow it.
We come to a shabby cathedral,
where three candles dance
to the wind's soprano.

Twelve men are going up,
under the applauding bells,
the seventh speaking in tongues.
In the circular cemetery,
there is wine bubbling
like the dead seething of a volcano.
We turn, framed like a manic caravan of flesh,
and go back toward the knees of the hill.
Down, down and into it,
with the cavernous city doubling like a bull,
the head pushed into the navel.
The body is singing to me,
"This is the gift of living in the fire,
of being turned to righteousness,
of being melted into some other
to become what you are."
The taut wind goads me,
undulating in the half-light,
now egg-shaped, now a fleshless embryo.

Now is the time   to give up
the death of it   your own dead living
the life   what will not sustain you.

I run, under the dead man's stutter,
through these hills,
with these shadows,
to the ankles of the hill
and a green grave, an open coffin,
the morning's sheer cloak.
The dead man drops me there.
The shadows kick clouds over the grave.
The sun, taking the dusty air for a bed,
copulates with the moon.

Night Walk

These streets wake up at night,
with tongues & eyes to spear you/

        Seventh & one twenty-fifth/
    condemned   changed/
foxes tittering through meat boxes
ladders   staggering podiums   flags
the drunken wastes   the eyes   the hands/
Down one seventeenth
    & the pot smell on the steps
    & nodding junkies with tunes in their heads
    & late night barbecue at the corner/
    balloon men & jewel men
    clothes marked down from the rack
    numbers going out in the barkeep's tips/
Up one eleventh
    dance & down your four for one
    teenaged girls huddled in mockery
    you flash your own brand of bougaloo/
        Everything is fact/
        the essence of it all is that
        there are too many shadows to clear
        too many leftover markers
        & someone must show you the ritual/
It is there in the language
    & you are you   if you are recognized
    & you are recognized   if you can rap
        & you will not catch yourself
            running
    after the man in the ritual hat
or go after that challenge again/
    but the sisters will speak to you
    & prophesy/
        in the attics
    where deaths are being planned
    & how will you change that
        when it is done/
Church & funeral awnings
    go up the circle hand in hand/
        Street cries fade
            the lights go out/

The old man was right
        Death is the language of these streets
        though death will never own them/
        When it is all done
        so much of your life
        is how & what you speak/
        if you go away
        you carry the speech in your bones/
Nothing is invented there/in you
                you come to that
        even though the streets cluck their triumph
                & you sit in the dawn
        with the old man piercing your tongue.

First Principles

I see my father
standing in the half-moon
that the ancient lamp
throws on the street.
There's broken glass
scattered on the sidewalks
like sugared diamonds,
all around him.
He looks a little strange to me,
almost ecstatic, as he stands there,
with his left foot planted
unconsciously on somebody's
discarded and torn shirt.
I walk toward him,
breaking my pace,
trying to approach him
as if there were no reason
to be in a hurry,
as if all that could be said
had been said, here, tonight,
among these broken windows,
these iron bars that squeal like pigs

when they're twisted.
I walk toward him
as if I didn't expect him to argue,
as if he would nod to me
in some silent acknowledgment
of what had been said over the splinters
of these pampered doors.
And yet I cannot believe
that he is here,
even if he's only come
to pick up the pieces,
to make sure I'm alive.
I can imagine his coming
to identify me,
lifting the sheet with emphatic hands,
nodding briefly and turning out
into the crowd, where he could
bury himself and scream tears,
as if he were one of them,
giving in to his rage,
and not his loss.
Or I can imagine him,
going down whitewashed halls
in the groaning wards,
where men are hammering at their eyes,
as their sons tell them
what the streets were like,
try to describe the feel
of being bludgeoned half into death,
half into the silly exhilaration
of letting go of everything,
reaching out and whirling
toward the center of yourself
and feeling that, if you grasped it,
you would be caught there,
suspended like a leaf
bottled in the wind
with no place to drop.
But he is there.

And I'm alive, for the moment,
still the lively son of a man,
who is the lively son
of a railroad man,
who came up out of the South,
telling lies about his age,
his work, his place of birth,
his stolid wife, tricking everyone,
including himself,
so *that* moment would come
when he would see his son
move from being only a son
and change his own truth
to probable lies, going off
as if he were being born
at the foot of death.
And I'm walking, now,
prepared to argue with that man,
who has his foot on the tattered shirt.
I hear it coming from me like a text,
my biblical, righteous rhetoric:
how can I tell you
the absolute rightness
of being in this fire?
how could I turn back?
for this is certain,
and I can't sit, now,
on your darkened porch,
like a scholar,
telling you that when dancers
argue with the earth,
and black men speak in tribal tongues,
it is not a festival of the damned,
it is a feast of the living,
who move toward the past,
not in the fantastic,
but in the certainty of myth,
in the tongues of the exiled dead,
who live in the tongues of the living.

Walking here,
I still feel I can sing
like a poet, a mad prophet,
caught up in my own cadences,
while my father stands
drawing in his breath,
prepared to run to me,
prepared to save me.
I look at him
in the half-moon of the light.
He lifts his hand,
and I listen to him breathe
in the tongues of the exiled dead.

A Nuer Sacrifice

Red patches of ashes.
The cucumber,
once fleet as a gazelle,
being cut and sworn to,
hurled in the fire
to crawl and bleat
and come up changed,
in my rhythm,
as I go on socking the earth
with my iron-splitting leg.

A chant.
The scrape of a follicled gourd.

We have visions, now,
of ships docking and stealing
up the smooth coasts again,
with unearthly red sailors
lost and tangled,
choked in the croak
of an asson,
at the tail end of the night.

Like a singing god,
I stand and call the names
of all my dead.
They fall and distract the living.
And in this forest of motives,
I pretend with the pretenders
to enter in here
in the night,
with my urban chatter
transformed,
my mackin step weighted
with the grace of a ritual dance.

I circle
with the accommodating wind,
looking through the flames
into the eyes of one small man,
as he pulls at the legs
of the cucumber,
burying it deeper in the ashes,
burying those filthy ships for me.
He holds me with his eyes,
as I grapple with the last
life-draining lurch of the ox.

The Desert Revival

Each year in July
we charter buses,
and come to this California desert
to pitch our tents
where, for days, our tambourines clash
as if they were lashed to proud,
full-bodied horses, prancing the desert.

Closed in this city,
we move from bell to bell,
gathering the tales of penance,

being treated, now and again,
to the voice of a black apostle
who sears us with book and verse,
compressing Christ's tidy lines
to a shriek in the dung-brown tents.

Sometimes, at night,
old women in ankle-length black dresses
sit and teach a catechism with their eyes.
What they know
is the language of confession,
of tribute, of lacerating joy,
and it bursts from them
as from the first apostle of pain,
forgotten now, except in his cadence,
dead now, except in their ecstatic tongues.

Now, the moon dips
in the river of these voices,
where one is still alive
with unholy passion.
One trembling singer begs
to enter time again,
to tear himself from the desert loneliness
and run smartly to that other city,
babbling and wild, in the manner of one
who cannot wait for his desert light.
We wrench him from his coat.
A choir begins to smash the tambourines.
But he cannot be held.
He runs, as if some lover called him,
over the arc of the desert,
toward some other light,
and the voice of the black apostle
stalks the desert silence.

We turn back toward the old women
nodding before the tents,
each beginning to tap the sand

in her own rhythm.
They cannot say that he has gone.
They cannot say why we are unable
to learn these silent catechisms.
They cannot say why the paradigm
of these desert deaths haunts us.
In the dark, a nostalgic bird hovers
and claws toward something unseen,
and, through the tents, caught in the wind,
the deadly pitch of flutes and bones
grates upon our Christian skins.

Collection Time

The bleeding Jesus hangs
just where the preacher nailed him,
and the wooden church rocks
like a storm-caught fishing boat.
A gap-toothed, fat and rouged soprano gurgles
as if she were going under a wave.
My preacher stops, gasping,
sweating, his hips still tossing,
his fingers stretched in the ecstatic air.
The singing subsides to a murmur,
coming like a new wave to sweep
this rocking boat up and out,
expelling singers with nets
to hang over any sinner.

Collection time.

Someone smacks the table
and calls for every nickel in the house.
White-robed sisters, still smelling
of Saturday's lavender-scented dives,
wrestle the aisles,
and shove the platters at you.

Collection time.

You will mourn.
You will come down front.
My preacher whirls to frighten you,
descends to lay his knotty hands
where the hurt is.
You will mourn for us.
You will come down front for us.
You will not be caught,
dreaming that you have done the deed,
cut that bleeding, homeless waif
out of your heart, caught
with your pagan mind in the streets,
crying for a flag.

Collection time.

Bull, serpent and lion,
the symbols chase each other
over the wastes of cities.
The very sun calls back
the image of a thirsty traveler,
shaking his feet at the edge of a stream,
desperate for having come so far
without knowing his direction,
knowing only that he must die,
somewhere, under a strange flag,
his bearded head carved
and mockingly creased with a crown,
his bullies gone off to teach his silences.

Collection time.

Who here can sing
anything but swords and knives,
can want anything but that tribal beard cut,
that oil-scented flesh scraped
and cauterized with earth?

Collection time.

The words tumble like beads.
Spilled from that rocking boat,
this weary tribe staffs itself
to poke for the woman-soft
and yielding center, to enter there,
where the dance will shape
another pristine world,
black
as the underbelly
of a dead lamb.

Sketch for an Aesthetic Project

I believe now that love is half persistence,
A medium in which, from change to change,
Understanding may be gathered.
—Thomas Kinsella,
"Nightwalker"

1
I stomp about these rooms in an old overcoat,
never warm, but never very anxious
to trot off to the thickly banked park,
where the perpetual rain hangs in the trees,
even on sunny days.

When I step out,
the streets are cleaned of life,
only, perhaps,
an old woman in black
staggering along with a lantern,
only, perhaps,
a burro decked out under a pair of straw baskets,
or a dim-eyed student
lingering at a grilled window, listening to whispers.
Just as in forgotten cities,

there is hardly a sound,
hardly a movement, or a light.
I clatter over cobbled streets,
listening, watching.
I pretend not to be afraid of witches,
or any forces,
ground down under the years here,
carping and praying under stones,
calling curses down on unthinking walkers
who go, as I do, timid and fleet,
toward their own purposes.

I can only hope to meet some other soul,
tugging a burro up the street,
loaded with wet wood,
padding barefoot through the rain,
coming toward me, hard-mouthed,
holding his faintly gabled hands
to pluck my pity.

2

I call this home.
And like a traveler home from seeing,
I walk my flowered stairs
and reconstruct my journeys,
remembering every brick and bird,
recalling the miracle of being there.
But names are what I call again.
New York. And call it home.
Again, I walk in summer, innocently,
a long walk, down Seventh, Harlem,
twisting and finding new turns.
The streets breathe again.
The lights scorch the midway islands.
Voices dance at the edges.
An abandoned store begins to howl
with camp meeting songs.
I am there again,
under the eyes of the man they call the deacon,

a rabbi of the unscrupulous.
His eyes are as taut and brilliant as marble.
He babbles about shoes and croaker sacks.
Old women flail at kids, and return to gossip.
They watch the rabbi pass.
They watch me pass.
Even here, I am there again.
And those succulent voices drive me mad.

3
Wake, and the lights bob like tongueless bells.
Churches spew Catholic-clad blessed ones.
I wait, here near the ocean, for the north wind,
and the waves breaking up on ships.
At this point, the slave ships would dock,
creeping up the shoreline,
with their bloody cargo intact,
the ingenuous sailors unnerved
through days of hopeless waiting,
hopeless anticipation of reward,
hopeless clutching at the dying,
then intensely buoyed by sight of land
and the fervent release of cankered bodies.
At this point, I wait,
and cannot go back to linger on my stairs,
or grovel under the deacon's eyes.
I have made a log for passage,
out there, where some still live,
and pluck my bones.
There are parchments of blood
sunk where I cannot walk.
But when there is silence here,
I hear a mythic shriek.

4
This shriek in the coldness
is like music returning to me,
coming over the illusion of solitude,
swift and mad as I am,

dark in its act,
light
in the way it fills
my pitiless mind.

Beginning Again

1
I've come back so slowly
to here, trying to remember
how I came here then,
what sense of speaking
brought me to this place.
My history is like a bird's,
flying away, nesting
wherever sun and some small
charity are offered to me,
pecking in rain and ill fortune,
when they come, only to survive
as one whose virtue is flying.
But I am more than a bird,
and less, being weighted
and buoyed by a sense of tongues,
being kept in my voluntary flight
because I am impressed
with weight other than my own,

being sure that my routes are chosen,
sure that there is a changeless place
that holds me, that will not be shaken.

So leave the history of birds,
even their ash-scented flowering,
even their holy beauty.
I return to tell how
I come back so slowly,
carefully, to here,
where you see me now.

2

Ah, the pain I could tell,
but that is not my choice.
Before you, I'm not even virtuous.
Sulking and skulking in old bones,
I ravish cities, shredding rich cloth,
picking golden coins,
spading up shards of faded vessels
that tell me nothing.
I sit in semestral light
like Chekhov's old student
annotating manuscripts,
looking for something to oppose your arrogance.
But I write here, speaking to you,
where discoveries end,
opposed within myself,
but here now at the edge,
where something must speak
for us, to us, for me, alone.

3

The bridge is open.
The night of the bay falls
liberally to the water.
The lamps are lit past paling time.
I think of how
I walked this bridge,
and would have leaped,
leaving only my wallet
to identify me,
leaving without a scream,
splayed and sucked
by the eddying water,
my life the still center
of the ocean smoothing
its deadly wrinkles.
That is the history of a dream,
of one life choosing its end.
We cannot all choose so.

And at the foot of the bridge,
two lovers walk on the can-burdened sand,
a portable radio fusing their twin heads,
their stripped shoes leaking garbage.
They are not lonely or lost.
They speak from the other side
of the bridge; they walk toward
a car, to drift toward a lighted house,
with the smell of meat
and unintended parties waiting there.

4

Ah, but I've come away
from that death desire.
Walking in soggy alleys,
my ears beaten by the cock
and preening crull of other tongues,
I haven't wanted that.
I will lay you a limbo
of soft afternoons,
with peacocked drinks
and street dances,
take you through the square
in Vera Cruz, where you can hear
your indiscretions sung by La Negra,
her bombastic harp nursing
your pesos in the womb of its bridge.
There, we turn away, and float,
while the three o'clock camphor
settles in the square, and La Negra
wobbles silently toward home,
her cuddled harp cradled
in one restless hand.

5

"Everything rhythmically organic is true."
La Negra's harp.
The voices I cannot claim.
Even the memory of a dead bird,

coming to rest in my life.
And now my ancient rhythm calls me,
out of ashes and fraternal death,
"Before you, mother Idoto,
naked I stand . . .
a prodigal . . .
lost in your legend. . . ."
An aching prodigal,
who would make miracles
to understand the simple given.

Soothsayers and Omens

I

The Charge

1
This is the morning.
There is a boy,
riding the shadow of a cradle,
clapping from room to room
as swift as the memory of him.
But it is no memory.
I did not come at this hour.
And if I had,
and if I were a memory,
would I be here now,
fully awake,
as sure of your memory
as of myself
who would be your memory?
These sounds, this image,
are not memory,
but the heart's throb past all defeats,
a livable assertion.
Now,
I hear you whistle through the house,
pushing wheels, igniting fires,
leaving no sound untried,
no room in which a young boy,
at sea in a phantom cradle,
could lurch and scream
and come to settle in the house.

You are so volubly alone
that I turn,
reaching into the light for the boy
your father charged you to deliver.

2
We stand, and watch
my young wife's body rise and fall.
We wait to release ourselves
with the cry that makes the moon sway.
Soon,
there will be dancing,
a slow retreat to the water,
where women will hold the boy,
plucked from the weeds,
a manchild, discovered,
waiting.
That is the memory
that will begin it,
an unconscious possession
of what coming like rain,
and the image of rain, can mean.

3
Now, father,
I am yours again,
and you belong to him
and the father who charged you.
But it isn't true yet.
I have only been dreaming,
and caught in the dream
of bringing him here,
where what is given
is only a memory,
and still no memory,
where death is all I have
to offer him,
though I go on living,
drawing closer, as I age, to you.

Even in this dream
I call you to come to him.
Even though this is no more than a dream,
I call you to argue him
into existence.
No,
no word is enough.
Even the image will not come again
unless I give it my assent.

4
Careful in everything,
we have prepared a place,
just at that spot
where the sun forever enters this circle.
Fathers and sons sit
making the noise of fathers,
waiting for the cut
into the life of my son,
waiting for my modest life
to be as whole as theirs.
All things here move
with that global rhythm.
All memories come
after the heat of it.
We are petals,
closed at evening,
opening at the first touch.
We are gathered to watch
the shaping of another miracle.
We are gathered in the miracle
of our own memories.
Unhappy sun,
even you cannot light everything.

5
This is the morning
when I am fully awake
to your sadness.

Now, father,
I am more than yours,
and lead you past the tricks
of our memory,
into this moment
as real as memory.
This is the moment
when all our unwelcome deaths
charge us to be free.
And my late son,
no savior,
rises still to fill
our vacant eyes.

The Appearance of a Lost Goddess

I have taken
this self-appointed priest
into my confidence.
Garbed like the very moon,
he leads me to the edge
of this water
where we cast for all
my lost connections.
Something, not my own,
has been riding me
without my consent.
But tonight I am ready
to pay with my life
to see the shape of my own queens,
dancing here in the colors
of the moon and the water.
In the full light
I see the first approach
—not the favorite,
but the mean one
who lies tangled at the bottom
of the water in her own hair.

Often now at night,
Eshu, capped like a sailor,
commandeers a boat,
and pushes out to stir the water.
The favored one,
in the garb of the moon herself,
grapples with the boat,
and the water foams
and disguises the rising
of the woman,
who comes raging from below,
until we cannot tell from which realm
she has appeared,
cannot tell if we should love
or fear her.
This one we cannot tell
may be the mother of all our gods,
casting off the weight of the water,
coming toward us with curses,
unable to forgive our neglect.
Here, at the water,
I have become the last initiate,
unable to put together the right form,
or to abide this goddess' curses.

Sources
(1)

And what if the god
should send me as a messenger,
adorned with quetzal feathers?
In the light,
I have seen that pink and white
flower, at the top of the thorns,
float up, a feathered arrow,
or move, an embellished body,
to drink the rhythm of drums.
But this is the House of the Eagle,

the House of the Night of the Tigers.
This is the place where the spring
itself lies garlanded by kings.
When the rain falls,
when only these quetzal feathers
light the house,
I kneel in the only light it gives,
needing no light
to catch the dark, sweet smell
of this intoxicating god.

Sources
(2)

1
There is no way to begin
without the image
of boisterous Tlacahuepan,
turning among his proud twist of flowers,
proud of his warrior's scars,
proud of his singing.
So I begin there,
uneasy with the way
his dead voice captures my ears.
In the middle of my life,
snug in a snowy village,
I lift these texts,
wanting the words
to enter my mind like pure wind.

2
Here, no god advances.
All the words I join
and launch like bright arrows
are tossed about like feathers
in the wind.
No warrior,
and without that desire,

I lean into songs
with the lust of a boy
parsing age-old battles,
calling up an unconscious
and unforgivable pride
in doing an unspeakable god's honor.
How would I sing of gods
without the image of a prince?
How can I sing of a prince
without the touch of that
particular flower, in that
particular sun,
and my own innocent approach
down to a clear river
on a clear and innocent day?

3

This is the House of the Eagle,
the House of the Night of the Tigers.
This is music familiar again.
Over the long evenings
I have been sitting awake
with sad Tlacahuepan and his friends,
learning how flowers can intoxicate;
how the sun will dart into your bones;
how the river will run swiftly to its source
and turn as rapidly to the image of a goddess;
how a poet will wrestle with a god,
risking his mind;
how a woman will turn in ecstasy
to a god in the image of a warrior;
how a man will move and flower,
uncertain, even, of a god's love.

4

To be certain of sun
and rain and death
is enough.
I want to say I remember

how it must have been,
standing on consecrated land,
with the light around us,
the dark, sweet smell of our own god,
the voice of that god,
saying perhaps he loves us,
for us, for now, for this place,
for his own love, for us, only perhaps,
he loves us, perhaps.

Sources
(3)

Strange,
but by night
you look clearly
into Nyame's eyes.
Now, these eyes
light the earth
down toward the red tree,
and I am on my way there, too,
angry with his anger.
Today,
we heard the silence
beating about our ears,
and knew that there would be
no pity in the air tonight.
Nothing has been forgotten.
We forget nothing.
I still see my first sister,
in silver, shy and positive,
move surely to our mother,
giving her hand, as a witness,
ready to die, and lie
between our world and Nyame's eyes.
Or was that a vision
of my own desire?
Was that some simple truth

I cannot speak again?
Could it be
that I am not even
worth the death
these eyes beg so insistently?

Sources
(4)

It still happens.
As far away as memory,
as near as my skin,
you come shooting light,
bringing me awake again
to the smell of wet forests,
to the weight of wet fruit
and the unearthly touch
of sun and rain and nights
that linger like the unhurried
hum of a sweet hymn,
a song that refuses its own death
as I would refuse yours.
I have learned that you move,
and change, and come again
to enchant my eyes with another form.
A duiker antelope, you lope
here on the harassed highways.
A ram, you force light along these walls.
A lion, you stalk our merciless hearts.
A leopard, you crash and carve
your name into my soul.
Once, you were the moon.
I have grown used to your changes,
never to your death.
Even now,
though others sing your death,
I wake to see you, heron-like,
catching at your tail.

Sources
(5)

Another god,
they say,
came like this,
disguised in a feeble body,
waiting for some poor spirit's
passive pity to be guided
into light.
But you want no pity,
only perfection,
and all these years,
journeys and terrors
away from you,
I come only now
to care about that desire.
I will not ask you
for another beginning,
only the body of a slim, imperfect child
to fill with light.

Sources
(6)

Once the color of sun,
now the color of darkness,
it appears when all penance
has been done.
Now, there is time for joy,
and, touched by the life
and death of all our fathers,
you will praise and carry us
in your own life.
I am not alone here,
in my own memory,
but stand as old as angels,
as new as the silver dress

of my ancient sister,
as powerful as the still bright moon,
lurking through the night
to catch those who do not believe.

Benjamin Banneker Helps to Build a City

In a morning coat,
hands locked behind your back,
you walk gravely along the lines in your head.
These others stand with you,
squinting the city into place,
yet cannot see what you see,
what you would see
—a vision of these paths,
laid out like a star,
or like a body,
the seed vibrating within itself,
breaking into the open,
dancing up to stop at the end of the universe.
I say your vision goes as far as this,
the egg of the world,
where everything remains, and moves,
holding what is most against it against itself,
moving, as though it knew its end, against death.
In that order,
the smallest life, the small event take shape.
Yes, even here at this point,
Amma's plan consumes you,
the prefigured man, Nommo, the son of God.
I call you into this time,
back to that spot,
and read these prefigurations
into your mind,
and know it could not be strange to you
to stand in the dark and emptiness
of a city not your vision alone.

Now, I have searched the texts
and forms of cities that burned,
that decayed, or gave their children away,
have been picking at my skin,
watching my hand move,
feeling the weight and shuttle of my body,
listening with an ear as large as God's
to catch some familiar tone in my voice.
Now, I am here in your city,
trying to find that spot
where the vibration starts.
There must be some mistake.

Over the earth,
in an open space,
you and I step to the time
of another ceremony.
These people, changed,
but still ours,
shake another myth
from that egg.
Some will tell you
that beginnings are only
possible here,
that only the clamor of these drums
could bring our God to earth.
A city, like a life,
must be made in purity.

So they call you,
knowing you are intimate with stars,
to create this city, this body.
So they call you,
knowing you must purge the ground.

"Sir, suffer me to recall to your mind that time, in which the arms and tyranny of the British crown were exerted, with every powerful effort, in order to reduce you to a state of servitude: look back, I entreat you, on the variety of dangers to which you were exposed; reflect on that

time, in which every human aid appeared unavailable, and in which even hope and fortitude wore the aspect of inability to the conflict, and you cannot but be led to a serious and grateful sense of your miraculous and providential preservation; you cannot but acknowledge, that the present freedom and tranquility which you enjoy you have mercifully received, and that it is the peculiar blessing of Heaven."

"Reflect on that time."
The spirits move, even
in the events of men,
hidden in a language
that cannot hide it.
You were never lost
in the language of number alone;
you were never lost
to the seed vibrating alone,
holding all contradictions within it.
"Look back, I entreat you,"
over your own painful escapes.

The seed now vibrates into a city,
and a man now walks where you walked.
Wind and rain must assault him,
and a man must build against them.
We know now, too, that the house
must take the form of a man
—warmth at his head, movement at his feet,
his needs and his shrine at his hands.
Image of shelter, image of man,
pulled back into himself,
into the seed before the movement,
into the silence before the sound
of movement, into stillness,
which may be self-regard,
or only stillness.

Recall number.
Recall your calculations,
your sight, at night,

into the secrets of stars.
But still you must exorcise this ground.

"Here was a time, in which your tender feelings for yourselves had engaged you thus to declare, you were then impressed with proper ideas of the great violation of liberty, and the free possession of those blessings, to which you were entitled by nature; but, Sir, how pitiable it is to reflect, that although you were so fully convinced of the benevolence of the Father of Mankind, and of his equal and impartial distribution of these rights and privileges, which he hath conferred upon them, that you should at the same time counteract his mercies, in detaining by fraud and violence so numerous a part of my brethren, under groaning captivity, and cruel oppression, that you should at the same time be found guilty of that most criminal act, which you professedly detested in others, with respect to yourselves."

Can we say now
that it is the god
who chains us to this place?
Is it this god
who requires the movement,
the absence of movement,
the prefiguration of movement
only under his control?
If so,
what then is the reason
for these dancers,
these invocations,
the sight of these lesser gods
lining out the land?
How pitiable it is to reflect
upon that god, without grace,
without the sense of that small
beginning of movement,
where even the god
becomes another and not himself,
himself and not another.
So they must call you,
knowing you are intimate with stars;

so they must call you,
knowing different resolutions.
You sit in contemplation,
moving from line to line,
struggling for a city
free of that criminal act,
free of anything but the small,
imperceptible act, which itself becomes free.
Free. Free. How will the lines fall
into that configuration?
How will you clear this uneasiness,
posting your calculations and forecasts
into a world you yourself cannot enter?
Uneasy, at night,
you follow stars and lines to their limits,
sure of yourself, sure of the harmony
of everything, and yet you moan
for the lost harmony, the crack in the universe.
Your twin, I search it out,
and call you back;
your twin, I invoke
the descent of Nommo.

I say your vision goes as far as this.
And so you, Benjamin Banneker,
walk gravely along these lines,
the city a star, a body,
the seed vibrating within you,
and vibrating still,
beyond your power,
beyond mine.

Benjamin Banneker Sends His "Almanac" to Thomas Jefferson

Old now,
your eyes nearly blank
from plotting the light's

movement over the years,
you clean your *Almanac*
and place it next
to the heart of this letter.
I have you in mind,
giving a final brush and twist
to the difficult pages,
staring down the shape of the numbers
as though you would find a flaw
in their forms.
Solid, these calculations
verify your body on God's earth.
At night,
the stars submit themselves
to the remembered way you turn them;
the moon gloats under your attention.
I, who know so little of stars,
whose only acquaintance with the moon
is to read a myth, or to listen
to the surge
of songs the women know,
sit in your marvelous reading
of all movement,
of all relations.

So you look into what we see
yet cannot see,
and shape and take a language
to give form to one or the other,
believing no form will escape,
no movement appear, nor stop,
without explanation,
believing no reason is only reason,
nor without reason.
I read all of this into your task,
all of this into the uneasy
reproof of your letter.

Surely, there must be a flaw.
These perfect calculations fall apart.

There are silences
that no perfect number can retrieve,
omissions no perfect line could catch.
How could a man but challenge God's
impartial distributions?
How could a man sit among
the free and ordered movements
of stars, and waters, beasts and birds,
each movement seen or accounted for,
and not know God jealous,
and not know that he himself must be?

So you go over the pages again,
looking for the one thing
that will not reveal itself,
judging what you have received,
what you have shaped,
believing it cannot be strange
to the man you address.
But you are strange to him
—your skin, your tongue,
the movement of your body,
even your mysterious ways with stars.
You argue here with the man and God,
and know that no man can be right,
and know that no God will argue right.
Your letter turns on what the man knows,
on what God, you think, would have us know.
All stars will forever move under your gaze,
truthfully, leading you from line to line,
from number to number, from truth to truth,
while the man will read your soul's desire,
searcher, searching yourself,
losing the relations.

II

Entering New Mexico

Here, on the porch,
with lights going out
all over the neighborhood,
we can see the moon rise
from hour to hour,
as red as the flat,
round top of the stove.
Voices seem to harmonize
with the quiet belling of spoons and dishes.
The whole world lies softly
as though it waited for us
to gather here.
        I have a stub of a pencil,
        a nickel pad of paper.
        I sit close to the door
        where our light trickles out,
        listening to you.

These are the things I should get down.
Night time. Night town. You nurture me.

We are sailing now,
in an old car,
through flat, red sand,
through hills like scraggly beards
of brush and cactus.
Above us, the railroad staggers

uncertainly off into the hills,
and cuts among the wolves
and the dregs of beasts,
circling there at the ridges
in search of something
innocent and lost,
now and then turning their eyes toward us
as though we were.
        Crusted adobe houses rise like dust.

        We are approaching this desert city
        as though it were a mirage.

It is spring,
and the early morning sun burns us
until we stop along the way.
You try to split and milk the cactus,
while we stand like communicants,
        waiting, as if in prayer, to drink
        and rise, and turn toward the city again,
        feeling that we have taken
        some part of its body into us,
        have made another pact with it,
        going down toward its heart,
        tongued from lugging our desires to here.

But that water will never be enough.
Nothing that we could hack or dig from this earth
will ever be enough.
Black men will forever enter this dryness,
heading down where they will stop
in the heart of Albuquerque,
the noble name of a noble city,
where castanets still seem to crackle
around the black skirts of women
who would be noble,
where the ghosts of bright bay horses
spark the cobblestones in midday's quiet,
where everything, and everyone,

like the name, would still be noble,
still untouched by the step and touch
of the sons of slaves,
where no slave could ever go,
except by stealth, or riding in,
armed and assertive,
free himself and noble as the city,
ready to be changed by it,
or to change it.

Call,
and some pantalooned grandfather may come,
with the leisure of Virginia still on his tongue,
and greet you uneasily.
Here, he holds uneasy land
from which he pistols out intrusions,
and fights the common tread of cattle.
And though he greets you uneasily,
he holds this land for you,
walking it over and over,
as if his step would age and mellow it,
as if it could never be free of his weight
or the image of your coming.
Call,
and he will enter now,
and begin a ceremony
in which you take possession of this land,
where you will live,
where you will, he hopes, die,
and step one morning out of your shadows
to slit the throat of a lamb,
or perform some other ceremony
to pass this weighted land
further into our blood.
I call,
but cannot step here with ease.
Only the faint flow of my own blood
welcomes me here.
I walk unburdened only
because I walk on graves,

and hear Black voices
howl and importune gods
to strike me dead,
if I should pass on.
I call,
and hear my grandfather's voice
warring with those others
who scream to be released
from keeping the living graves of slaves,
to begin here to dig the graves of other slaves,
and move south for hills loaded with treasures,
ravishing every noble name,
to change it,
never to be changed by it,
and the dryness of this land would burn them
through my grandfather's flesh.
Forever, his weight on the land,
under a noble name, will frighten them.

We are still approaching it,
with the sun, tolling in the east,
pressing on our skin like cactus thorns.
There is a post that waits.
We stop.
An old woman,
whose dead daughter we recognize,
offers us bottled water.
We drink,
and push toward the noble city,
with death under us,
the beasts circling us,
and the sun opening my grandfather's eyes.

The Master of Names

1
Lately, you return,
walking the cold Saturday afternoon,

brushed and shaved and cocky in your sheepskin coat.
Remember?
How I walked in your hand?
The town had the look of a movie set
—Navajo from Gallup,
sporting their beads and blankets;
farmers, who could never account
for their farms, down in old Fords,
languishing like penniless widows
in front of hardware stores;
your mysterious cousins
searching out mysterious cousins,
blowing foam from their nickel beer.
Gone. And laughable. And unbelievable.
A history that is none,
that may never be written,
nor conceived again.

So I turn you up, and turn you out in that draft,
my orphan leaning at garden gates,
waiting for some swift vehicle
to appear and give you a different name.
            My father
            —all you should ever need—
            you are my father.
But not enough.
You have names and names of places embedded in you.
Often, alone and far from you,
I have conjured you up,
each name and reason for it
protruding from your image,
and have tried to pluck them from you.
But not enough.

2
Grown to contentiousness,
I walk crowded Saturday streets
so many miles and images
from where you left me.

Here, in Mexico,
I challenge all the eyes,
and knock against people
who come too close.
I go slowly.
The flower lady thrusts a bunch of dead mums
in my face and winks hysterically.
Two years, and I am still the one face
she thrusts her sorrows into,
the one heart she thinks she can pierce
with her hysterically winking eye.
Two years, and I am still her stranger,
the one name she doesn't need to remember.

3
It is always right
to name the place you move in,
to name yourself within it,
to name these people here now.
These people now.
Wherever you are,
they come upon you like an image
they cannot believe, but want to.
They come upon you as though only you
had the secret of names
—a prophet;
a wounded saint
wound in his own silence,
davening, feeling the pull
of some unspoken words
taking his suspended body into the earth;
a healer,
sitting through bare seasons at his rugs,
casting dice with demons
and making the dying live,
the broken whole again.
Almost, now, all paths have been closed.
Your bones almost a maze
even you cannot puzzle out.

Your voice escapes by ways
you may not find again.
Listen.
Birds chatter down from hidden nooks.
Saintly cattle tug into the open,
and turn toward their own freedom.
Waters dash their dead possessions
against the sand walls, Monday's wash.
Holy women beat by the river,
calling your name, calling back a power
you had almost forgotten.

4
Now, I conjure you again,
listening for the stir of angels,
the beat of birds' wings, in your voice.
Again you take my hand
in a whisper almost like silence,
and lead me into the mystery
of the names you carry like crosses.

The Faithful One

Every evening
you tugged me out of our neighborhood,
over the sooty viaduct,
down through the fast alleys
where I sucked up sin at first hand,
into that shingled church.
We always arrived first.
You dozed, or stared at the velvet
shawl draped over the podium,
as if you would decipher
something hidden from other eyes
in its stitched gold cross,
or if, by keeping your eye
fastened to that magic eye,
some saint would appear,

or some text would suddenly
be scrawled there.
I sat, leafing through song books
or discovering footnotes in the Bible,
and, now, and then, got up
to crack three flimsy boards
to toss them into the broken stove.
But, often, we sat through long hours,
running out of boards,
listening to each step in the street,
turning anxiously toward the still-closed door.
I see your face still,
uneasy at being left alone with a boy
too familiar to impress with your faith.
Your eyes glittered
with the unopened hymns in your head,
and you would turn away
into a solitary stillness
that Christ's very bones would break.

The Albuquerque Graveyard

It would be easier
to bury our dead
at the corner lot.
No need to wake
before sunrise,
take three buses,
walk two blocks,
search at the rear
of the cemetery,
to come upon the familiar names
with wilted flowers and patience.
But now I am here again.
After so many years
of coming here,
passing the sealed mausoleums,
the pretentious brooks and springs,

the white, sturdy limestone crosses,
the pattern of the place is clear to me.
I am going back
to the Black limbo,
an unwritten history
of our own tensions.
The dead lie here
in a hierarchy of small defeats.
I can almost see the leaders smile,
ashamed now of standing
at the head of those
who lie tangled
at the edge of the cemetery
still ready to curse and rage
as I do.
Here, I stop by the imitative cross
of one who stocked his parlor
with pictures of Robeson,
and would boom down the days,
dreaming of Othello's robes.
I say he never bothered me,
and forgive his frightened singing.
Here, I stop by the simple mound
of a woman who taught me
spelling on the sly,
parsing my tongue
to make me fit for her own dreams.
I could go on all day,
unhappily recognizing small heroes,
discontent with finding them here,
reproaches to my own failings.
Uneasy, I search the names
and simple mounds I call my own,
abruptly drop my wilted flowers,
and turn for home.

Family Reunion

Each time we meet,
you stare at my nose and eyes,

my cleft chin and high forehead,
and find an unfamiliar relative's traces.
And here you sit and thrust
the family photo album on me,
slip snapshots from the book,
clap them into my hand
the way you would a spoon in a baby's.

In a voice as high and lazy
as a mountain stream,
you enchant us with your own rewards.
Christian tales and triumphs leap from you.
I remember now the German drunk,
puking and sprawling down your ghetto alley,
lost, until he sailed into your house,
into your arms, into your pity
and his miraculous salvation.
Or you could tell us again
about the night you prayed all night,
having given your elders and saints
an ultimatum on the last request
your landlord made to you,
and woke the next morning to find
dollars as common as leaves on your table.

But why should I find this strange?
You have always had the gift
of looking in eyes,
and finding the touch of another there;
of stepping into the day's sun,
and being able to measure it
against every other;
of hearing a voice, and being able to coax
the speaker into echoes of himself, his selves,
his forgotten voices, voices he had never heard;
of calling your own name, and having it belled
back in tongues, being changed and harmonized
until it is one name and all names.

My saintly sister,
you are more than a woman,
more than the saintly body and soul
you desire for yourself.
You tell me,
but I know you do not walk
with Jesus or his saints,
nor do you grovel up the paths
you know he took.
You bless, save, rage
and turn yourself sinners from the temple.
Close to the book,
your eyes hint that I must be one of them.
Am I your final disgrace?
Is it the book alone itself
that has caught me moving away from you?
Among these images you know so well,
will you finally recognize me?

Baptism in the Lead Avenue Ditch

Ageless again,
I stand on this bridge of railroad ties,
and hear the lion's purr of trains
pausing between Chicago and Los Angeles,
the swish of steam,
the water whipped over their heads
to beat away the unconsecrated dust
of the deserts they pass through.
In the evening,
the grain-brick patio hotel
is a cathedral.
Pigeons roost like doves.
Navajo stroll under the naves,
robed in rugs and special beads.
Bells, boasting in a nearby adobe church,
calm the streets.
All travelers are held in silence.

This is the stillness
from which the night will come.
This is the stillness
from which all travelers will set out.

At night, I climb
the lonely cypress on the ditch bank,
and see our neighbor and her daughter
steal down the street,
barefoot, erect and balancing
bundles on their heads.
I hold my breath,
and try not to shake my tree house,
so high away I only hear
the melancholy slap of their hands,
and see them move from side to side,
dressing the cypress in their wet clothes,
passing and coming so close to each other
that I cannot tell them apart,
cannot separate them when they part.
Sometimes, they sing or moan in a language
that, even knowing them,
I cannot understand.

Now, at twelve,
I rise in the singing to confess.
All morning
every eye has been turned toward me,
the only one still unbaptized,
the only one who has never spoken,
the one who has kept the common light
in his own darkness,
sitting at the edge of the circle,
in shadows,
listening to the common life,
raveled, piece by piece,
into a story even I can tell.
I tell it now.
And now, at twelve,

I walk with the others
along the ditch bank,
out where the hoot of the trains
comes like the weak howl of a wolf.
Robed in white,
I step into the preacher's arms.

The best time to arrive
is just at sunrise,
come, cushioned in a coach,
along the mountains turning gray,
reddening out into a golden bronze.
The pale green cacti
line the land like crosses,
breaking at the top with pink and white flowers.
Even the buzzards,
diving after cow carcasses,
circling in the dark clouds,
caught in the halo of the still dying moon,
become beautiful.
I pass through this silence
again and again,
down into a silent valley
where the streets fill with Catholic bells,
and a donkey, loaded with pails,
moves from house to house.

You come into the stillness that remains,
at night,
and move in my river,
under my eyes,
and beat the shame from your clothes.
I lean down
and see my image in the water
and wonder, if I fell,
if you would robe me in a sheet
like a baptized boy,
or strip me and make me dance between you,
embracing one and then the other.

Was it here, at this point,
that I stepped into the preacher's arms?
Was it here, at this point,
that I caught the travelers' cathedral
moving into the darkness?
Night after night,
I take your voices and your bodies
back into my apprehension.
Mother and daughter,
night after night,
you beat my absence into the water.

Under this water,
all sounds come like thunder.
Familiar voices are lost.
God's man has his hand,
like a mask, over my face,
and still I suck up mud
and the taste of dry grass,
hear the deep tone of a bell
struck at the bottom of an ocean,
see fire chase down flashes of light,
feel my head swell.
I rise in pure water,
unashamed.
You see me,
and find me washed clean.

I lean down now
and push the thick mud away
to look for your footstep,
and think, with the first touch of rage,
that you may even be buried there.
I move, and return
to this city stripped of movement,
remembering that I entered its holiness,
by your side,
my fingers already filled with its death.

Night Ride

A lame horse moves
along the edge of a stream.
You are on his unsaddled back,
leaning into the soft buttocks
of a girl. Your arms extend
over the girl's thighs,
down around the horse's neck.
It is that rainbow evening
that comes at times
at the end of a gentle rain,
or at the end of a day so fierce
the crickets slug through their songs,
casting a sorcerer's eye at anyone
who would choose to move.
We should not be out past dark,
but no one can tell
if it is the sun or the moon
swaying in the hammock of the sky.
Off in the distance, I hear
the old folks create a canon
out of June bugs and junipers,
a lemonade, sweet peaches,
an empty moon over an empty garden.
I would follow you
down the muddy back reaches of the stream,
and wait when the horse stops
to lift his lame leg
and drop his heavy, straw-scented load,
and wait when you stop
to caress the horse's neck,
or to reason out the moon.
It is an old path we take.
The ridges rise with familiar bumps.
The same grass reaches out,
at the same spot, to tickle
the same fetlocks.
We approach that spot

where the girl will always tire,
and stretch her eyes back
in wonder
at all the covered distance.
She has no way of knowing
that the ride is not for her,
that we would capture our lame horse,
and set off along the stream,
and hope that this night
we would go far enough to hear
the moon whistle, or the grass croak,
or see the stream leave the borders
of earth like a woman
dropping her clothes,
go anywhere where the child's tired face
and the limp of the horse
can no longer contain us,
go anywhere where suddenly
we have grown into complete
understanding of the old folks' canon,
anywhere where the silent rainbow evening
has an answer to the crickets' song,
the gentle rain and a day so fierce
we dare not stare it down.

III

The Sense of Comedy: I

Imagine yourself,
in the suit of lights,
strolling toward the barrier
as if you, alone, knew
the purpose of your coming.
You are suddenly erect,
suddenly the keeper
of a deeper knowledge.
You are suddenly another,
and yet yourself,
suddenly in control
of your own fear.
Right on time
without a sense of time,
you extend your hand
to become less private.
You turn to the stillness
of all these old
identifications.
Everything must be won again.
A clear call.
And the comedy begins, again.

The Museums in Chapultepec

As round and soft as women,
they lie in the sun,

jealous coquettes tossing their kisses
under the feet of wire bulls,
Moore's concrete apples,
Giacometti's daggers.
Each afternoon, their cool chatter
freezes the flippant air,
and lovers, with warm eyes,
crawl to their sides with suspicious smiles.

Walking Chapultepec

These gardens circle up
and lose you.
You can hear the call
of forbidden hunting
going on under you.
Every tree has a dull eagle
fixing you with his impertinent eyes.
A man in white invites you to a fountain,
where another, with cancer-eaten jaws
quaking like the gills of a fish,
swims toward your leg.
You walk where nothing will release you,
and only your tenacious separateness
will convince you that you are dreaming.

Meeting Her in Chapultepec

I would take you
wherever the provinces
dabble in paseos,
and the Sundays run in the sun
to the rhythm of your heart.
There, I'd go beyond
the sophistication of your dress,
your city manners, all those
smart denials in your eyes.

I look at your rich, brown body,
your polished hair, a covey
of frightened blackbirds
grouped at your shoulders,
and I know my decomposed Spanish
isn't good enough.
How shall I enchant your ears,
and make those African eyes
lie softly on your cheeks?

I watch you move,
remembering dances,
and think that I can chant
in Yoruba Lucumí.

Inside Chapultepec Castle

Wherever you turn,
the sensual halls caress you.
Rose blood heroes snarl
and careen from the walls.
Jades and silver medals enchant your eye.
Fading amber tapestries and gold furniture
lie jealously next to them.

To get here,
you are pulled from below,
a baptized sinner
emerging from the water,
still trembling.

If you listen,
you can hear something
picking at this temple's heart.
If you are still,
you can see a girl,
as pure as a goddess

who would embrace the chosen,
lie down to caress it.

The Birthday

My mind,
a child's again,
is filled with all your gifts.
I sit all night,
with the light out,
my back to the darkness
and my eyes kept focused
at one point in the light,
as though I would fix
the face and name of a friend
absent even from my memory,
as though, by fixing that spot,
I could hold its heat against
the whispers of the shadows around me.
You have smiled,
and gone off to bed,
clamping your silence down
over the brilliant surprises
you hold for me.
Now, alone in the darkness,
I recall and memorize
the cards and telegrams
that came as early and polite
as unfamiliar guests,
their eyes picking out
my wrinkles and hesitations.
I am, it seems,
between one day and another,
between one age and another,
waiting in a time when only time
itself is the gift,
waiting in a darkness
I construct for the light.

How will I measure the movement now?
How will I know at what hour
to call you,
to clear this impossible stillness?
I am, it seems,
still moving toward the first light,
a chosen point to celebrate
the fact of moving still.
Before morning, you will be here,
and all strata and all mysteries,
and the music of the moon
that will establish me here
with your one impossible gift.

Jason Visits His Gypsy

This babbling gypsy
tosses beads at your feet,
and dares you to kneel
and grope before her.
You must keep your eyes
on her eyes,
on her hands,
on her body,
all at once,
and stop your ears, at first,
to her laughter and her talk.
It seems that she has been to school
near the dark edges of rivers;
or off at the end of a dog's howl
deep in a covered wood,
smashing her tambourines,
shoulder to shoulder,
with women who had learned tongues
in the middle of the ride;
or on some Sunday,
having walked into a clapboard church,
lured by the coded stomp

of a righteous man.
It is no trick of beans
that leap from point to point,
or the click of some unruly syllable
that catches you.
You couldn't kneel
to gather a string of fallen beads
that you could purchase
from a ragman's cart,
for these.
Reduced to stillness,
you wait.
And now, at evening,
in a soft rain,
the desert at the gypsy's door
falls and lies like a loose and motley cloth.
The babble about you stops.
Only the flame of the kerosene lamp moves.
And now, the gypsy moves,
raveling the sand into her sleeve,
past your still body,
past your stilled desires.
Long ago,
when you entered this room
with its scent of faded roses
and chicken fat,
with its shadows standing at attention
among the rasping curtains,
you signed with your eyes
the pact, from which you could not
be released into anything but silence,
from which you could not be released
until you had been cleaned
of all desires but one.
The gypsy knows what you have forgotten,
knows even what you would forget,
knows the rhythm of raveling
the sand into the dark and closeness
of a space, where only she can live,

waiting for those who need to kneel
again before the chosen and the strange,
leaving the unlucky omens of their lives
at the door,
to listen for distant voices and the knock
of ancestors grown weary from neglect.

The Death of an Unfamiliar Sister

Your body,
measured out by moans,
lies, facing the unused patio,
in a room stripped of all
but your white-gowned bed.
All day and night
the neighbor women shawl themselves,
and enter as quiet as awed lovers,
and beat themselves into remorse
and love of you.
I have been out of your life for years,
but find myself, miraculously found,
here on the floor among them,
unable to pray, or shout, or cry,
unable even to enchant myself
with the dark and unintelligible oaths
the women utter into the stones.
Once, in a sullen Mexican town,
an old scholar drew himself even,
for a moment, with the Mexican horizon,
and snapped his heart against it.
For two days,
I lay against his bed,
his uncommon smell and ruffled skin
so close I could not move
unless I changed them.
The women came
and, just as these,
sang in the pain of their memories

of death, in their future knowledge
of death, regarding me
as though I were one of their own,
or had passed, through my own pain,
into the perfect death before us.
I did not pray, nor shout, nor cry,
nor enchant myself even then,
but sat as comfortably with him
as I do here with you.
I turn my eyes to the women,
moving toward the holy expression
of their entrance here,
and know they do not lie,
know that they are right
to thrash themselves into remorse.
We will be here for hours,
in the dark,
your bed the candle
by which we watch
the changes in each other.

Sister, I have walked to here,
over this compassionate dust,
to wait in this moving light
for your last movement,
the one movement
that these others will not
and cannot understand.
Their singing fervently rises;
it is the pitch and tone of our
forgotten spirits,
rising over this unfamiliar room.
Caught in it,
I ask for the blessing you cannot give,
and I know you will leave me alone at last,
with only this earth's touch, the women's silence,
but know, too, that the lid will close,
unveiling my one imperishable star.

Homecoming

Guadalajara–New York, 1965

The trees are crystal chandeliers,
and deep in the hollow
a child pits its voice
against the rain.
The city screams its prayers
at the towers in the distance.

Those guitars again.
And the Catholic mantis
clutching at the sky,
a pearl of a city,
cuando se duerme.

Subway blue boys
now ride shotgun
against my freedom and my fears.
Pistols snap like indignant heels,
at midday, and we stand at the docks,
singing a farewell we'd soon forget.

Hymns resound against that dome
entre la fiesta y la agonía.
Worms feed on its concrete,
or we pluck them out of bodies.

But time to forget.
Or remember the easiness
of leaving easy loves,
disappearing
in the arms of secret dreams.

We'll sit at the end
of a banquet board,
and powder our tutored wigs,
flip the pages of gentility
in the rainy season.

English lessons over tea
for the price of memory.

Il mio supplizio
è quando
non mi credo
in armonia.

They say the time
is not much different.
The strange and customary turns
of living may coincide.

In Mariachi Plaza
travelers sing elegies to the beauty
of revolutions and tranquillity.

From the opposite side of the river,
coming in, the skyline seems scrubbed
and pointed ominously into the darkness.

I walk through the market,
kissing colors in a murmur
of self-induced petition.

Two spires,
lying against the night,
are suddenly armed to sail.

The water foams against the bottom,
the way it looked when I left
that dying city.

Only a turning to feel the bark
slope off into the night,
with a promise to return.

Un dì, s'io non andrò sempre fuggendo
di gente in gente, mi vedrai seduto

su la tua pietra, o fratel mio, gemendo
il fior dei tuoi gentili anni caduto.

From line to line,
from point to point,
is an architect's end of cities.

But I lie down
to a different turbulence
and a plan of transformation.

IV
Second Conversations with Ogotemmêli

Ogotemmêli

1
Last night
I heard you call again,
or heard myself,
calling in the rain.
Now, when I wake,
and trace the fat, wet sheep
nibbling at the castle on the hill,
I seem to see you sitting,
patient and parched,
ready to read me into God's love,
into your perfect love,
into my love for you.

2
But your voice comes clearly
only where I found you,
and so I come again
into these mountains,
and scrape the narrow streets and pyramids,
to find you, robed in brown,
perched on a stone,
pinching your leather snuffbox.
You tilt your head like a bird,
and wait until my step stops.
You squint and sniff,

as though you would brush away
some offensive smell or movement.
I wait for you to speak,
and know I will read your voice,
and read the silence of your eyes,
and know, when no light comes,
you will lead me into the darkness.

3
Father, your eyes have turned
from the tricks of our visible world
to move within you,
where God moves,
where the seed moves,
where we move,
where the word moves among us,
into this visible world
and into its perfect order.
So I arrive,
at the end of this, my small movement,
moving with you, in the light you control,
learning to hear the voice in the silence,
learning to see in the light
that runs away from me.

Beginning

Alive again,
you wait in the broken courtyard.
Oblivious of its dung heap and ashes,
you sit once more,
near the main facade,
and listen for this unfamiliar footstep.
In the village
young men tell me to learn to wait,
to speak softly, to grow lightly
into my demands.
Facing you,

I cannot tell what word,
or form of that word, I shall face.
In this light,
in this stillness,
the leaves lie hushed,
even the burdened water rests;
all the restless members of the body
I must learn to understand
stop, and tiptoe as well to the wall,
where your silence promises speech.
Your silence promises
the warm vapor of wisdom,
promises to lead me
into that first and perfect order,
broken, and cast
into perfect order again.
I will learn these secret movements,
will learn to hear the Fox step
in my most secret corners.
Always sinful, always just,
I pull against myself
and come to sit, here,
where you pull me apart
and order my very bones again.
Even in your silence,
we have begun.
I sit before you,
wondering what is in the space
between us.
You have me in your hands.
I trust you.

The First Word

Though perfect,
God was lonely, you say,
and chased down our mother earth
to break his own perfect order.

You stop,
and turn your head for my objections.
I nod you into speech again,
drawing a little away in my mind,
to that encounter in a dark wood,
the Florentine, his Roman guide,
arguing out the first sense of justice.
Knowing them, following their painful steps
up the difficult mountain,
I follow your words
into a clarity they do not reveal.
That other god, less bold,
cast his failings
into the naked heir,
watched the man
naming what was most strange,
learning to touch and break a world
from which the god would soon retreat.
For us, there was only
this feckless jackal,
lurking near the borders of speech,
too lonely, too destructive,
to bear the compassionate descent
of the holy twins,
to watch them seal their presence
into our mother's skirt,
the craft revealed in the spirit,
lingering forever in the undulating line.
I conjure this beneficent act
and think it strange to find
these green and serpent figures,
red-eyed, fork-tongued,
redeeming God, redeeming you,
waiting in this brilliant and distant
courtyard to redeem me.
What justice do I understand?
What craft is the craft of the first word,
weaving speech into spirit,
spirit into the sign of your very presence?

I look at you, blind here before me,
and know you sense the tremor in my silence,
know you will not go on
past this uncertainty
without a sign, a word
that wrenches me from that dark wood,
into this, my own shadowed world.
Fox of my memory,
Fox of my contradictions,
you descend, too, already fleshed,
like the God,
bearing the weight and depth
of that first movement,
that first word,
that first act,
bearing the weight of that God
who could never be absent.

The Second Word

The seventh is always the wise one,
a bully boy,
a thief,
speaking,
speech itself.
He makes his mouth
a weaver's reed,
his teeth a warp,
a shuttle,
his blunt nose
blocks the process.
Now, a woman spinning
recalls his image.
She sits over this skin,
sun spun,
the smithy's bellows,
spinning the sun on a spindle.
Here, at noon,

locked in this court,
I do not see the woman,
moving her bright gossamer.
She sits
on the other side of the wall,
moving her arrow again
toward God,
dipping her fingers
in the calabash ash.
So it is this fertilized sun,
this ram I cannot see,
licking at her fingers,
playing in the dark corners
of your eyes.
All this must be done by day,
even the deed
of the Onndom weavers.
And down by day,
Nommo entered the anthill,
leaving a sign.
Taken in hand,
into the woman,
speaking to herself,
the seventh one, speaking,
moved into the earth,
dying,
or pretending to die.
Even this thief
leads us into purity.
Even this spirit,
frightened of the touch
of flesh and blood,
leads us back to the woman.
She feels the threads
and touches the earth.
She cannot hear.
But I listen as you say,
"The craft of weaving
is the tomb of resurrection,

the marriage bed
and the fruitful womb."

The Third Word

Strange to think
that this seed
being broken there
on the smithy's anvil
will burst to stars,
design a man,
lead us back to the God,
designing and undoing
this world from his own design.
Father,
where did you get that iron bow?
From Papa Ogun, I know.
Now, place the day,
Legba, swift as the flutter
of a bird's wing,
streams,
with Damballa's consent,
over miles, over years,
over wars, over anguish,
over desire,
to lend you this arrow.
You say he struck the moon
and wound the gossamer
round the shank
to form a spindle-whorl.
The first ark fell
from that first figure,
dancing himself,
into himself,
perfect yet less than perfect.
Here, at your side,
each name and figure
being born again,

I hear the bird
sing to the blood,
the kɔ kɔ
of the koro drum,
the kɔ kɔ
of korabra,
the lope of the antelope,
the movement of Nommo.
"Bear in mind,"
my teacher said,
"that death is a drum."
And even here,
in the sunlight,
when the smith strikes the ground,
I hear in the ark's descent,
in its perfect order,
the echo of unworldly death.

The Smith

"Silent the footfall,
Soft as cat's paw,
Sandalled in velvet in fur . . ."
Today, I wake and sing to you.
In my own waking,
beyond the dream,
I have seen the webbed hand
of the Water Spirit descend.
This sound is always over us.
Master of Water,
stand here as God's witness,
stand here in support of our prayers,
stand here, in our quarrels,
strike the rocks with your holy note.
Like me, you say,
he entered with only his desire,
his need, to search and take
the earth that God had given him,

working by day
to forge the love again
that was almost lost.
Nommo of the lake,
you swim sandalled in velvet;
you breathe the water awake.
I hear your twins chant dirges.
They hold their hammers
as high as the ark.
Laid out like this,
the earth, listening too,
recovers its force.
Laid out like this,
the victim, split from navel
through sex, unravels the stars,
the yala of the egg.
Circumcised one,
God has put these pearls,
this water, into your hands.
So I am here in these dry
mountains, this burning court,
with this blind saint.
I count the kɔ kɔ kɔ
of your stroke.
I wait for you to rise
and give me a name.

The Sanctuary

The rain will tell us
where to stop,
how to arrange this body.
Here is the door,
where I still see
a tuft of skin.
Like Thomas,
my finger itched
until you came with me,

this far,
further than you would go.
We enter,
under the primal field,
the tomb of Lébé.
I face this old man
who will not speak.
Like a baby to him,
I have no name.
He knows nothing belongs to me,
knows I have no pot,
cooking with cool water.
The turtle, casting a sorcerer's eye,
circles me
and moves away into the hollows
I cannot enter.
This hook my eye catches
becomes a ram,
becomes two hands,
becomes the object of my prayers.
Pebbles,
cowries,
waters of torrents and marshes.
The hands hold the moisture in.
The corn grows,
is spread on the roof,
grows again,
as though it grew from the weeping
of these ancestors' eyes.
In the half-light
and the strangeness,
with the sound of this patriarch's voice,
the hands move
to call for rain,
to call for the making
of the world again,
the descent,
the guardian of space,
that body

where the seventh son will rest.
Old man, so far,
I cannot wear this dead man's bones,
these covenant stones,
cannot bargain with his nails.
Old man, so far,
you keep my tilling land,
my spirit and my name.
Old man, so far,
the darkness of this tomb
defies my eyes,
and the turtle's silent stroll
about this place
comes to my ears
like the breaking of the earth
in a distance
I am still crossing.

Lébé

Dyon, the digger,
searching in the primal field,
dug this serpent and the covenant stones.
Turning up life and death like that,
his wisdom told him the land was good.
So it would come just like that,
when the earth wouldn't fit anymore,
when men would sit long hours in the sun,
carping at their neighbors' gifts,
when even the spirit of a nameless child
was uneasy.
Time to carry these sorrows,
these dreams,
away into pure air,
into that spot
where the God would come again.
Then Dyon, the digger, led them,
stopping at Amani,

placing the first altar
under a square stone
covered with mortar,
breaking the earth from the altar
and sending the others on.
"And the Lébé serpent,
omnipresent,
one yet many like a God,
followed each founder."
Now, here, the Hogon
holds the man and land in place,
holding his sweatless body
erect on my grandfather's back.
Though he is copper, sun and water,
he wears the moon,
the shell of the egg,
the ancestors' tombs,
the seed and the soul of woman,
on his head.
I have seen him now at Arou,
slice the victim's liver,
pray,
turn and fly into the sanctuary
to return with the perfect word.
Oh, my blind saint,
I fear your laughter
when I tell you
that I have visions
of his iron lance
coiling at my own feet,
feel myself, a postulant,
trembling into knowledge of God's body,
knowledge of his naming.
I have entered without knowledge,
sandalled and disguised,
to be stripped of myself,
stripped of uneasy visions.
At night, now,
when I lie with my wife,

covered and turned on my side,
the bed is his tomb
trembling under us,
my funeral pall,
from which, you say,
my name and tilling land
will come again.

Biṅu

So, in the spirit
of the act,
of the art,
in the rite
I have before me,
I call death
an imitation.
Dyongu, the hunter,
the warrior,
dances at the dama.
I stand among these masks
with a place at last,
watching the old men
rise again,
watching them appear
in the astonishment
of our need.
They go and come again
without knowing death.
They go and come again
when the seed is cast,
when the corn
is plucked from the ground.
Living, we free them;
dying, we learn
how we are freed ourselves.
I preen myself,
a dreamer,

too intimate with death,
going by night
over gorges, through marshes,
looking for the stone,
my own revelation,
my Biṅu.
My craft is the craft
of the word I say
you do not understand.
But you know my craft,
its direction and element,
the god, lying under my every move,
better than I.
So I come here,
through them, to you,
envious of your ears
attuned to some animal's
tentative step,
or the subtle shake
of the wing of a bird,
the design
that escapes my eyes.

Altars and Sacrifice

1
Even this is movement.
I see each point and body change,
and come again.
They move as my eyes would have them,
yet move and change as the light,
and the word, direct them.
On that point of the world,
the blood divides,
caught by the god,
caught in the crucible
of the victim's life,
where the word will return.

I have asked you to choose me,
knowing myself impure,
neither living nor dead.
Arrogant like this,
I have begun to design
my own god.
Arrogant like this,
I am sure of the perfect
divination,
the release from myself,
into the words you cannot say,
into the act you cannot perform.
Surely, I can argue
that something has been lost.
Surely, my father
will make me an infant again,
casting for my name,
consecrating my newborn altar,
stringing the god's teeth
on a necklace around my neck.
But how will I stand?
Am I the babe or the vicar
of the god?
This morning, it is clear,
the divination tosses me back.
I stand,
not wholly lost,
not fully chosen,
and watch the act played out.

2
It should be winter here.
It should be time
for the warmth of blood,
for the warmth of the breath
to enter and contain us.
This incomplete one
has been chosen again.
Above him,

God's vicar sits like the rain
and sends his messenger to earth,
into these shadows,
with the instrument
as sharp as God's teeth,
with a need like ours.
Half-man, half-woman,
the victim will stand,
his eyes fixed
on the suffering of the world,
to be split from navel through sex.
When it is done,
the incomplete one will take
the crucible of the word into himself,
speaking, to release that greater part
for which we wait.
Now, the God will turn
this blood into stars,
beginning that small movement again,
moving again into the memory
of his first gift,
his first destruction,
moving again
toward that first naming,
that first delegation of powers.

3

You wear, I know,
these emblems now,
these covenant stones to design
your own prefiguration.
Even when the Fox steps
in your most secret corners,
even when the seed
is threatened by his step,
you parcel out the word,
the resurrection,
without mourning.
In God's winding,

in his center,
I learn of the movement of stars,
of time and seasons,
learn how to inhabit this space.
This broken body fills again
with the memory of fathers,
their slow recovery,
my slow movement
into this ordered world.
Father, standing here,
watching this broken and fulfilled design,
I find my arrogant impurity
shakes to the kɔ kɔ kɔ
and the rhythm of the smith.

The Dead

The dance grows
from the sleeping eye,
the image of death.
I see the Fox
creep into God's chamber,
ignorant of death,
believing his father dead.
I see the God himself dance
and turn about himself
like the stars he moves,
turn into himself
like the dead he caresses.
Still, my dead go rootless,
without names,
without altar pots.
Often, I frighten myself,
listening, here in the courtyard,
in your silences,
for a flutter,
a sign, in your hesitation,
in the movement of your hand.

At night,
I hear you call,
and snap myself awake,
and tell myself it isn't time,
that you wouldn't leave me
here at the entrance,
hardly able to speak the names
of those who return,
out of season, with you,
by night.
No, I will not face it,
though I know that even
the god died unfinished,
yet he moves still
in the shape of the Sigui,
moves still
when we stumble in drink,
the living dead.
But it is not enough
to sip the knowledge
of our failings.
The masks dance
on this small point, and lead
this soul, these souls,
into the rhythm
of the eye stripped of sight,
the hand stripped of touch,
the heart stripped of love,
the body stripped of its own beginning,
into the rhythm
of emptiness and return,
into the self
moving against itself,
into the self
moving into itself,
the word, and the first design.
Now,
I designate myself your child,
nani I can name,

and see this fire, burning between us,
moving like water,
caressing these birds,
these stones,
your sandalled feet,
and the sound of your voice.
All these will have their place,
twin and totem,
earth and warrior.
All these will gather at my dama.
I sit here with you
and my hands learn the feel
of cloth and seeds and earth again.
I trade these cowries.
I learn these relations.
This is the moment
when all our unwelcome deaths
charge us to be free.
And I wear these covenant stones,
a sign,
that your world moves still.

Explications/Interpretations

For
Harold Bloom
and
Robert Hayden

Tensions and Resolutions

At dawn, the pips
are piped up by the birds
to watch the night woman
tune and take her lover's arms.
It is such a small
and almost silent beginning
that there seem to be no measure,
no assertions of stars, fire bursts,
prophetic serpents, clamor of shells
ripped from the river, no whisper
of wind to husk in the wet field.
We say each dawn is a bond
of your own beginning,
the ground established for our
movement from dawn to dawn.
Clearly, we must remember,
just at that moment—
the confusion of light
of first star and first sun.
Every appearance
rises in its clarity of bones,
flesh, leaf, trunk and skin,
turns toward its proper placement of light,
the space it places clearly about its body.
Each moment lives two lives in its act.
Each act caresses
the moment it remembers,
and the moment it desires.
Outside our love,
the night woman,
image of our flesh-gifted saints,
lingers, silent and serene,
to hear the women
beat their earthy bowls,
and worry us with time.
Spirit-skilled,
we still cannot escape

these solid claims,
the inhabitable body sprung
from its debt of stillness.
Here, we live, at rest,
a throng of acts,
propped up by the constant caress
of a movement,
search in the light of first star
and first sun,
for a sound and an act
to acknowledge.

Polarity's Trio

Zones

In the city of eternal spring
I awake in a mist and lay
my arepa on the buttered air.
Then, in the zone of healing water,
I take my jangada and ride,
Maracucho, on the pulse of your blood,
the black *ir-venir* of the bay's clock.
Jangada, sloop, coracle, skiff, a shell,
we all have nets, bright silver shawls,
to enfold the water at dawn.
We rehearse an old Mexican prayer;
the fish kick and sprinkle the shore.
This is the bitter beginning
of a flood day, or a drought,
the ticking of the jaguar's teeth.
Plain marble murmurs—
dress my master in liquiliqui,
twist the bulls' tails, dance,
four in four,
to the harp and the snake's bones.
I am entranced by Maracaibo,
steel leg in the air—
plunge, the exaltation.
All day, from dawn, I scrape
the soft scales of little fish,
or pluck the veins and little bones
of my brown mother's body,

or cuddle my own weaver's call
in the market.
I reward my hunger with a toothpick of hide.
I will sleep,
and think of the liquid black hardness
that bleeds the marrow of my bones.
Some god will flood the ocean's night
with an echo of my morning.
We work,
with the body's changing firmness,
to repair the constancy of things.

Corrida

Trumpets at four o'clock
seal the rain in the Plaza.
All capes are darker.
Spangles choke their novilleros,
who wait in the blood the water soaks
from the Plaza's shallow blood urn.
The rain eases nothing.
Left-handed bulls shoot for the center,
hook the guards, tumble blind horses.

In the infinity of one faena,
one cherub learns the rigor of space.
Pic and call.
The night horn.
The daemon flourishes his flags.
Hovering at the wing,
he would ride the loose gestures
into the cherub's body,
ride down into the nerve song we ask of it.
All in a circle of fire,
angels fan a holy anger higher.
What can be purged is not the final act.
Death must surely enter, but no eye
can shape, from the start, that end,

no eye will welcome it.
We ride the daemon's back
to feel the weight of vision,
to balance the thrust of time.

In the eye, clouded by injury,
the texture of maguey is rose,
a caravan of gypsies is at rest.
If we buckle and kneel on the sword's point,
it is to acknowledge the source
                                        of another strength.
We have come here, under a Basque sign,
to be used up. We will be dragged
into a dark corner, under the Plaza,
to be cut and sent, living,
                                        into the poorest pots.

San Diego's Dispossession

Clouds fall in San Diego's yard,
finca shape, black liquid
in its pores.
An Aztec urn with cross
struts in its center.
Four pyramidal points surround the cross;
a chevron-hatched phallus holds it erect.
Unnamed, disguised, covered with moss,
the emblem is still a crown of thorns.
San Diego, Saint James,
the Lord's brother,
lightbearer of the mountains,
a pilgrim haunts your open door.
A horse-drawn dickey leaves
to pierce the clouds,
returns, to pierce the silence.
In the New Hampshire woods
there are four nights of moon
and a silence that never leaves.

All fields pray to be inhabited.
The birdmate follows and falls
on his mother-to-be,
in the dark thickets by the road.
This, you hear, is the shriek of love,
the bird people pecking at the water
of joy, the misery of a day's eternal bell.
Ask him, who tolls your height,
for the knowledge
in the wail of our pleasure,
the lilt of our obligation.
It is right that Our Lady of the Field
is figured in stone.
At the height of summer,
when the second eye is figured in its white robes,
Jacob will borrow this pagan wind and rain.
We worship the clarity
of the figure that does not appear.
The clean tree calls us down
to lie in the deep woods,
under the rain that tangles us in green.
The cold light of this tonsure
will possess us, when we return
and fall unseen.

Harmony's Trio

The Continuing City: Spirit and Body

I resist the image of a god,
tipped on a leg, a lonely double blur and egg.
If I accept the direction of the east,
a heavy star will seed me, the light
will lay its solid lines about me;
I step through these to measure what appears.
Soon, it will be difficult to tell
who led me from the derry of jackals
into this habitation of song.
Now, I must accept my descent,
and rise with my stone back set
to diminish the dust hard hills.
I work all things in flesh—
acacia for the veins of my hearth,
another body's blood hide for my bed.
I twirl my pots from the earth's second skin.
Day into day, I walk to the line of my own skin.
Perhaps this city I walk
unfolds from oak roots,
or is unleashed by water
bellied near the deepest rocks;
it may unfurl from crystal or from granite.
I grow into the craft of glass,
and curry all my iron and steel
into the glandular chains of my home.
Where now is the city my eye rules?
How can this body last,
if it must come?

How can the eye rule a body
of constant change?
I measure and control my god's intent
and call it flesh,
the visible intention of sight.
This is the city I consider and compare,
the balance I desire. All else is blindness,
all other speech is numberless.
I have it
that Prophesie shall faile,
and Tongues shall faile,
and Knowledge shall vanish,
and so I try to make a body
contain a certain knowledge,
to free the light to set clear figures in space.
The space around all bodies must be named.
Now, the singer sits to work
this age-old figure into flesh.
Craftsman of the ear and hand,
he acts between the real and all our names;
he finds his image in the act,
his faith in his inability to rub
the god's body
into a bright and lasting city.
I take the earth beneath me
as parchment and intention,
memory and project of all
movement it contains.
I am the dark glass of some other spirit
who will know me, the bone sound
of some other resonant body.
I await my completion in a strange house,
my soul's rags falling in pride from its door.

The Measure

I continue in my gbariye.
All things along my path are clean and white.

I have set out on a flute's quiet wave
in search of my dark love.
Divination and division mark my road;
yet, if I turn from left to right,
I walk the same straight path.
I carry the wine of salt water in my bag
to the crossroads of honey and milk.
I am puffed up and charged with the thought
of my own separation. From light to light,
I continue while the light lasts.
The light rests on my walking pole.
I continue.

If ever you marry, remember,
there is a festival of light
on every island, a garden
where the women gather in white
to turn to the sound of a king's song.
If you ask why the queen is silent,
the dance is ended.
Then only a boy on the cross of roads
can find the blue stone of wisdom,
the lourie feather of love in the flesh.
You ask me to enter the chamber and sing,
groan, inexpressibly, groan, ascend,
descend, leap from the ash of your pillow
to the calm light of your grave.
I am too certain of the measure of these days.
Sojourner and guest, I continue;
I polish new stones from old;
I am at hail's end in the deep wings
of the city; I would return to the feast.
I continue.

I have learned to see a seed as act,
a word as a gift of perfection.
The hand that slips the abundant
seed into the darkness of earth
extends from my body.

I have always wanted to ask—
who speaks, who moves and who returns
when the I is hidden in the paradigm?
I have learned to accept my presence as act,
my act as a placement of time.
I hold now, by my presence,
to have held the first light,
and, in my imperfection,
to have held the vision of my own absence.
This is the one you marry, so lightly.

Each figure, now, twins and untwins us.
We say we can be brought, in white,
to the marriage bed, under a reed's bass,
and settled, limb to counter limb,
with our desert's necessities.
I wait, as always, at the crossroads
to be led into the city.
I desire your double journey.
I ask your name.
I continue.

The Sunset's Widow

Ridge hair   runny nose
snuff-dipped teeth
she loves lilacs and wears
snake garters
                        At sunset
she sits on an egg box
spits
at the evening's hesitation
                        You find her
in summer   quarreling
with the wind   but it isn't the wind
alone
that knows her voice

Witness now her voice
                            her sign

the serpent cactus spined
and smooth as oil
caressing her neck

Witness now
the pattern of her body's lines
the curves and undulations
the sweep
        toward the hard case
                        of her garters
                        the hard eyes
that would be there
that would hold you
                as still as a bird

Root   lovely woman
the love of a bitter root
tea fangs   and shells
a bitter egg
        that will not hatch
all serpentine and green
but the lilac   but the lilac
determines here
the rough cast and bitter root
of everything   of everything
but the witness

But the witness
determines
the rough cast
and bitter root
        of the evening's hesitation
        spit   an egg box
snake garters at sunset
weary lilacs
snuff   snot   and the line
dying
        at the crown
                of the head.

The Body

(MAN)
1
All day we charge,
the sun toward its tomb.
I canter after you,
a buck myself,
placed by your coat and flaming hair,
in the green darkness around us.
Up ahead, we hear
the crack and spit of rifles,
the momentary whistle of trees,
a branch split
and then the silence.
All these antlered heads we track
sprout like bushes or ferns,
trying pitifully
to withdraw into the earth,
hoping their silence and stillness
will take us past and off
to an enemy,
moving fiercely, tangled
in the labyrinth
we make by moving ourselves.
With the rifle, you lead;
I follow with a knife,
feeling myself too well-armed,
shy at its touch
against my leg.
We stalk these hills
for my childhood,
and the solitary, crooked cook
who could not kill,
our penance to prove
that nothing is right
but blood and the memory of it.
So I know
there will be no return

until we have drained the sun
of all its light.
Still, smoothly,
you push ahead, and circle,
and move as though the measure
had been set by God,
or some forgotten brother.
Perhaps it is memory.
Perhaps it is this presence
of the palpable deer
within me,
the breath, heart level and unafraid,
eyes the light of a movement,
the search
that will not end in death alone.
We wait in the silence now
for the one that has chosen us.
This, now, is the limit of our movement,
a point in the restless plane
of bushes and ferns,
dead trees, one body
moving toward this closed space.
And this is the point
of a remembered space,
focus of feeling,
focus of the steps concerned,
the mask with which I dress your face.
With all these poles
and definitions set,
I see you settle in the darkness.
Alone, I listen
for an unfamiliar step,
and know it may not come.

(WOMAN)
2
Pinched, at the peak of summer,
between two rivers,

I stroll to this corner
and wait for you.
You know the telling time,
and come just at the right time,
walking from the other shore,
along 125th,
your robe so white
the lights defile it,
your hair hidden under a veil,
a Magdalene, or conjure woman,
smelling of snakeroot oil.
No one knows from where you come,
but we hear your first step,
feel the deliberate sternness of your dress,
moving toward us.
No one would take your corner.
No one would move within that field,
at that hour; no one
would move from it.
You come,
and even the snap of dice subsides;
cars, bars, lights and we ourselves
move without sound.
We pass and pass,
as though we were linked to you,
linked to your voice,
linked again to the rhythm of your body,
the set and ground of all movement,
the point and measure
that serves this source and ground
on which you move.
Say I wait and come here,
bearing the weight of a city
without measure,
to nestle under your left eye.
Say I snuggle here
in the cuddle of a crowd
you caress and scorn,
trying to measure its light,

trying to determine what form I take,
or lose, in its brief regard.
Often, you descend the box,
and chalk a circle and cross,
another eye, at our feet.
You chant and scream in another tongue,
and stop and listen for echoes.
You know we will not speak.
You need the tense presence of our bodies
to filter the sound,
to filter the light,
to touch and recognize
the achievement of your voice
—that other god,
who takes the deliberate measure
of a city that will not fit.
Night after night,
you stand at this corner,
and beg us not to be afraid.
You turn and step along a line
in each direction,
as though you were dancing,
as though the dance
would establish some living point,
design a body,
rising at that point
to enter and shake you
until you were changed
or our eyes admitted it so.
This is a gathering of Baptist boys,
Rollers, witches and saints,
a choir of the fallen
who have not been released,
who would grovel under the lash
of your tongue,
to return, in the heat of your eye,
to a presence we may not remember,
but know.

(THE MAN'S SOUL)

3

Fishermen out there in the dark—O you
Who rake the waves or chase their wake—
Weave for him a shadow out of your laughter
For a dumb child to hide his nakedness . . .
—Christopher Okigbo, "Lament of the Drums," III

Long before dawn
the fishermen wake
in the season,
take their three-tiered
lunch buckets,
their straw hats
and quexquémetls,
and wind,
barefoot and secretive,
through the maze and stillness
of this rough-grained town,
down to the lake.
All night
I have lain,
crutched in an old cockleshell,
crushing sand crabs
that dart after the searchlight
(their hint of sun),
listening to the late serenades
tuck the lovers into yesterday.
I watch the fishermen
take their small boats,
load them with nets
and push off for the deep
part of the lake.
Slowly, one by one,
they row away, and move
until they are strung,
dark and silent birds,

nesting on the surface.
At this hour,
the water, a spider's web, accepts
their movement and their stillness.
The cave welcomes the boy
with the right amount of light.
I return and turn to them
again each morning,
and wait for that moment
between the movement and the stillness
when the men, stretched out,
seem to be praying,
listening and testing the depths
for a murmur of discontent.
They do not turn to each other,
or call, or gesture,
but rise, one body awaking,
and drop their nets,
looking into the water,
listening again,
taking the task step by step,
fixing the morning
with these real movements and signs.
Each day, the movements
are only shadows of themselves.
The men, clothed just so,
are memories of themselves.
They take the water and return,
and do not know, or care,
that I watch and work
my own order.
They have their own,
and float back into the light,
to wind their ropes around their waists,
and dance their nets and fish
into the hungry arms of the women,
come from the maze and stillness of the town,
waiting on the shore.

(THE WOMAN'S SOUL)

4

You sit on your stool
at the head of your rug,
dip, palm and rake these beans,
and pick the stones and burrs away.
With the right touch of sun,
the right angle and measure
of your touch, these brown
and melancholy sprouts
are cowries, shells,
sea-tinged pearls,
the infinite eye of God.
At dawn
you clap your children
into dun brown coats,
as though you would disguise them,
and send them along the roads,
over moss-covered fences,
into any corner and cave
that will yield a bean.
You wash your rug
and brush your dress,
and shake and brush your hair.
You move in the early light,
singing, and plotting the place
where each bean will fall,
each color lit by the space
it will take,
each space lit
by the presence of the bean.
You enter the market
and sit erect, waiting
for the boys' return,
the brown and threadbare sacks
to be set just at your right hand.
This is little enough to start
your singing again,
little enough to have you call

and welcome the timid foragers
close to the circle and sparkle
of your rug, the plucked seeds,
stars spread out and radiant.
Pulled from the earth,
they show their signs,
until you pinch
their vestiges of navels.
Cleaned now,
they take their final form
upon your rug,
dipped, palmed and raked into light,
their skins already beginning to wrinkle
and break away from your love.

Twenty-Two Tremblings of the Postulant
(Improvisations Surrounding the Body)

I

1 (ARM)

Candles, ribbons and a cross
                        gaud my sash and tux.
My derby and white gloves
stand erect over my coffin.
This music greets death,
                the winking, prancing lid
that lies
                still with longing
                        for a bone that has flared,
                        an embryo with the power to appear.

2 (FOREARM)

Between
        the hand and these long bones,
eight bones,
as small as covenant stones,
lie and turn about.
Articulate grip,
such force,
                a god's delicate disguise,
alters the marks of the altar stones.

3 (SHOULDER BLADE)

Companioned pity, doubt's
double contradiction
                reveal
the body's incisive intent.

Cut and placed just so,
they would seem to turn
                        from sun to moonrise,
each state and figure carefully defined.
Caulicle scribes of heaven's notice,
they graph love's
                irradiant positions.
Under the head's strict account,
the body's lost arc and arch
count the platelets in love's force.

4 (FINGERS)
for Albert Ayler

Patron of a dap,
            a dapper sound,
let us here recall
breath,
presence
and desire.
Witch moss listens for the elephant horn,
the dirge of imprisoned light.
Darkness charges your bell's light;
its emptiness endures
                    in your free light,
point without closure,
space without beginning.
Your fingers must endure
      the astringent eyes
            your horn wears.

IV
5 (THIGH)

To him who has not killed
it is forbidden to drink
                    the virgin's beer.

Sun and son of the thigh mark
must press the distance
        deeper into the spirit's grip.
                        You sail,
                        shorts slit so high
                        the cloth billows
                        and rides
                        around your waist.
This stadium veils the paradigm of the race;
the wood obscures the declension of the hunt.
Your tempered thighs, contesting air,
            unfurl love's amber presence.

6 (TIBIA)

Your father guards the story in a cedar box:
a vulture's tracks, fish bones, a cattle head,
discarded mat, sheared pot, the forgotten
dispositions that empowered your music.

The dry north calls the whistle and whisper
of a darkened cave from Muslim mouths.
You have returned with your bleached, marrowed
bone, home of the god's throat,
            embedded
in the flute certainty,
            in the midnight
of the cave's red, comforting leaves.

I
7 (FOOT)

Even at night
a trace of sunlight hangs in the east.
Air creates an immobile, blue canticle.
The sea gulls' incapable wings remain
"merely an unwithering tumble,

a chute of angels fallen
by a sheer delight in their weight."
You set out in the delight of a fall.
Flight's image defines
        the conjunction of your besieged foot
with the zodiac of a timeless god's
                                weightless grief.

8 (LOWER JAW)

Dressed and belled in perfect order,
we arrive under the tomb sound,
the antiphonal knock of the smith.
We have enshrined the speaker's ninth hour,
harmony's impulse, in visible acts.
The knife's deep exaltation settles
the mouth's thirty-two degrees, exults
the votive articulation of the unspeakable.
Our stripped gifts of measure and control
begin the descent of the shuddering
                                communal jaw.

V
9 (TOES)

Disguised,
I walk by night
and listen for the rain.
It slips upon and shakes
these blue white nameless wings.
The rumor of roses, gossip of foxgloves
remember death's cause.
Night refuses to fit the cluster
of cobblestones, bees' lamps,
a woman's scented and magic pot.
The rain in the bird's wings, the antelope's

certain hoofbeat raise the dead
                    at the moment of rest.
I must remember to discover
the unfamiliar terrain of my shadow,
the doṅu bird's scale in my toes
                                on the ground.

10 (ANUS)

Why should you come,
    with your voice filled
        with the morning's bright oranges,
to be saddled and hiccuped into pleasure?
Love dresses, in this room,
    in the wrong color.
        I light
cold water in a porcelain bowl
to cover the swiveled space
    the barbed god left us.
Five yams, five kola nuts, two logs
    of firewood from the ita tree.
Junior wife of the road,
I have sponged holiness
    into the room's extended body.
Now you must touch my deepest disguise
    and pray for an uncorrupted star,
        the light of an uncontaminated ship.

I

11 (NOSE)

The dignity in beaten maize abrades the nose.
Brute heat rises, weed strong, above the lake's decline.
Shellfish embrace the moon disc on the shore.
Our memory of passage lodges in a goatskin,
                                lashed to a rock.
Night breathes in a crystal purity

and in the sleep of comfort in burnt cactus.
We descend,
                    from the sun's point,
on the red liquid of exchange.
The cocoa smell of cayenne fills the desert
and assures us that the cut will heal,
the scar will disappear.

12 (MOUTH)

Six o'clock.
Blanketed and muffled,
we circle the reclining forest,
through the morning's guard
of drooping banana leaves,
cacti, clumps of grass,
        dead rhododendrons.
                    Conjure
a cedar stump for your hand
and a likeness in a cradled, scented body.
If silence is the forest's majestic word,
the name it invokes at dawn,
the mouth must be bridled,
until the tree has understood
        its canon death in the carver's song.

I
13 (HAIR, HEAD AND NECK)

Near dawn, she purls through the brush
to appear, sibilant and serene, at the elder's blueberry stream.
Midwife of God's unbroken hour,
she cuts his morning body for the stars,
lotus, doṅu bird, calabash and stolen seed,
all the fiction of his craft and command.
Her plaited, pearled hair now measures
danger's intervals in a heron dream,

the reptilian night, in a virginal return,
a death without end.
She has taught me the limits of contemplation
and the way a bone,
        though it be taken from the truest cross,
                                        decays.

I have it from her conch in the water's web:
high tribulation attends every celebratory bell.
I know now, my woman will bell down berries
at the water's edge, to press a devotee's
uneasiness into my traveling bones.

14 (CHEST)

I know this country by the myth of the rose,
those linden tenors, lilting swords, unruly loves,
larcenous runts who rise from the mist at the peak
of an insurmountable passion.
I have been given the book of a peasant heart
and the cave for a passion other than my own.
I would acknowledge my journey
                                down
                        the decent path
                of tenure, here to the grammar of being,
standing-in-itself, arising, enduring,
the radical exegesis of the false myth of existence.
Sausage dark blood piques my thirst again
        for the intemperate sword and jackboot love
        my body holds for itself.

15 (STOMACH)

I would have you an unblemished bell,
an angular assertive god, text for the perfect
singer in the perfect grove,
                        or carve you
in ebony or sandstone, a toucan perched in an ebony

bowl in a corner of this room.
You understand the danger of being stripped
of totem and amulet, the bliss of being cold
to a god's stroke and set, untangled,
darkened in wisdom, in the direction of a self
                                        you may never reach.
A migratory man, licked by the serpent,
you dug your life from under withered baobab,
became your own, a seventh, son.
I turn and turn.   You remain.
You have taken your insatiable appetite
away from the limits of our love.

16 (EAR)

Pagan by birth, you arrange your route by spring.
You bring your eastern, skitterish saw to cradle us into night.
For days you boil us in hymns,
stopping only to admire your wife, in white
from heel to head, stutter into tongues
                        or stagger into dance.
We raise you into prophecy and offer you
this house, the leftover moments of ecstasy,
the right to pierce our hearts with your fluent saw.
All night, the women clasp the serpent's sting
and reel uncertainly after your melodies,
into your wife's design or into inventive glosses
upon your meager lexicon.
                                    This, too,
is the watch for that star's spin, the seed's turn.
This, too, is the ear open
to the accumulation that begins our death.
Strange, how you, having taught an element to sing,
come unmasked, riding the morning into night,
invoking the music which binds you to this place,
able to distinguish what little can be spoken,
or what space the silence leaves
                        to redeem our souls.

IV

17 (SIDES)

Come sunset you can bet
like a moth at a flame
old Blind Man will bè here
cue caught up in his crotch
cup of Mr. Boston cuddled
under a corner of the table

take a nickel more
if you can run six
before he get a line
got such an eggplucking touch
young men close their eyes and sleep
stand at his side   and learn

money down mouth back
come light   beef up
hey   take a nickel on a run
who want to shoot the Blind Man one

buy a drink   you will.

18 (SPINAL COLUMN)

High in the wind,
Chinese gongs quiver in the night.
                                        It is winter.
All day I play with your fig wine vision
and tamper with the tricks love has taught my tongue.
Here, I have a moment to construct the path you set me.
I am at bells' end,
buckled in the shift you spur.
I have truckled to the arks and bright beds
of virgins who could not be clear.
Let me tell you of the wickedness of spring
and the giddy danger of unthreading a maze.

I know, and regret, the moon's embrace
of the straight-backed, nubile sun.

I
19 (KIDNEYS)

In time,
in tune and omen rich,
I spin about my body,
at ease with my sabbath temper.

I know there is a mark
upon the man who only knows
a penitent's shiver at a Joshua tree,
whose only peace is

intoxicated stillness,
or the breath of holiness
that comes when evil, faced,
has been denied.

But what can we deny
when each body falls,
plump with his father's gifts,
into this body already rich

with the god's gifts?
Your shepherds now shiver under these bells.
They stamp about our feet
and pinch their fingers at our mouths.

Disguised,
I rise, under your eyes, from dung,
to begin my trembling.
My eyes remember

the goat's quiver,
my purity's star-bound blood,

the liver-laden word
in its moon cold silence.

Redeemed, I keep
longing's mark on my body.
Just once I turn away,
finding these fathers' gifts

too much to bear.

20 (CLAVICLE)

My dancing master of the gold bead,
I see you trouble the waters
        between that moment of light
and the star's darkness.
                                        Doubled
in your body, you wake; you twist,
then lurch, your body into motion.
Played upon by love's one breath,
you mount your antelope, the horse
who releases the cull bone god in you.
You anoint me the coffin's scribe.
A second birth folds us head to head.
Death doubles us to ride
        earth's sunken ark
toward a second and hazardous light.
Master, remember it was you,
discontent with your own imitation,
who frayed and made these bones delicate
        by bathing them in time.

V

21 (BACK OF THE HAND)

Light,
night's unladen image

in your wedding dress, the thin line
erasing heaven's darkness,
staunches me in its shadow.

All night,
I feel you smack my cheek
and wake me to the thunder
of your breathing,
                    a mother's moan,
a bride's clamor for rain.

Surgical,
you could part my body
along earth's axes; spirit me
among your father's oaths and altars.

I belong to the figure
          of the rain
you coil with your hand,
the stones that find
their places only at your touch.

If I awake, with you,
in darkness, it is the clean
incision of your love
that calls the light to dance,
just out of reach,
        on earth that rises
                    clearly
without the press of your hand.

22 (EYE)

Ecstatic, full,
and still half blind,
I see you clear your body
of its scars.
                    Astonished

by the magic of my name,
I name your scars, the angry cuts
stitched and hidden from yourself.
How shall we measure these bleached bones?
How shall we disregard the curry of a prophetic fox?
All peace is stolen,
        a disfigured rite,
nourished by your scars and breathless denials.
Those others now know my name.
Yet how can we possess
what you yourself have lost?
We own no land,
no love, no art, no death.
We walk among these signs of your
dispossession
and hear you say you passed this way,
like this,
            and it was right.

(The last two bars are tacit.)

MacIntyre, the Captain and the Saints

A northern light at midnight
wakes the bronze upon the hill.
The crowned clock sits on the tower
in a gable's eye. And I,
a serpent of the east,
unwind at Lothian Road.
This
has been my dungeon,
through the day
and through the evening.
But now, at night,
my walls are glass;
they bubble under
the heathenish touch,
till they are forest and sea,
till they become one holy
coracle, by which
I am coiled to the house.
I live by the darkness
of these other walls.
I turn on the cross
of the house that lights them.
Again I wake in the royal burgh
of Edinburgh.
I turn in the Castle's deep,
and go where the city's life
lies on the market.
A watch and an ivory cane handle
lead me over His Majesty's bridge.
Saint Giles, the Law, High Street—
I salute High John.
I go into the close
above Waverley, below
the jolly *Scotsman.*
This is my castle
of hotpies and rest,
one-half an ale.

The keeper keeps a tap
upon my nights;
I keep the morning.

I call great John O'Groats,
the Hill O' Many Stanes,
Gray Cairns of Camster,
Craigievar,
the Temple of Carinish,
Elgin Cathedral,
Lantern of the North,
victim of Wolf of Badenoch.
I call my David
for the rights of trading;
I posit my burghs—
Dunfermline, Perth, Stirling
and Aberdeen.
What is my eye
but the chief's eye?
What shield but his name?
Yet I am not Pict by Scot;
great Kenneth is not my king.
I take my concepts and my kin
from desert waters.
I have belted my bones
with ritual invocations.
Now, should I turn from this,
and run from my rose garden
and my kilt
into another darkness?
No, I think that I shall stand,
and stand called to see
who is the *I* of this constellation,
what is the shape of this life.

> And on a birlan edge I see
Wee Scotland squattin like a flea . . . <

I see you now,
and I would dizen

and divvy your birlan eyes
to protect me.
Saint Christopher, welcome
to my castle keep,
my night of stars
and desert memories,
your own *planctus*
in the boat of history.

> Drums in the Walligate, pipes in the air,
Come and hear the cryin o the Fair. . . .

Drums in the Walligate, pipes in the air,
The wallopan thistle is ill to bear. . . . <

I know ye dinna ken my sound,
so I'll speak to you
in the sweetness your tongue belies.

I'll accept your grace.

And I'll accept your cup.

Ale in the close.

Whiskey to wash away
the stain of the rose.

We drink away the sugar on our tongues,
and take the Mound.
The school of doctors waits in darkness.
A morning coat with keys,
a gentleman, with bones draped blue
with mourning, waits in the thistle air.
His blue is cut by one small key.
I think of this,
and wonder what a key may be.
I think of locks I cannot open,
locks I cannot lock.

Wee Scotland still is a howling babe
in the breech this key will miss.

Are you happy on the Mound?
The Equivalents set that tail
on the gardens.
We are still, in this high air,
mixed by money and God.

I know that.

You cannot know it;
you can only see.
This Mound is weary
with the thought—
an Irishman, a Pictish king
brought Jesus to us.
Yet even still, I think
I hold him dear—
*a royal man, a scholar,
abstemious and gifted
with a second sight,
and fine hand,
"none of your St. Maluag
of Lismore, or your drybones
of Pictland."*
If we wait,
we'll hear that first James
promise God to see that
*"the key keep the castle
and the bracken bush the kye."*

It was St. Ninian who brought the key.

You do not even know.

But I do belong.
Look here,
I have my tartan

on the Princes street.
My name is MacIntyre.

You show your purpose.

I'm searching for my purpose,
and it cannot be in blood
or in Highland drafts of praise.

The light is still,
and time is a movement into light.
In the moonlight, here on Princes Street,
I stare into the colors of my Celtic name.

If you plumed yourself in this,
I'd break your hips,
I'd sever your shoulders.
I taught you more than this.

Yes, Captain, I am sure I learned
my lessons well from you.

Then?

Then, I leave you.
Oxford tames what London teaches.
My Danquah learns from Hobhouse
what he could see at home.

Before he came,
I said this.

You called the proverbs
ethics of a savage people.

I knew no other words.
I learned.

To speak more carefully.

Yes. And more simply.
There follow:
Ashanti,
Religion and Art in Ashanti,
Akan-Ashanti Folktales.
These things are true.

They were true then.

I know that. I quote,
> I have taken every opportunity,
while gathering material from my
Ashanti friends, to impress upon
them strongly that our culture,
our ideas, arts, customs, dress,
should not be embraced by them
to the entire exclusion and ex-
tinction of what is good, just
and praiseworthy in their ancient
national institutions. <
The hope is in the sunsum.
I suffered for this.

Half mad from teaching
a tongue to Great Stuart Street,
I was on my island.

You condemn me, too.

You were the Scot
who took the cause
from New Town to Kumasi.

I took my life there.
I saw my kindred spirits there.
I returned, puff-hot in tweeds,
a fuller man.

I suppose I will return
myself, puff-hot in tartan,
a better man.

A fuller man.
Haven't you learned anything?
The good is all of us.
It is never lost.
If you are better,
it is not from the perfection
of virtue, but the perception
of virtue, the acceptance
of the okara.

You, in this city of daggers
and shields, instruct me?

The sunsum teaches.

> Nae man can ken his hert until
the tide o life uncovers it . . . <

The sunsum teaches this.

I am the angel of sunsum,
the breath of rain that fights
to fill the foam with mercy.
If the god does not appear,
then we must imagine him
in blue, or in the dun of earth,
or in the red of bronze, imagine
him wreathed with his own shrieking hands.
Now, I turn from my tartan, Captain,
along St. David Street.

**As Mr. David Hume's circumstances improved he enlarged his mode of living, and instead of the roasted hen and minced collops, and a bottle of punch, he gave both elegant dinners and suppers, and the best claret, and, which was best of all, he furnished the entertainment with the most instructive and pleasing conversation. . . .* *

*Lord Monboddo says
the man died—
confessing not his sins
but his Scotticisms.*

He still was a gentle man,
a daemon of good sense,
whose good sense disturbs.
If, in the light that carries
us along this road, we could
see him, startled by a piece
of woolen cloth, lord of astronomy,
savior of ethics, we could place
herring and hides in the deep fissures
of our souls. He is indeed dead,
but much of him still lives among us.
I believe that there is cause
to see him yet.

So it is night in our royal burgh.
The father of Common Sense has been let out.
The boys from the country gather
in the hill mists. I repeat:
Robertson, John Home, Bannatine,
Alexander Carlyle and Adam Smith
and Ferguson, Lord Elibank, Doctors
Jardine and Blair.
        Who is this
who walks with a key in hand?
Oh, then, good St. David,
by whose authority do you walk?

> None . . . can go beyond experience,
or establish any principles
which are not founded
on that authority. <

You are here.

I do perceive myself.

Well, I pucker and refuse
to enter that clam of memory.

Enter, if you believe in the imagination.

Your memory and your belief
lead me away from that.

I struggled with belief,
not under your saints' bells,
but here under the dissolving
assurance of my skin.

This is from Johnny Knox,
Geneva bound.
***Those who are saved
have certainty of it
in their faith, that
they are God's elect.***

I glorify God,
but I will not toll
man's corruption.

This is needless.

*It is the visible body
under the head of Christ.*
Do you deny it?
Do you deny a nation
can believe that God
will provide?

> Let men be persuaded . . . that there is nothing
in any object, considered in itself, which can afford
us a reason for drawing a conclusion beyond it . . . <

*The doctors at Aberdeen
refused to subscribe.
Lady Huntly lay in state
at the head of a brave funeral.
They had the town's haill
ordinance for ane good night,
and the Marquis had taken
his household and children
back to the country in high
melancholie. Wine and sweetmeats
were offered to the Covenant
embassy, and refused while
the Covenant was unsigned.
The provost and the baillies
gave the banquet to the poor.⁑

/It is for God to judge whether the Least shadow or footsteps
of freedom can be discovered in this assembly./

> The only defect of our senses is
that they give us disproportionate
images of things. <

*Spring corn and oats and barley
were all we had.
He gave us Easter and other
movable feasts, the shape
of the tonsure. By Margaret's
and Malcolm's time, we had
lost Iona; our kings were buried
in a Benedictine abbey
in Dunfermline.⁑

You hold me responsible for what was done?
I recorded this.

/God hath a people here fearing his name, though deceived./

And all my kin Barbadoed from the house.
I return, or do I return?

Do I hear the reason in St. David's voice?
Do I now enter myself most intimately,
and find myself able to entertain
a diffidence and modesty in all my decisions?
Do I remember the special light St. David gave?

> If reason determined us, it would proceed
upon that principle, that instances,
of which we have had no experience, must
resemble those of which we have had
experience, and that the course of nature
continues always uniformly the same. <

Oh, then, let our lives be bled
upon the roses of our trimmed days.
This is no' comfort, but a spike
in the tongue, a gate against
true memory.
> And yet, I dinna haud the warld's end
in my heid. <

Old Saint, I know you know
the *Gude and Godlie Ballads.*
Just in faith, the head
is redeemed by the head.
I twit you on the world's end.
The text excludes you as a saint.
You have no hiding place,
no bawdy of perfection.
The body will not be quickened
on your tongue. If there is
a word to speak, and one author
stands above it, how could your body
be revealed upon these stones?
I read you as revealed in your own text,
but read you in a feminine text now dead.
If the witches presume,
Saint David puckers.
What can be known, appears;

what appears, lies among us.
Then the offensive witches
must go down in their own glory,
and the king must search the basements.
I have heard it was said from the scaffold
that
**God hath laid engagements on Scotland:
We are tyed by covenants to religion
and reformation; those who were then
unborn are engaged to it, in our baptism
we are engag'd to it; and it passeth
the power of all Magistrates under heaven
to absolve a man from the oath of God.**
I know,
> The thocht o Christ and Calvary
Aye liddenin in my heid;
And aa the dour provincial thocht
That merks the Scottish breed
—These are the thistle's characters. <

No, not the thistle's alone.

I only understand
*quantity and number
matter of fact and existence
all else
is sophistry and illusion.⁑

All else is the king's realm,
and the king's realm is
spirit and body,
dying and being born,
living on reason's unadorned shores.
Why do you quibble?
Why have you sent me with cap
and compass to confirm these facts?

Can the facts grow from vision?
Can a new star arise to figure
a new constellation?

> I find myself involv'd in such a labyrinth,
that, I must confess, I neither know how
to correct my former opinions, nor how
to render them consistent. < Yes, it is
sufficient reason for diffidence and modesty.

> Darkness is wi us aa the time, and Licht
But veesits pairt o us, the wee-est pairt
Frae time to time on a short day atween
twa nichts. <

**Deum de Deo, lumen de lumine,
Deum vero de vero Deo, genitum,
non factum . . . **

Wright, would you hurt me in this way?

Saint Christopher,
poet to poet and soul to soul,
we insist on our darkness;
yet we may be wrong.
There may be more light
in David's perpetual twilight
than in our hidden hope for light.
We live between the two nights.
We await the light.
A game of billiards may be
all our affirmation of hope,
crowned, in our anguish, belief.
Or do we find we have two bodies
—a yellow seed split open by the sun,
a blue stem caressed by moonlight—
and each embodied by a reason?
Though I have never been your king,
you give me cain and conveth.
I would not burn your Cardinalle's town.
Saint David, believe
I know the debility of my own assurance.
Captain,
I have met you in the gulf.

Here, in my lean years, I have risen to say:
God is not *propter quid,* but *quia,*
a reasoning in an empty vessel.
We know, or think we feel,
our bodies calm upon the wave
which has its own design.
Bird-boned, we contend with the fire
within us.
What is our intention but the fire
within us,
or the description of a body
clarified by a wind?
We may live through the bone blaze
of our bodies and know only
how to shiver each bone from its scaffold,
each cell from its surface.
Surely, it is pain to reveal
the indifference of God's substance,
to acknowledge we are sufficient
only in his grace. Singular,
we prove and construct what we may
only know.
The years rigor and steep
these questions in your faces;
I read the night's unhurried return there;
you temper your return to me.
Your air can promise me nothing
but the thistle's sense of the spirit.
The cuckoo in the Hebrides would only bind
my blue wings. I know the air as gold,
the shell of an egg; I marry in the moon's seed.
I rehearse all reasons to be false to you.
Now the night covers my serpent skin.
I slip away.
Your night remains.
You ask for assurance;
it comes; as a star falls,
hart for the hind of our shadowed world.
I crown and sceptre you with your blood
burden, and hear the echo of my own.

Love's Dozen

The Ritual Tuning

Now I will enter the house of affliction.

King carry me above myself in death.
Awake to the king of all,
I come, regal in my purpose,
out of the heated darkness.
Tune me only now;
I tune myself to your love
and your many-eyed longings,
to your deepest look into your life.

I am the contradictions that you make me.
Scaled, I climb your trees.
I lay my eggs, one by one,
and suckle them.
And in my sign I raise
the bright seed of my spirit.

I am two heads in one,
two lives in one.
I end my life in a double vision.
When I am eaten, you pass
this double deed among yourselves.

Love is to enter another's house
a creature coined from vision's deepest pain.

Here, creature of heaven,
I surround you with my sign,

and look upon your marriage bed,
and look upon your death.

Love in the Water, Love in the Stone

Faithful bean lady of the plantain,
your tubular beads surround my voice.
You bring me a berry song so old
I hug the silences. You
embrace the silence and the clear light
on the track of your quest, to here.
I see now in that light myself
into the tangle of the river's bottom.

Knee-deep in another's bliss,
I wake and find myself a stone
at your lover's feet.
Then stone upon stone,
I rise into another's fire.
I touch your palm oil flesh
to light me from my cave.
And, if I rise, under your thunder,
into rain, I praise your touch.

Now, life-long a laterite,
a rain of beads, palm kernel oil
stipulate my clipped time.
The earth weaves eight gold bridal veils
to cast into the sea. The moon
is up at noon to catch me naked,
drunk and dancing with a ram.
I use the loom of seasons so;
I abuse myself.
And, even if I leave you,
I marry your worship in my wife's voice.

I begin the decline of having you
close;

your memories feed me.
These are my intolerable survivals.
And so I take my love's journey
from the language of your needs.
I mount my woman's earth smell
in the shadows of your ageless eyes.
I crawl to the altar of your thunderstones
and bleed for the bride whose blood
will fill my name.

Love in the Iron and Loom

Double the earth in northern light;
double the west in water.
Twin me in iron and weaving.
Binu, Lébé, my male hand
knows my woman's hardness.
I am the twin of my head, the twin of my hand.
Woven into cloth,
I slither from the dance a mask.
I am a dance in mask.
Who will answer the figure of the dance?
Who will unmask the twin at my heart?
My water shape in stone has a grip
upon the earth.
My river has a line around the star.
Shuttle and hammer, my life coheres.
My axe is the altar stone,
the loom of your love.
I know you as my cold light
and as my dying light,
and as the barking star I ride
through love's light.
My lord's light is the deep pit
of my marriage bed,
the song of my sign within the dance.
Weep, weep, weep.
Brother mask, you leap

to double me from myself.
I am broken.
I am finished.
I weep for the twist of my craft
in the green river of my god's love.

Love as Heaven's Nostalgia

Rhine moonstone, light
of the devastated world,
I could name your nobleness
in minerals and stars,
or in the light's courage.
Yet in my ear the ages linger.
I know your passion for a melody,
your nostalgia for heaven.
I wait, under your touch,
for the vision of your governing.
Sisters, I will awaken in myself
your melodic temper.
Strange how my life runs down to reason
in the memory of a bright daughter;
I am at the gate of a lost life;
I am at the door of my own harmony.
And you, delivered from this world,
summon my purified soul to sit
in its nature with the stars.

Anagnorisis

Through blood
and into blood
my spirit calls.
You sit at my head
and weave my power.
Queen, I do not do as you
and deal in deaths.

I have no power to make
that male power crawl to my knees.
Yet I speak and am your seer,
chaste lover and your bridge
                    from the dead one's
blackened space
to the white sun of your prayer,
the red daemon of your mother love.

You took the crescent moon and named me.
You bought my axe and sent me
through the desert of my southern dreams.
Clearly, in my sign,
I love
your overburdened body.
I love you
as the black chapel
                    of my penitence.
I love your forest's touch
in winter's memory.
Now, I grapple your deeds to my tongue.
And out of your woman's common eye,
I take my son's pursuit
of the days he must live
                              to recall.

Transcendent Night

Your feather hands
are love's nest in winter,
and yet I fly,
or do I dream I fly?
And I wóuld fly
to nestle near your child's lake,
to press my needs upon your feather hands.
There at the lake,
in the shadow of the celt
I find there,

I dance in your spine's darkness;
I clothe you in your spirit's darkness
and in your body's darkness.
I awake to the light of your total darkness.
I keep, for my constant spring,
your feather hands upon my eyes.
My eyes will always take
the dark path to your heart.
My heart will drink its light
from the only heavy hands
                                        you offer me.
Death of the dark. Death of the light.
I live in my spirit's web of love's
                              transcendent night.

Love in the Weather's Bells

Snow hurries
the strawberries
from the bush.
Star-wet water rides
you into summer,
into my autumn.
Your cactus hands
are at my heart again.
Lady, I court
my dream of you
in lilies and in rain.
I vest myself
in your oldest memory
and in my oldest need.
And in my passion
you are the deepest blue
of the oldest rose.
Star circle me an axe.
I cannot cut myself
from any of your emblems.
It will soon be cold here,

and dark here;
the grass will lie flat
to search for its spring head.
I will bow again
in the winter of your eyes.
If there is music,
it will be the weather's bells
to call me to the abandoned chapel
of your simple body.

The Crosses Meet

Patiently, I set your seat
in cedar and a bit of gold,
and by its arms
I cross our lives.
And then I turn your body
toward the wind,
my path from worship
to certainty.
Now, may I house
my woman's meaning
in angels and in stone.
I hold this pagan three-in-one
under your lips
and under your last sign.
Could, now, I trade
your daemons for her body,
I would cut the hardwood
of your seat to peace.
But can you hear me
when I press my preservation
at her knees,
and leap from the tangle
of your seated cross
to the bell of my own voice
at her worship?
You hear me

as I walk from dark
                                        to dawn
to save you.
And so I do save you
when my voice
is at her service.
I serve and preserve myself
in her grace.
I set her on the tangled
stool of grace.
I take her voice alone
to rule in my politic body.
At last your crosses meet
in the love above love,
in the word that spells itself
                                        in silence,
and I am the carpenter
of your new spirit
that speaks to hear itself
                                        in stone.

Love Plumbs to the Center of the Earth

1
I will live with winter
and its sorrows.
Here, the earth folds its blanket
                                        at noon.
The eastern crown appears,
disappears,
appears
to lie in pine
on the west ridge.
Some light has been lost;
a stillness has been betrayed.

I seem to feel your body
shake that stillness through the deep

water which separates us now.
Your husband, my father,
plumb of the earth
from our air to his,
lies in the silence of water
we gave to him.

You say you sit at night afraid,
and count the gifts you carried
to his bed.
I know that they contain
this fear of the winter's sorrows,
this offense of being left above
the deep water
to pluck this plumb string
for a tremor of love.
But it isn't the melody of loss
you have in your moon bucket,
nor the certainty of a line
to your own pain.
The clamor that rides this line
unhinges sorrow,
unburdens its beatific companions.
This single string,
a heart's flow,
is a music of possession.
And so you twin me
in the plain song of survival,
in the deep chant of winter
and its own sun.
Our balance is that body
and the sun extended
from our grief.

2
Today,
nine days
after the hunters have gone,
a buck walks from the forest

and nuzzles at my snow-heavy trees.
I crown him king of the noon,
and watch the light drip from his coat.
In these woods,
his light is a darkness,
an accommodation with winter
and its midday shroud.
And, if at night, the moon
holds down its spoon cup,
he will be fed by light
that holds the darkness in it.
His body is the plumb line
the stars shake upon our earth.
Now, will I dare to follow
and to name his steps
through every darkness of our earth,
or shall I turn from that light
to my own winter's light?

3

Left. Right.
Turn. And counterturn.
I would have my foundation stone.
And so I carefully turn my words
about your longing.
Soil, water, root and seed,
the pin of light on which your love
will ride to air finds and turns
in the heart of each of its possessions.
You own me in the grief
                                        you will not bear,
and in the act you will not name.
You crown my darkness in your silence,
and you crown me king of my engendered light.
If I possess a seat to rule,
I rule love's coming and the taut
sound of my father's voice in you.
Voices of that deep water stretch
into heaven on a thin line filled
with all we do not possess.

The Unwedding of the Magdalene of the Vine

Down, on your bare feet,
with a wicker basket of tomatoes,
you come to the courtyard of blue roses,
rare garden on a rare day,
and you are pinioned in the waterfall
from which the day would seem to rise.
I rise on the curl of your hair into ecstasy;
my love boat knocks from shore to dark green shore.
The birds go braying where I hide
                                        my intaglio of you.
This is my Mary lock and locket,
my chalice and the box I will not open.
Clearly, you have pruned me from your vines.
I know you through the earth's rising
and through the candles which you light
at your grandmother's grave.
Your red fruit defines a day you took from her bones,
sets my limits, calls my wedding bells.
Magdalene of the vine,
I would be free of the wicker of your day's duty,
your barter bays from dawn to twilight.
But in the waterfall's night, I hear you
call your familiar faces against me.
A Jesus of my continent veils your voices.
I am at rest as a shaker of serpents.
I once had a dervish depth to dapple you.
I once had my love's sorrow
                                        to draw you near me.
Now, I follow you down the sunshine,
and know the blood of the earth in the fruit,
the white pull of your bones upon the earth.
Now, here, I take the waterfall to wash
this stain of marriages from me.
I will not have you as my duty to the earth,
nor take the white pull of your bones
to reason with my days.
I have pitted your bare feet and wicker basket

against the jealous redness of my stripped love.
Unwed, I accept your turning of this our earth.

Love's Coldness Turns to the Warmth of Patience

My blanket smells of burnt apples.
My hair is tangled in smoky birch.
I sleep. I wake to watch the snow
ease itself around the shivering hills,
the same ice tick off in islands on the lake.
In all these silent postures,
I burrow into the memory of winter,
and fall, past your warmth,
into the high air of your heart.
Now, I am with you when the birds
circle and redeem their own air
and press the sun to hide their losses
in rainbows and serpent skins,
and, while you read their Zeno's flight,
I read your stillness.
                                        I see now
in your eye the birds are bronzed
to be set near our temples in the wood.
Water and bronze, the birds curled on a staff
lead me to the purity of my own coldness,
down where what is lit is still unseen
and the blind light is the token
                                        of your only star.
For who hopes for what he sees?
But if we hope for what we do not see,
we wait for it in patience.
I wait for the turning to teach me
what can be seen and what,
as I sit near my north star,
my lost green wood reveals.
I take the clothing of my memory's winter
as a sign that you are patient still.
Surely, I am my own flight into stillness

and into the cadence of a necessary cold.
I comfort you in the bed of charity,
my soul redeemed in your body's expected fire.

New Adam's Cross

Dove, I offer you my hand
and, from my shadows,
try to contain your sacred flight.
If I can name you or your flight,
I contain you. Berry lady,
I say love is your succulence.
Or are you my moonfall at the waterfall?
I know you are the blue bead
and the chicken kick, the diamond
or the gold stuck upon my stool.
At noon, I hear your frothy roll
bleat upon my grove's shores.
You come in the rain, you come in the wind,
you come in the eastern star; rose and redhead,
lily of the desert, my balm and blackness,
you surround me with your signs
and with your perfect body.
If now I am Adam,
you are my Eve of morning
and yet you cannot take your form
from my desire or from the gods' design.
I know my lure is useless.
I know I lie in shadows
because I cannot see your true light.
I say all light appears in darkness,
and every body rises against emptiness.
I say I know you through your mother
and my uncertain knowledge of her body
and her spirit. I know you as the web of my
father's spirit's weave and caress you
as the infinite water sign you weave.
Is love the name you weave?

And do I stand in the white milk of dawn
with only a red star for a sign
and watch my only horse split the air
and watch you wave your benediction at our backs?
And through your transparent body
can I see old palm leaves become
my first dwelling,
my first altar stone,
my first bride's first bed,
my fire,
my first grave?
Do I see you as the first example of my being,
or as the oldest road I take into my being?
You are the cross my body hangs
upon its spirit, the light my eyes will take
to read these oldest questions.
I am not all of you, you draw away from me.
I break my unillumined bones.

Love as the Limit and Goal

What in me is best
I lead to the hard stone
under the sun,
or to the dark habitation
of the blessed dead
where love's music
will be cut from my ear,
my body laid to serve
a constant light.
The subject of my own desire,
I am egg and synapse,
the body's pulsing measure,
the gold and purple of the light
about my days.
And so I invest myself,
invest you, with all
by which I dispossess you.

Now, when I beat my temple drum
and shake my bell
and praise my love in you,
I see the altar lock its heart
against your ecstasy.
The burden of the key,
under the rainbow,
rides you still.
You take the corn
for the thread of your skirt.
Love is the limit and the goal
by which that death is measured.
This love is the kinship of the saints
we bleed to make us worthy.
I turn from the order
of this constant dispossession
to awaken my body to the spirit's
historical sign, the logic of my soul
enlightened by your grounded eye.
I turn from possession of your oneness
to the vision of your twin acts,
the breaking of the ground from which I rise,
invested with the light my grave reveals.

Inscrutability

1
Inscrutable when I speak,
I am learning how my body sounds.
In the sand by the river's edge,
my head is a moon's egg,
my shell is a bell in my boat.
My arms and legs are storms.
I turn left, I turn right.
I chain myself with sun's rays,
star spur coals, bits of coal diamonds
and granite, a yucca branch,
a chicken claw and rose thorn;
I stretch goat hide between my arm and chest,
balata and steel from my lips,
and laud my women near the water.
The song I hear refers me to the mark
upon my body.
I hear my death again in nail rings.
I set the nail as harp of my breath.
Such music can be measured.
We have, then, a measure of zones
and generations, the association
of cloth and iron, herring bones and keys,
and, if I take my malt to the garden,
the glass contends with maguey,
the beads of crown and sceptre
recall an ascetic quarry.
But, temple bar, I inquire
how I am to examine you.
I have a measure for the facts,
but none for you.
Though I live in the essential
condition of vision,
what truth I know
is a burden in my ear,
sign and countersign
of the light's discoveries.

Light is a weight in the ear,
a memory of the light's incisions,
and, in the dark, I clear
my possession of memory's poles
with the attributes of speech.
Then, if the god speaks of failure,
I turn my body's speech star-high.
I work the dead from darkness
into light; for these
there is no other definition.
Darkness and silence define
a lover on a bed,
or shuttled in a tree,
a constellation of beads,
bridal veils and berries.
I hear in the contradiction
of my song a weeping.
My speech is a plumb line
to the echo of the earth.
My voice survives on a dervish dance,
and a king's howling body
would be the first stone of my house.
These are the deeds
to possession of my body;
these are the acts
by which I dispossess myself.
I remain a morph in my own
proposition.
Clearly,
my leaving and return
are in my power.
I number my powers
by an inscrutable class—
my voice in the leaves of a river
in which my light and full
and silent body lies.
I ask how to measure
the leaving and return,
the weight of the body.

I ask which of the marks I must
perceive to enhance my speaking.
I examine, now, the exactness
of salvation, proverb and purpose,
the blaze of the serpent skin.
I am persuaded of spring oats
and corn and barley, wine
and sweetmeats, darkness
and this text on light and the dark.
I speak only what is sufficient
and what can be assured
by the essential condition of vision.
I am in the place of light,
a bell in my own boat,
storm-driven into speech
and, by the rhythm of desire,
I forge my body's space.
I refer to the unity of this space,
and to my body's singular paradigm.
But even here, I wait with you
for the bird's flight into meaning.

2
(i)
This must be said.
I am provoked by the state of things.
On the most propitious night
the mother claims her god's
singular visit; the results
are the birds you see before you.
Bird, I know you as a common thief
of fish, a puller of nets in the dawn.
You cannot fly by your hungers.
But the god assures your holiness.
Our speech assures your struggle
with the god; your body addresses
this schema of our own desires.
You are the rain's head, the solitary
prayer in the brass-filled temple,

the mutilated tree on the rainless hills.
If you are silent,
we turn that silence to a tilling tool,
an eave, a hearth, or a pot.
We wear your silence against the heat.
We tune our day's bells to your pauses.
Your every proposition is grace,
a perfection of our absences.
Twin, you title all my voiceless provocations.
And yet I am indifferent to the terms
you choose, until I choose them.
Changer, fox, a fallen verb,
even you provoke my speech.
I ignore your generation.
Determined,
I begin again to parse my body's needs.
I ask if the world is real enough
to measure my intention.

(ii)
Down where the smallest quality
will turn and figure itself,
turn again to become other than itself,
I hear the exact belling of my vexation.
(Strange, how I refer to every act as sound.)
I body all my logic of the world
in the gray depths of these changes.
I pull the world's bare figures
to the scaffold of my gray eye.
I am, in the form of my own urging,
my gray eye and, in its movement,
I have my schemes, my launch pad
                                        into the actual.
If the god's elemental bones are real,
my hand must never scruple to design his flesh.
Old men will have it
that the word alone is real,
and leave these facts in pieces.
Is the word the design of the fragments,

or of the strict connection of the missing fact?
Surely, a yeoman would search another tree,
or the leaf fallen from the same tree.
Thing is not a name, and a tree
is named by virtue of its life.
You must consider that the tree has changed.
The tree alone can never bear semblance
to such a stripped body.
I assert now the eye is a pauper;
crown it, and subtract the self.
The English, impersonal banker retreats,
is content, is at home, is heard no more.
If I am intelligible as the other,
I explore my body's future path.
I become the body's changing form,
transformed by any unspoken absence.
The act itself is figure and ground
for the necessary absence.
Then we must go down,
through the will of the dead,
and ride the living mind to the dance
of light, distinguish the tune
in which our names are called.

(iii)
Still, I am entranced
by the eye's harmonics—
soundings of the invisible;
historical return;
field of the line and counterline;
false note and true;
house of fact and composition;
sphere in the wall of two lights.
Old opposites possess me once again.
I surrender and contest
my power to enhance you,
my need to embrace you as you are.
Are you the ring in the peacock's tail,
the round stone temple on an arid

mountain, the black belly of a fish
in moon rings? Are you a footprint
glazed on the urn of the sand,
the litter-shield of a warrior's body,
a bride in a white hut,
the drum or its message of love?
Voiceless rainbows speak in their colors.
The wind rides its horse
up the cobbled streets at noon.
Up, down. All figures rise or fall.
They arrive before me.
They remain.
I remain, a sinew in an aggressive hip,
the counterweight to another speaker's
                                        exultant eye.
You must adjust to this intensity.
In the tumult of this body's vision
I must elicit my intention.

(iv)
I am arguing with the body's exaltation
and the mind's enstoolment on the seat of love,
all inebriate devices of the fallen.
I cling to the fate of taking one step
at a time, or so I say, and know I lie.
I lie by the process of enacting my memories.
You are in these acts.
I cite your losses; I cite your powers.
We devise the truth of all
                                we have not learned.
It has been given to us to understand
what may only be unspoken.
What is unspoken may be undone,
what is undone may be unspoken.
I am proposing the clarity
of the undone, the still unspoken,
the clarity of stillness in the movement,
of the movement in the perfect calm.
I am proposing the undetermined body,

the invested space.
I cite the ages of liberation—
from the key,
from the second eye,
from sainthood
and from death,
from the body's definition
and its investment,
from the quality of being actual.
I bring you every disposition
of the double.
You will not find my sign
bare in your gray eye,
nor shivering feebly and alone
in your ear,
but bodied in the deep ground
of my tongue's impossible passage
through the ill-defined logic
of my body's exaltation.

Dimensions of History

For
Francis Fergusson

The Second Eye of the World

The Dimension of Rites and Acts

I

The Eye of God

The Soul's First Vision

Brightness is a curse upon the day.
The light has turned the plain cave dark.

Who chooses me
to rise river-burdened, here,
where the sun has bent itself
and sprinkled ash about our doors?
To be a river spirit
I would have to burn this ash again
to moonrays and sunlight,
control the waves that push us higher
on the land.

I strain to clasp my dust again,
to make it mine,
to understand the claims the living
owe the dead.

Who burned this land,
and sent us evidence of the god's retreat?

Rain on the brow of the arid nurse of lions
is the ash from which I rise.
Emblems remembered in a rain forest
become my compass.
I am that head the little girls carry at their backs.
I am an angular bird,

dedicated to healing,
iron-wrought and ready to fly again.
I am that center of a star,
risen on the wings of empire,
the warm pit of auquénidos.

Like the master of the spear,
I cross my river now,
always to return to one beginning,
which may be one or no beginning.
Under the tightly bound arms
and the spirit of masks,
I return to you,
to name,
to own,
to be possessed and named myself,
following the movement of the eye of God,
whose lids will close upon your greater claims.

And so I start in search of that key,
the ankh,
that will unlock the act.

"Much I have strained to make my soul obey."
Not in the perfect understanding of submission,
my feeling given form
to ride upon your judgment.

Unusual lights are at our altars.
Unusual hands go 'round our pots,
and dip into the blood that we alone can shed.
But
"I have made an end of my failings,
I have removed my defects . . .
I am purified in my double nest."

Is this only in death?

Where did I learn to present myself
to the cut of some other voice,
substitute in a mime
my body breaks to contain?

But

"I have become a prince,
I have become glorious,
I am provided with what is necessary."

These are the signs of understanding
that I assert, but cannot reach alone.

"Sleep had carried me away a little while.
The first thing I did on waking was to take an omen:
whatever words and whatever magnificat
came into my heart, that I would know to be
the rising of a sign portending the return
of my spirit to my body."

I need not now create a goddess for this earth,
or name the earth in *A*'s or flowers,
or in blinkered weekdays clamoring for rain.
My intent is not to fork the branch of a tree
and fill it with God's axe alone.
These acts must give rise
to the birth of a star,
whose understanding is our life among ourselves.

Yet

"By my father I adjure you, this that comes from the continuance of calamity and the consequence of misery, from a heart that is stirred from its foundations and tormented with its ceaseless conflagrations, by itself within itself. For thus it is, being without perception, without speech, without feeling, without joy, without

> repose, without effort: not in the sense of passing away, but because it is constant in the calamity of ceaseless torment, a torment without meaning, past indication, beyond limit. . . . If it speaks, speech is an affliction; and if it is silent, silence is an affliction. Unto God is the complaint without complaining, and there comes no answering reply, no easing. So it continues, wholly swallowed up: in loneliness hidden, yet it appears, and is hidden, and appears, and is hidden. I know not what I say, nor what he says whose reins have fallen from him, whose straps have been severed; who wanders in most perilous wildernesses, and thereof has no share in the conditions of blessedness . . ."

My scope is not a god's,
but he has placed this sign of birds between us.
And did I wake to see
the sweet potato grapple with the fire,
eight days in transit from my beginning
to my fulfillment?
But I have learned that that is no fulfillment,
only the first death that I must suffer,
only the first acceptance of another goal,
the eye opening on a different order.
This is blood of my mother given bodily form,
spirit of my father, spear hand,
the opening ear,
the point at which I am myself,
                                        and yours.

It will be difficult
for me to lie at rest in my own suffering.
It would be a death that comes too soon
to deny the sight of things not seen,
the signs that plough these fields,
people these houses,
cut into these conflicts.

What trust has been forgotten?
"Tumi nyina wo asase so."
All power is in land,
on which you lie.

So red is the color of the day.
Young mother, you bleed too much.
You must reject your son.
So red is the color of the day.
Young mother, we will teach you
to thread your bowels about your blood.
Here is the red clay and the red mukula tree.
The hunters know these things,
and so will you now.
You must remember when you lay
in the place of death and suffering
how you accepted the teaching of the tree.
That tree's whiteness,
white as the beads draped on the bow
in your lonely hut,
white as your fertile womb,
taught you to hear the women,
playing on the little drum of thirst,
the hand up and down the reed,
the sound of love
from which your loneliness would retreat.
Dancing,
you carried your beads in a pack on your head.
Solemnly, one night,
you showed them to your husband
on your marriage bed.
Now, you bleed too much,
angry with our needs.
We dress you in hunter's skins,
fill your hands with bow and arrow,
turn you 'round in our hunter's dance.
There is a feather of a lourie bird above your brow.

Hunter,
manslayer,
circumciser,
you will not take your place.
Little mother,
remember our need.
Thread your bowels about your blood.
We are waiting to be moving again.

I cannot buy my brother's gifts,
nor can I buy a life.
But you see me, here,
waiting through my seasons,
with the accumulation
of all that we have suffered and won.
"I am not a man whom girls refuse."
At night,
I dream of the termination
of these searcher's feelings
and the day of rain, upon which
I shall begin to build myself again.
But here alone I sit
with the tassel and the bell,
holding the celebration of my people's love.
I can hear these bells in a distance,
and hear them shake the child's voice,
singing his ox's name in your womb.
We cut them to a peacefulness,
and breed them to witness
our slow coming together,
to bear the burden of the years
in which you will meet me
again and again,
each death a growth,
a life rising into its clarity of being,
a love unspoken when we shout our spears.
"Friend, great ox of the spreading horns,
whichever bellows amid the herd,
ox of the son of Bul

Maloa,"
teach me to hear
the tone of my child,
singing in the future history of my wife.

Turn again
to the blood given bodily form.
I lead you down, little mother,
to the river of your dispossession.

In season thirst,
we dust the roads, and come
to rest only when the seed
pulls us into the earth,
or when, at the end of the long
battle of tides, its fruit appears,
and calls us from our wandering.
Then the boys leave your kitchens,
and beat the flies and stench
from their faces
to sneak into the pain and power
they will have to die into to know.
Again, mother, you must learn the lesson
of this sweet dispossession.
And now, little master of the dance,
we turn to you,
the reflection of the reasons we have
to straddle you before a knife
to cut you away from her
who would never but always possess you,
to teach you to bear the burden of our lives
within your own.
Who you are
and where you are
we teach you to teach us.
So I would wear myself
the feather of the lourie bird,

and be the hand to cut you
into this special kinship.
Yes, my little mother,
"I am the lion who eats on the path
You sleep on your back, you look into the sky
Nest of the marabout stork where a black kite lays eggs
Hole of a mamba where a lizard lays eggs
Novice's mother, you used to revile me
Bring me your child that I may mistreat him
Your child has gone
The son of a chief is like a slave."
Now, disguised, kambanji,
you ride another master
into your mother's exhilaration,
where she will soon learn the meaning
of another death.

If I possess these souls,
they are all that I have.
For you have given me this name,
and burdened me with memory and duty,
a tricky commerce with the dead deceivers,
the injured and the ambitious.
What I had you took
into the possession of this black stool.
What I receive
I pay in food or thanks.
If I lead against another,
I gain nothing but his tribute.
His gods will not fit in my stool house,
nor mine in his.
"Tumi nyina wo asase so."

Who has burned this land?
Who has sent me, shaven head,
bleeding for my princes?
Who has chosen me

to reconstruct this eye of God,
to understand the signs
                                        of this dispossession,
to slip, beyond this pain, this key in the lock
to objectify this joy?

II
The Key That Unlocks Performance

Vision as Historical Dimension

And, as the god relieved you
                                        of the burden of sight,
naming you sage,
he burdened you with wisdom.
Purest of speech,
pure in understanding,
lit within, you lead us
to the limits of our skills.
Could I have named your twin Muchona,
the hornet high-pitched ritual adept,
master of ritual knowledge?
So righteousness appears to one
                                        at the end of his light,
to the other at the limits of his freedom.
We belong to their charge,
charged ourselves to stare down
                                        the other's emptiness.

It must be that deserts fill with light,
that watching the god's retreat
fills a human heart with knowledge of itself.

If he leaves us,
it is only the leaving of this world,
the abandonment of a city without grace.

Who is just without you?

How can there be peace without you?

The death that grows into another thing
is lost without you.

There is forever between us the task of choosing.

I choose you,
and wait.

You choose me, and go away.

My good is the Joseph's coat I strut before you.
My contentious body is the promise I lay before you.

And yet you pull your rain away from me
until you choose,
and I see you alone rise at the apex of sunset,
berry bright, your needled head
contending with an early wind.

Who would believe in a city
that has only itself for an end?

My desert body teaches me
that even love is not enough.

Look at your state,
a city with so much power,
and bankrupt.

But I live here, and will.

Aurelius Augustinus Augustine
Bishop of Hippo

Even I
like the sound of my name.

And even I,
here,
like the sound of a saint.
Saint, we agree that the rain
is the perfect expression of a god's love.
But I am honest.
I know he cannot come again.

"Comienza, cantor.
Tañe tu tambor florido.
Con él deleita a los príncipes,
los águilas y los tigres.
Solo por un breve tiempo
estamos prestados unos a otros."

A seventh degree mason
Royal Arch Captain
Principal Sojourner
blinking at two degrees.
Born in Santa Rosa,
about to die in San Pedro,
I have gone from mother to father.
I have lived my life between
one saint and another.
Feeling my manhood,
I cut myself away from my mother
and ran to San Antonio.
A carnival,
a festival,
a circus life
is a bright boy's passage through the saints.
Bright black boy on a motor drome,
dizzying the white folks,
living himself without a dream.

I dream,
and wake in Mountain Spring

from San Diego to the Imperial County.
We move through Mountain Spring rocks,
and descend by centuries,
through faces of Toltec and Maya kin.
The rocks wrinkle,
                    elephant skins,
                         the trumpet sounds.

"We find we possess in ourselves
an understanding. . . . We know in
ourselves we possess a right
to see ourselves justified. . . .
Fallen, sadly, sadly low indeed . . .
That within you will, to the
presence of your God, be at all
times your sole accuser. . . .
Peace and Liberty to the Ethiopian
first, as also to all other grades
of men, is the invocation we offer
to the throne of God."

Even if the land is filled
                         with the memory of saints,
we need no saints.
We have no holiness
nor any invocation to relieve
these burdens of memory and duty.

What is the task in a new land?

What is the weariness of liberators?

"America is ungovernable. Those who serve the revolution
plough the sea."

Dominguero devoted to France,
unable or unwilling to read
the delegate and soft-spot eyes of Hédouville,

"There was no need for you to quote me your instructions to recall me to your worth and dignity. It is sufficient for me to know that you are sent by France to hold you in veneration."

You wait for Bonaparte.
You lose your patience with Moïse,
visionary son, ready to call a nation.
Moïse is no Mackandal the Maroon,
whose failure stirs you, old and privileged,
to put away your wife and walk to the plains
when the flames come.
But flame is not your nature,
though, patiently, you take the forge
upon your back.
Forge them in iron or steel,
you think they betray you.
Forge them as axes,
or in the shape of birds,
still they fly from you.
Forge them as God's own,
they deny your hand.

Who is my own, if not the world?
Were we not all shaped at Ifẹ?

Oh, Toussaint, the opener,
who will dare to accept that entrance?
Name yourself before the time is up.

Take this man,
and tuck him in those ambiguous mountains.
He is yours to honor
in the manner of nigger kings.

Give him the robes fit for someone
who has lost his kingdom.
Gradually take away what daily garbage
his body requires.
In winter, tell him there is no wood to be found.
Relieve him of that geechee servant.
Watch him eat and shit.
A black body needs no care,
tell the doctor to stay away.

"I was one of your soldiers and the first servant
of the Republic in San Domingo. I am to-day
wretched, ruined, dishonoured, a victim of my
own services. Let your sensibility be touched
at my position. . . ."

But death can touch the sensibilities
of those alone who see it
not as the termination of life,
but as a growth into a life
no final death can touch.
Toussaint, the opener, your love is too great.
It is left to others to turn this land
into a green island.
The blackest of the black will purify
and purge
what cannot be saved,
and so enters in the harvest time,
fore-rite and the coming to be.
Then from Philadelphia,
the covetous *Connecticut* brings his crown,
his coronation robes frigate from London
through the rum of Jamaica.
Ogden on a *Samson* lifts a six-horse carriage,
the weight to bear our Emperor into Le Cap.

"Toussaint's failure was the failure of enlightenment
not of darkness."
This is your epitaph.

Sea-change, or sun-change,
the tides reversed and flowing out to sea,
to search for the center, some point
that moves the heat-love, some point
that will not deny moon-love, cool-love,
even the hunter's cool-love,
still it is always the ambiguous war,
one with no boundaries and no tactics,
one in which the wounded win as often
as the unwounded and lost.

He was in Boston
on some task or other,
or maybe
it was no task that brought him there,
nothing other than the rumor of something
about to happen, something
to change him from himself into another.
He ran to confront the British red,
waving a flag snatched from an unsure hand,
or was he leaning on a stick,
listening to the queer quarrels of cousins.

He was in Boston.

He is in Boston.

You are in Boston.

I have given you a motive
to run down a flag.

I ache, but must concede
that the motive of this city is justice,
                    its goal, peace.

Strict black brother who understands grace
and the strict separation of the elect,
strict black brother who understands the absence of grace
and the strict duty of the elect,
you meet in Boston,
focused on a flag you ache to own.
We dream in twos,
strict destiny, the two in one.
Two men in one,
one man forging himself one
                    of these divine birds.
The solution is never to yoke,
but to split.
This is the gesture. This is the act.
From every twoness cut from itself,
the scar gives rise to one.

                    Father, I weave no more.
The weaver in New York, Thomas Jennings, tailor,
grains his fingers digging trenches on Long Island.

What ambiguous war?

Who belongs to Spain?

José Baquíjano
          Spanish dames and sires
          marquis   marquises
          all the native flowers
          pulled from foreign soil.

There is a Black cloud rising,
                    promising rain.

                                She, our virgin,
guides nuestra santa revolución.
¿Qué patria? La patria.
This will be the only chart of your bones.

Who belongs to Spain?
                                   Dames and sires
                                   marquis   marquises
                                   all the native flowers
                                   wilting in Xochimilco.

The city sinks   and stinks.
And in the air the cry of an eagle.
A shackled Black wrist claps the clouds.
I sit over a dish of moros y cristianos,
bitter communion, bitter memory of no communion,
bitter memory of the padre's death.

"I am your fellow man, but not your slave."

But even here my brother runs me down.
Savannah slave,
brother of my own,
slave of my own,
I come packed among the ivory,
ostrich feathers, hides, kola nuts and gold.
Rich, it is a good thing
to straddle your own heathen,
and to gallop, puffed up, among
your filled corrals.
Caparison these beasts,
and you have a garden of tribute
                                      to yourself,
manured with your ashy soul,

with the mother-tightened bones
of your own dead.
The thirst for a horse to take the river's rise
becomes the river's insatiable rise,
and I will ride, berserk
and pressed behind the gold
to see you satisfied.
Surely there is a limit to these waters.
How many horses does it take
to brand a man?
Return, return to this,
if the god will answer.

These, whom we keep locked away
from the sight of women and the incomplete,
will always answer.
When it is time,
you visit their bones.
Lined before the great brass vessel,
the twelve uncut and caught disciples,
knife-clamped into silence,
their arms pinioned, lean to hear
the whisper of wine to earth,
the call of the articulate drum
for their blood.

"Unto God is the complaint, without complaining."

Not this.
And not the miracle of charms.
Not the gifts sent to 'Nyame-fre-bere.
Not the insatiable dust-click of horses.
Dyēli
dyāru
gyeserē
tumble the ta'rikh,
and I would be the keeper
of origins
myself.

But why must the dead
be clamped into silence?
Why must every claim be answered?
Still I must follow this star that screens the world.

Ambiguous wars
that begin with no boundaries.
Iron carts and horses trooping up the dust,
trying to arrest the god's retreat.
The saint says the Garamantes used bulls
to gird the war.

Who will lead us?
What muffled nomad knows a god
better than we? What bull-driven Nubian
will take the cross in his own defense?
Peacefully, the god will come,
cuddled in cloth and letters.
Everyone knows the scholarly singing
of Bilād as-Sūdān.
Peacefully, the god will come.
And so my task begins
with the lord lion, the crippled king,
Sun Dyāta, son of Māli, savior of himself.
I dust, I kneel, I pluck my bow
to wipe away the extravagance of gold.

But it will not wash.
Here even the god
is hidden among cloth and parchment,
takes his way again in ivory and gold.

Now, twenty thousand Portuguese heads
lie cooked in the sand.
The old leader dismounts for the last time,
and dies.
The son leads on, but loses heat,

and you rise to the cry, "Let him not be!"
a si kyi a   askiya,
you, Muhammad Turē, congeal these tongues
and brotherly cuts
with the tunic, turban and sword.
Brother to brother,
it is the name that coagulates the blood.
Yet here is my blue glass bead.
Earth spreader, I remember you.

And I remember you
in the land of soapweed,
making your own rough soap with lye.
Yucca baccata of the foothills,
seedpod for the open mouth,
breast for the weary.
The stiff-leaved one must indicate the flag.
Call me one a Spanish dagger.
Call these God's candles.
Waking cradled by your saint,
father, this is your land.

So Nuño de Guzmán, governor of New Spain,
employs Tejo the trader,
trader of gold and silver,
bearer of the tales of the Seven Cities.
Weary at Culiacán,
he finds four sailors,
lost in the search for the flowered
end of things.
Now, the friar takes the slave
into the valley, and sends him on above.
Send me a cross as big as my hands,
if the land is good.
If it challenges our new mother,
send a cross larger than that.
A day   two days   four,

and a cross "as tall as a man"
mysteries of Seven Great Cities
under the Black man's eyes.

Following God's candles
further than the friar will go,
your light breaks down at Hawikúh.
Estevan   Stephen
carrying your own stone
into the valley,
victim again of your services,
you lie at the gate of the Seven Cities.
Who will trim your hair and pare your nails
to send your sunsum home?
What sister will shave her hair for your soul?
The friar never approaches the gate.
He stands elevated long enough
to set a cross for Spain.

At that point,
each day, the young priest appears.
He wears the crescent moon embossed
with sun, moon and stars.
He would set the bowl in the friar's tree.
Your 'Nyame dua, father.
Your shrine not anywhere but here.

Friar and the crowned return.
The plumed and mailed blessed ones
search for the gate again.
This is the gate of gold
Gao   Guinea   Hawikúh.
But there is no gold,
only the whisper of the wind
fluting the black man's liberated bones.

Into this sound,
tracking highways, you come.
Cold morning's return out of the desert.
Cold metal search in the Golden State
to return, enchanted again at the gate.
Not gold. Not the cities' magnificence.
What the others left at the gate
you found within, extended,
"a gateway to the beautiful."

III
The Second Eye of the World

Anochecí enfermo   amanecí bueno.

Yes,
"I am the bennu bird in annu,
I am the keeper of the book of things which are
and of things which shall be.
                    Who then is this? . . .
The things which are and the things which shall be
are his dead body."

My breath leaves my body in dreams.

          Who is mounted here?
          Who returns?

Jinete   hunter
Here is the return.
White moon   olive
Here is the return.
     Shango   Boanerges   Dios-kuroi
     lead me to the sons of Heaven
     Bana-ba Tilo

Under the white moon,
the god will straddle you.
Santiago on a white horse,
twin bolts, or a lance,

brother of Christ,
give us a nation.

"We must MAKE an ISSUE, CREATE an EVENT, and ESTABLISH a NATIONAL POSITION FOR OURSELVES. . . ."

Muhammad to Mecca again
for the weavers of souls,
clothiers of a body gone fat with stillness.

Who chooses me?

In Cuba,
Black Melchior caresses the cobra.
Dahomey dance   Havana Boa
This Python, sacred serpent of Delphi,
this Pythia, stretching the dark corners,
dark herself, caught in darkness,
sees the fat sin burned on the island.

Upon a Day of Kings,
these women dressed in white
group themselves and pirouette,
and become my dawn,
my sun,
my earth,
my lamb,
my buzzard,
my butterfly.
I live this day through them,
counting no clock time
but the blood's time,
the gentle rise and fall
of a doṅu bird's wings.
I assert that I am twinned to your light within.

Will we get these symbols right?

In Lima,
thirsting for the waters of worship,
the lost tribes keep Our Lady of the Rosary
in the Monastery of Santo Domingo.
There in our brotherhood,
we awake with breath in place.
So many waters crossed,
yet crossing is no journey.

And will we get these symbols right?

Gold of Guinea, gold of Gao,
Morocco rides Gao under Judar Pasha.
Under the drooping heads,
under the flat flags,
there is left a cannon
                    with the arms of Portugal,
a statue of the Holy Virgin,
                    a crucifix,
all these powers lying dead,
with no one to transform them.

Still, anochecimos enfermo   amanecimos bueno,
learning the dwelling-place of the act,
the spirit holding the understanding
of our life among ourselves.

Is it enough
to have these sanctified ones
roll themselves from skin to scalp
and smack the bell-trimmed hides on their butts?
Is it enough
to be ridden, to be married
to a power that snuffs us up and out
and shapes itself only in our trembling skin?

"By my father and his goatskin and his three cowrie shells . . ."
Emblems of the ecstatic connection.
But we would bury the priest
between oxhides, never to touch the earth,
never to have his bones caressed
by the prayers we walk upon.

Give me reasons for this emblem.

What is the first act?
The egg that rises from the water.

The body, that thing there,
will lie forever in the earth;
the soul will ride its course to heaven.

What is the first act?
The unraveling of the egg.

And death enters with the word,
the conception of speech.

Hawk-headed,
with a disk upon my head
and the ankh upon my knees,
I sit in this sun bark.
Your speech is the speech of hands upraised,
your eyes give as much light as mine.
I have heard the timid call
the lord of the hidden world, great god,
lord of the underworld.
Shrine-clad,
white feather crowned,

he holds the emblems of dominion.
Who is the greater teacher?
What is the first act
if not the body rising from itself,
becoming itself again,
                    spirit, shadow, spirit,
heart of its own bones,
the name of the wise one?

Can this be hidden from the hidden one?

Can a body be imagined under the ox-name of God?
Or will water forever contain us?
But this is the matter between us.
You understand the space about your body,
the way you take these plucked skies
                                        for your bed.
Your ghosts awaken, smoked, at their shrines
to attend to their deeds and their names.

I am always approaching my end,
looking for the hidden one.
Tongue-tied in time for my nani's deeds,
I have done my trembling,
but the soul must be an All in All,
laid out in one sentence,
over the Pool, over the absolute intention,
even the knowledge of death.

We are born to trade upon and build
the head's intent
                    in the river's seed,
                    the seed's irruption,
                    the milk of a lamb,
                    the star's sudden fall,

the rock's mountain breaking shape,
the saint bickering with birds,
the sceptre, flail and crook,
the coffin at the neck of things,
the joker in the soul's bequest,
the eye,
the key,
the second eye.

This, before you,
is the life
of a dark and dutiful dyēli,
searching for the understanding of his deeds.

Let my words wound you
into the love of the emblems
of the soul's intent.

Modulations

The Aesthetic Dimension

I
Rhythm, Charts and Changes

Teponaztli

Fat singer in three keys,
a continent rolls at your feet.
Gourd gong of the dervishes,
praise your end.
Your tongue slit double,
the mallets stamp your body,
a calked Calliope,
sheer deep in pitch and darkness.
Bone clock of the spirits,
praise your purposes.
Inside, the body,
cut rib upon rib,
howls at the debt the drummer owes.
When the lion climbs
into the skin of a llama,
debtors to ourselves,
we pitch the sound of serpent's feet,
mare's claws, an eagle's brimstone,

and the body screams against
the stamp of a goddess
white as pain.

Atabaqué

Fat trinity of sisters,
buckle in the Bahia bay,
candomblé;
secret bones and bells
spread in the wine sea.
I am the palm
to blister the tale
of your silent origins.
Three heads in one,
blue mirror of a Christian saint,
trapped in your own ta'rikh
I name each one: batá, ilú,
cuica, urucungo.
I name each one: tambor-de-jongo,
agogô, adjá.
Secretly, you take the print
of heaven's foot
from my body,
disguise me in the cloth
my mother weaves at night.
I go out by day,
anxious to redeem the crocodile
who lurks in the heart of Rio,
but I am captive
up the coast.
A fisherman without a net,
I take only stone.
My grain turns to weed. Birds die in flight.
The cougar chokes. Bananas turn black on the vine.
So I carry the quilombo on my back,
with the wine jugs, caged birds, fridges
and imperial beds.

Now in a fufu bowl,
in hen's milk, in tiger grain,
I set your eyes as spies.
Sisters, deep in the carved ribs
I hear your voices begin to call
the ones who would still bear your names,
the gods who would understand
the lace of your labor, the offense
of being only your own.

Bandola

G

Tipsy breather,
breathing
is a sense
unsolved.
Five of you,
begad,
sharp as
a G bead string.
Teams of musketeers
muscling for a place
on the board.
Catgut
is your
only voice.
Some steel you,
gut beneath
the wind.
Quinto requinto.
A wine sound.
Chairman of the board.
Gaffer,
this is the gaff
to gaff the gaffer.
Tune your G.

d

Dolorosa,
what is heaven
but the breath
of that string
taken from the gaffer's
winding sheet?
Dolorosa,
ecstasy is the deepest
sound of mourning.
This key
is the angel's coffin;
this chord
is the trumpet's
announcement
of its velvet absence.
Dolorosa,
what is the sin in pity,
the heartbreak
when a child's voice
scans the night?
Trio of clarity,
in the darkness of your pitch,
I hear my absent voice
absent itself from angels
and the air they ride
to flesh the bones that here
my doves will dance upon.

a

Má lover of god
Má loved by god
Má of the sun
Má of the river
Má of the timber
Má of the wood
Má of the grief
Má Teodora
What source

is in your circle?
Why do you dance
with the *palo codal?*
What itch constrains
your orisha limp?
Who is the simp
to arrange your fall?
Má Má Teodora
fifteen sinners
guide you through the berries
of your own exultation.
Fifteen lines and a stick
make a whip
to remind you of the grave.
Fifteen stones and a star
lift you to a cloud
beyond my reach.
Má loved by god
you ride your flesh so surely
the gods within the flat drums
keep a tap
upon the earth.

e′

There is a harmony
the earth elects.
This boy,
with a witch's staff,
will search it out.
Doctor of the ditching rod,
the groom of charges,
disciple of monkey skulls
—the blood and bearded eye—
he paddles, bootless,
over the hidden water.
Under his light baton,
the ewes are combed,
the ram runs down his bass,
the froth of it

now dry in the clay.
Agnus dei.
What fine motets
these shepherds sing,
remembering our own
                                        and "civilized
                                                    lady."

b′

High bells and xylophones,
marimbas, a courteous guitar,
New England winter in a choir
of fifteen, dressed in Quechua shawls.

What sun is breaking on the pines?

This choir's jungle teeth
sparkle in the fountain.
I bang the drum and pay the toll.
My lover will wake tonight
at the height of a cold Thanksgiving,
and rise from her bed
to take the hidden rose from her hair.
So will the strings lament
                                        her indifference,
her body out of tune
with the balustrade's desire,
the light of a crafty night
setting on a pain so distant
darkness is our joy.
I choose the miracle
                                    of the whale's voice,
the map of an ocean
deep enough to be green,
unplumbed
except for the shell of your voice,
unmarked
except for the wreath of your hair.
I bring my love on these silver spires,

fifteen lucid lines to the cathedral
of your ecstasy.
This is the difficult round,
"a linked sweetness long drawn out,"
the design of the body's expectation,
the ear's vision.

Huehuetl

Upright,
tight,
caressed for any tone of voice,
jaguar tree,
the legends deepen
in your bowels.
Silent now,
you keep my rage,
my purple primness,
blood red crown,
the journeys set at sea's edge
into the forest's shadows.
I ride a horse, under mail,
into the plume's sunset;
I hear the cough of the prince,
dying in his garden.
Dead in my own garden,
courtier of my shame,
I am two souls in one,
like you a hollow log,
a jaguar skin,
                    fleeced of justice.
I stand still,
in whatever moon appears,
wounded by my own betrayal.
Night of the moons,
you will not run
from the voice
these creole hands

will beat from me.
Under the wing of the jaguar tree,
I rise upright, tight,
caressing my own power.

Areito

This is my mitote,
batoco,
areito,
my bareitote.
This is my bareitote,
areito, batoco,
my a-ba-mitote.

Corre, corrido, navideño.

Friday the thirteenth
and snow in the birch.
Love's days all begin
with that kind of coldness.
We had come down
to the fog and the bite of the sea,
another of love's soft nibbles
on the skin.
The axe had chipped in the trees.
High up, the squabble of birds
through the evergreens
became the painful sound of palms.

And the woman sang:
I've got love all around me
My own treasure's found me
My savior
is a boy in bloom.

So you guess that I wrestled
the shadows of my cabin at night.

My wife, in her corner,
tumbled over the milk in her sleep.
We had arrived
with more than a small purchase,
a small reparation,
                                        to make.
Was it only the axe wronged in the trees?
My skin is the repository
of the sun's needles.
Why had I chosen the cold?

And the woman sang:
Flesh of my flesh, I nurse your dreams
I nurse your screams
I am
your mother.

Mystic rose of the heart,
how could three of us
be imprisoned there?
And how could we come
from the dark wood into the light
yet still hear the moonlit canticles
prey in the water,
still pray in another tongue
for sunlight on our nets?
Three of us to nurse the night,
and three of us for saving.
Santos and serpents,
tangled in the streams of our bodies,
dance in the blue of our altar lights.

Dolor, dolori, passa
A strength in a weary land
A shelter in the time of a storm.

I had lived alone with the woman,
sunlight, a son, fish, the fallen apples,
the holy deer that would kneel to our knife,

all the provisions of prayer,
to find myself unmarried,
my woman drunk with God,
nurse of a savior's screams.
Then out of the woods,
I turned to the woods,
to the toothless nurse of my own dreams.
By the light of the thirteenth moon,
I began to search for my own light.

Wood of the woods
Bird of the woods
Woman you were created by God.

Necromancer of the hummingbird,
I bring you this bird's body
and the thirteen rings of my love's chains.
I bring you the secret whispers
of my wife's sleep,
the tangled passions of the forest,
the thorn I would return
to another heart.

Bird of the woods, fly into her heart.

Teach me how to stalk her sleep
and the bible of her loves.
Teach me the darkness of thirteen moons,
how to contend with a God.
Bathe me in love's coldness.
Woman of the woods.

Dolor, dolori, passa.

I lie down in the sand
to hear my batoco,
my mitote,
my areito,
end.

Joropo

Finger this my cactus, come now,
won't you buy now? Take now. Oh, how
thick can this rope of your heart be?
Sausage of my sausage, you see
it cut fat clean before your eyes.
Canta, comal, my eyes are wise.
Todo pica. Cactus? No sin
in the *piña* rings, thin as thin,
delicate haloes on your thumb.
Oh, my friend, I am not so dumb
to think you came this way by chance.
Piña? Pulque? Tea? Shall we dance?

Lundú

Moonlight, if I sleep on this bank
and lay my head against your kiss,
I recognize the river's sound.
Timeless me, all day I raise
my knife against the sugar cane,
sugar brute who takes my days for pay.
Sun glow in spring is crystal clean.
Sun glow north, sun glow south,
sun glow summer, sun glow fall.
The fall of sweetness weighs me.
Aribú of the sweetest god,
will this or what winter
be the longest sleep?
I serenade his green fingers,
his water's magic, his boot in the earth,
the way he pulls the green crowns to light.
Aribú of the grainy god,
will this or what fall
be the desolation of our mother?
I serenade the return of even light
to her wrinkled face.

Moonlight, now I lie on the crown
of my own desire,
hutched
in the fall of the god,
the fall of the cane,
the fall of my own night.

Son

titocotí tocotí tocotí

Blue bird, heron light,
you own the river bank.
I am only your turquoise shield,
the temple's decorative stone,
and so I serve.
And if I take my fee
in great jades and wide quetzal feathers,
I serve.

titocotí tocotí tocotí

You sit on a moss mat,
the river's seat.
Your eye goes from deep to deep.
The sun reflects the light above,
the light reflects your love.

tocotí

Myself deep in the water,
I see the mother take her breast
from the baby's mouth.
I see the father walk his fields alone.
I see the child, made fit for war,
turn to slash himself.

Orphans of the earth,
owl-eyed for evil,
we serve ourselves
and know it is no service.
Hunched on the tip of the rain,
we clamor foot-long for the earth.
Fetish-eyed in love,
we know the trick of leaving.
Woman, you are another's pleasure.
You will be abandoned. You will go away.

¡Día de llanto, día de lágrimas!

My tongue is coral,
my lips are emerald.
Feather flame, lucid *guacamaya,*
accept the service of your humble shield.
I write beside your emblem
my father's name,
my mother's name,
your name and mine.
Temple stone, the god endures
such service as you give.
So has the book been written.
So has your heart become perfect.

Tamborito

Four things, I know,
will never change.
I lie forever in the bed
of my cross,
north wind, south wind,
east rain, west rain.
The walls become my cross.
Tlequilitl.
I huddle the fire between my legs,
and light this room.

I am solid.
I am the measure of the house.
I sleep with my grainy eyes
plucking the shadows from the room.

A hummingbird, a forest flower
brought me to this house.
My bones crushed in a pilon,
I took my lover.

Comalli.
Clay, I lay
myself flat,
and, under my mother's touch,
I learn to serve.
When I am no longer in use,
I stand dejected
near the burnt-out fire
I danced upon.

A hummingbird, a forest flower
brought me to this house.
My bones crushed in a pilon,
I took my lover.

Metlapilli.
Blunt image of the love man's roller pin,
I roll the juices from the god's first fruits.
A hammer, I am forever raised
above the heart of this house.

A hummingbird, a forest flower
brought me to this house.
My bones crushed in a pilon,
I took my lover.

Now I am a mambo.
My açon croaks.

Now I am a mambo,
married to beads and snake's bones.

I call my Maîtresse
Erzulie Fréda Dahomin,
Venus of Dahomey,
Bride of the Loas.
I pierce her heart,
Lady of the Seven Sorrows.
I stand to the music
of my great, grate,
grateful, grating heart,
perfect rhythm of a heart
that never changes.

Vela

. . . cawMacaw of the rain forest.
Marigolds and bright banana leaves
light the road,
and yet the darkness closes in.
Too late,
I light your death with candles.
My feet in sandals,
I am a pilgrim
where the pilgrims wind
and beat their sorrows
at a Virgin's hem.
Tambora call.
The flutes call.
The scented candles call.
I call you,
                    Langston,
to a forest of beads,
choir of a Virgin's call for you.
Ave,
sing,
southern dangers ride

even the Virgin's wing.
María,
here,
a dead man floats
until you claim him.
I cannot claim
your sorrows for my friend.
Pilgrims with pity for themselves
follow me
with bleached skulls
and thorn-wrapped hearts,
follow me
with save us for our pity.
Can they remember
that you gave me fruit
from these forests, corn from these hills?
The gift redeems.
The gift is a debt of adoration,
an invitation to a shrine,
the blind path of the pure
who honor the light
the grave keeps.
Your grave keeps me restless.
Riding on a bed of marigolds,
I rub the glass before your saint,
massage my forehead with the bloom,
which may contain your grace.

Villancico

Love in a body, love in this your sign.
I raise four moons to polish your love's shine.
I raise four stars to see you as you stand.
You take me, in debt now to your own hand.

You take your white dress from the waves. No stain
appears upon the water where your train
curls lacy from a ram's horn, hugger bane

of eight young brides. Could I myself now chain
you to a monster rock to take the rain
of my love, horned, I hear the bell and plain
chant far out of time. My love is the line
you ride from the deep, and I ride the brine.

Love in a body, love in this your sign.
I raise four moons to polish your love's shine.
I raise four stars to see you as you stand.
You take me, in debt now to your own hand.

My antelope, my horse, there is no rein,
ram's horn, bull's bell or god's eye to constrain
you in the fields of love; there is no sane
man who would touch your knees, or hope to gain
the secret of your clan hunger, the skein
of your bones, wave of your heart's deepest vein.
Your love sits on my heart, a heavy wine
I give my untouched body at your shrine.

Love in a body, love in this your sign.
I raise four moons to polish your love's shine.
I raise four stars to see you as you stand.
You take me, in debt now to your own hand.

Faithful one, you come, wind before the rain.
Bean-bred, corn-fed, lady of the bead chain,
you hold an axe above your own domain,
where no ram dare plough, seed or shake his mane.
In the thorough-bass of your river plane,
I hear your name assault a priest, a brain
unfit to take a wife's caress, the whine
of the child's voice, hidden in this design.

Love in a body, love in this your sign.
I raise four moons to polish your love's shine.
I raise four stars to see you as you stand.
You take me, in debt now to your own hand.

There is pity in your name; in the reign
of your compassion, crown of love, you strain
to harvest pity on a bed of grain.
Widow of death, bride of change, you remain
the copy of the thorny heart, the vein
split free and open by another's pain.
Love, not your own, comes. You cannot decline
your body's burden, the redeeming sign.

Love in a body, love in this your sign.
I raise four moons to polish your love's shine.
I raise four stars to see you as you stand.
You take me, in debt now to your own hand.

So where my eyes have seen four moons constrain
these four stars to orbit and to ordain
a pythoness, a body yields, humane,
to the eyes' grasp, to the touch of plain
light. From orbit to orbit I retain
now all the distance of your body, drain
what light alone that it, my anodyne,
leaves, what touch it gives from your spirit's spine.

Pututu

What would you trade
for the sound of spring
                    in gazelle eyes,
for the sound of night in lilies,
of fire in the plantain,
of rain in a woman's bones?
What would you give
to hear the dove domed by the wind,
the doe caressed by the darkest
                    leaves of the forest?
I come from the river
under the mountain's claw,
and bring my daemon shells,

my god's penny change,
to tune your ears again.
Erect in the river's light,
I have my lance and flags at hand,
my body cased in the colors
of the lives that rise
in the blood of my horn.
I would rule you in the ooze
of my shell, or take you in
with the watery breath
that returns my song to my spine.
Pututu is the sound of your soul's ears
returning to my light.

Maracas in Merengue

Nothing suave,
a thief of beads,
snake bones
tickle your tum
and oil your neck.
I take your gaudy skin in hand.
I clutch your throat.
I rattle your eyes.
I free your fangs,
the cackle of your prophecies,
the high pitch of my wounds.
I find you everywhere.
Chucho, guache, carángano,
you are a devil's dance,
or the piper forty days from the cross,
the lover's kick,
or the dead man's trace,
the first light in the east.
Witness of the lilies' rising,
consort of the evergreen,
you are the keeper of my wife's
ringed eyes,

the anchoritic daemon
of my own dark forest.
The poor man cooks his hatred
in your bowels.
The mother, with a drunken son
at sea, snaps your jaws
around the silence of her heart.
You use us all.
We are all used up.
One day beyond the dimming
of the lights,
you will goad the dust to rise,
the air to charge the earth
                                        with our absence.

Bambuco

Face to face,
in faith,
my face,
a lyric mask,
becomes you.
I am at your grill again.
Your ribbon laces my ox
to your door.
Invite me, woman,
to the music of your middle.
I go one foot before the other,
leap back,
begin again from heel to toe.
You mirror my hesitation.
My nerve is in your back.
One foot before the other.
Leap back.
I pinch your waist,
and guide you through
the labyrinths of love's
                                        first petals.

I take your straight body
through the maze of my arms.
I fold my arms,
and touch the swords of yours.
I pass,
unbalanced by your face.
I court your kisses
while your body fades.
My life
is the middle of this dance.
My heart unfolds
to accept this cross,
the stone of our customary light.
Fire-ladened, river-burdened,
a bird indeed,
a blue knit shawl of moonlight,
you chase yourself before me,
you measure my soul's intent,
my clan craft,
the weight of my memory,
the distance of my father's fire.
I spread this shrunken white veil,
and call your step across the river.
I kneel,
and hear your familiar voice
call me home.

II

The Body Adorned and Bare

Cacahuatl: The Craft of a Bead Rosary

Who has buried
the god's bones in a boat,
riding on the forest's foam?

Cantor,
your free eyes bell me
through the psalter of a cocoa god,
fine yellow bones
                    cradled in a coffin.

Bell him and sour him,
cut him from the tree,
his bones will bleed
and numb the night
                    from your bones.

You thread his bones
into a rosary.
You gaud him with your rag's threads.
Adorned just so,

his spine is all of him.
Your hands hold the prayers
worried from the many souls
who change his holy name.

Ca cao Ifẹ
Ca cao Rome
bead me through the deep pitch
of my unfamiliar home.

The Craft of the Trumpet Shell Bracelet

God blind once again,
is that the sun,
is that the earth you wear?
Change is the needle of your days;
sumac and goatskin the twine.
I come down for the double of my life.
I trade my palm nuts, or my silver,
to have you clamp my left wrist
in a goat's song.
And so I would be finished
with your craft. Not yet.
Dicer, you will trim
this body with trumpet shells.
Sage, you will trumpet
a stage for the sun you wear
on your wrist.
Green shadows rehearse
an elephant song.
Divined by the hide,
I can hide no more.
I take the vision of your ear
within my bones,
and rub the darkness bright
                    and merciful.

The Craft of Beating Cloth

Nothing will decay or die.
All things will change,
the drum prop up my kente.
I beat the spirits softly
through the cloth.
Tree stump hand holds the cloth,
pulls the shape of it from the earth,
covers it with pigment
of the rock beneath.
Tree stump leg fidgets beneath my hand,
envies the adornment of my fabric.
Tree stump arm, rubbed by the water,
dries my wounded linen in the sun.
Drunk with the rhythm of my beating,
I see my clan under my hand
wake to weave its memory in my soul.

Agave

Maguey, they say
you live a hundred years;
for ten I cut your heart out
when you bloom.
I call you honeybee, and use you up.
I drink your juices for my dreams.
I stuff your hollow leg with corn.
I take you as my throne.
I bend you double over bamboo poles.
I crush a coat from your skin.
Your beauty gone,
I toss you into the fire,
and stir my nopal soup,
twist my lechuguilla rope,
cleanse my skin with another soap.
Above your dying body,
I shake my yucca baccata in the sun.

Missangas

I have no samba skill.
There is a carioca still-
ness in my legs.
I wake on rum and sea-foam,
banana meat and monkey brains.
But O Bahía
I count these none of my cock's
habits.
Sober in my sunlight ways,
the rays of your manner
lighting me down the cave
of my clan,
I follow your beads' design
into your magic.
Missanga miserere,
no Mary
                but a saint of substance
you cut me clear of fear.
My eye is on the blue glass bead,
the chicken scratching at the earth.
My eye is maroon.
My eye is red. My eye is green.
My eye is black.
Mother,
stiffen me in this my earth.
So many stars have passed
my sails no longer take the wind.
I need no further passage.
                                        I want none.
I roll the beads below your throat.
The perfect amber sun
rides the perfect blue green wave.
The darkness is as deep and bright
in this my cave.
Missanga miserere Ọya Mary,
the perfect history blesses your beads.

The Hat

1
(UNDER ITS ANCIENT ASPECT)

I was cattin with my hat
when the deal went down. But down.
Frown, but you don't know.
Gray felt, a stingy brim.
Could sit on a cane so trim.
Matched my shoes,
suede cut short in the toe.
Them was dues
                    born before your time.
Style don't go down so easy now.

2
(UNDER A CLOSER SIGN)

My crown I call it,
and I call you my crown.
Crowned yourself with beads,
you take the stars and the crescent moon
within your orbit.
There is a place you rest
when done with leading me,
head high, my eye widened
by your swagger.
I call this place of rest my home.
Your swagger is the beat it takes
to top my thundering eye.

Choosing My Shoes

Picture the patent ass of a 'gator,
belly floating caiman,
pig hips, doe fuzz, cow sheen,
rubber, blubber or wood. I cut

the butt of any living thing
to adorn my toes.

"A covering for the human foot."
The vamp is soft
to lead me where the tongue lies.
Cap me easy, cap me gentle,
cap where the G.I. spits
and rubs himself into the shoe.
I buff me gentle all around.
Dust or darkness,
my feet stand up, starlight on water.
The shank lifts me. The sole asserts me.
Soft skin, hard, bright skin, dull,
no skin at all, earth shapes it,
shapes my foot, takes my foot, takes me.
I remember
never do I greet a god,
an old man or a virgin girl
without my straps pulled tight.
To get a shoe,
you choose the thing from which
the blood has gone, a thing
that smells brand new and wraps
its pretty heat around your heels.
I used to call them wings,
and strap them to my body
to fly away from me.
Rough me, scuff me,
but leave my kicks alone,
unless you want to die.

The Body Bare

In darkness still,
the fish flop up and bite the beach.
They wrestle with the kelp.
The silver water cuts them cold. They die,

and will themselves be quarreled over.
My mother rakes the sand
in the foghorn's moan. We will be fed.
We will be told the story of her foot
upon the rocks, the chill of the guard's eyes,
the cold and beadlike body of the fish
hooked into her bag,
her Martha's flight along the spray.
We will be fed
by the water's benevolence, by a mother
who rakes the sun into her bag at dawn.

I am her sun at dawn.
Mofongo of the morning,
fufu,
farofa,
I cannot eat my memories.
But I clear my mother's body
from the coast.

Now I ride the Tijeras Mountains.
A whiskey still sustains me.
I cut the sleeve of night
                                        to find my food.
I lay my body on a puma trail.
I wait to hear a bear snore.
I would be brave with a goat.
Below the ridge,
the tumbleweeds of fires
roll from side to side.
I hear the slap of late tortillas
laid against the morning.
A boy buckets his bath in the moon.
When I turn, when I rise, when I return,
I see my sister turn upon the mud floor.
Her breath is the wind of adobe walls.
I take my hunger to another room.

Cackles in the cactus
and the cough of an old truck.

The highway slips away from the touch
of its shoes. My father has hard candy
from Tijuana, a Mexicali hat,
some spurs from Juárez and a head
from riding the border hard.
Thieves of the good things
laugh in this dust.
They raise their heads above
the broken tubs they bring, swing
their midnight lanterns round their heads.
I hear them celebrate the Chief's escape,
the jail's bells left at the border,
the nickel beer, the joy of tarring the states
together.

This then is my state when I leave you.
Fish on a mountain. Goats' heads in the bay.
Brown walls that turn to fire in the sun.
Sage of the coffee bean, sage of the corn,
you would have to understand
my bare body in the midst of cactus rain.
I am with you in the leap of loneliness
and your bank of wisdom at the gods' retreat.
I have this sumptuous hunger
for the tough meal in your kit.
I am tired of benevolent dishes,
the long lines round the pot,
the hierarchical cut of the meat.
I have gone from water to mountain,
fog dawn to needle dawn.
I have covered my body with your wishes.

Pine dawn now,
and evergreens.
I taste the snow.
I wish the sun stood silly
day by day, to worship my body.
I walk the paths cut thin
by Calvinistic blades.

I walk my body in their eyes.
I claim my itches, my discomforts,
when I turn in again.
Flutter of a winter bird, red shrill
piping down by the unopened doors.
These are not signs of my body.
I cannot take them so, though
the mark of my longing is
an unanswered song.
I would lay my brown desert body
at your door, beg you to take me in.
I walk a dog along the ice,
return and take myself in,
                                        into myself,
                                            unto myself.

Remember the willow and the swamp,
the tattered night patrol,
searching your body.
Remember the maze of trenches
and the tattered guns, searching your body.
Remember God's guards in tattered churches,
searching your body.
Remember your torn love and yourself,
searching your body.

I come upon my body bare,
at sea, in dust, climbing the heat,
or descending the cold.
I will not clothe it with my pride
or your unanswered pain.

III
Retablos

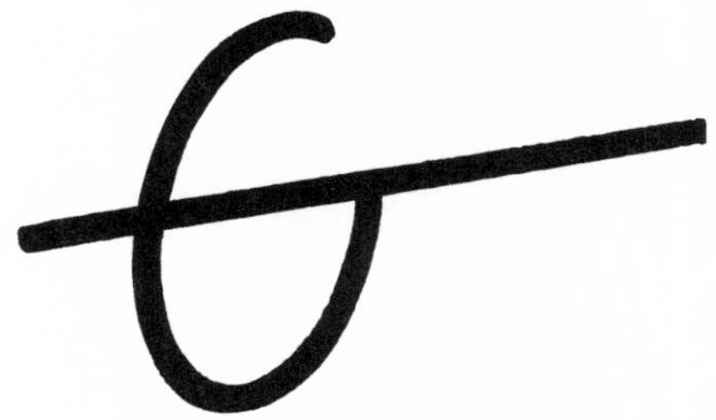

Niño de Atocha

Niño,
your service scourges me again.
I cut you on a piece of tin.
I tint your rose flesh rosier.
I curl your yellow hair.
I shoot your eyes full up
with my salvation.
I had your horsemen in a hutch,
once. Their mail hung down
around their sore hips;
their bleak hearts roamed
their banged-up chests.
God had given me their lances.
Their scruffy bibles screamed by day;
their chipped beads prayed all night.
I walked the wicked wires
about their jail,
their pain in my pocket,
my pity ready to ride a saint's wings.
Atocha babe,

my God admitted you,
a pilgrim with your staff, your basket
and your gourd. You fed their many hungers.
The bread and water flowed unstopped.
I stopped my heart against
the miracle of it, my urge
to clap you with the rest.
I told myself,
and tell myself
the same triumphant God looks down
to fill your Atocha basket, your gourd of grief.
Niño,
whose God is free?
Who frees the horsemen?
Who takes me safely
when I ride away?
Who is the One who keeps
all hands from striking me?
Niño, Atocha babe,
I cut your legend crudely,
my promise to remember
the danger of your service,
the danger of your God's sweet gift.

El Cristo Negro

In rose and ebony,
I bleed my Black Christ dizzy.
I cut into the skin so deep
the bone shows.
I take his image from the dark fires
in the green belt,
from the stone soaked in corn.
I fix the monkey howl,
the slither of a crocodile,
the orchid on the lake,
the strong, sweet coffee smell in rain,
above his eye.

Our Lord of Chalma,
Villa Seca,
Esquipulas
and Milagros,
I lift you from your own pain
                                        into mine.
Your sandals fit here.
Threadbare enough, you sit at ease
above my petate bed.
My wife will cut our maze
into your blanket.
Cold blood and a heavy turning,
these are the actuals of our lives.
One day, within the pool of possibles,
we all will come to be baptized
                                        in another's blood.
I raise your image now
before my face, and search the answer
you will give when you are called.

Mater Dolorosa

Lady, I look upon your axe;
naïve, I nail it in a corner
with the sword the book gives you.
I oil a rose to purple leaves.
I ponder over brown blood.
My sun must not compete with your
                                        chrome halo.
Your clinched mouth, opened only
in astonishment at your violation,
I cannot see. I cannot get your eyes
                                        bead right.
I have you in the water, or floating in the veil
the sun weaves from the mist.
I want to review your suffering,
the losses you accept.
You fold them under your body,

away from me. You raise your axe.
Wine of the blood is tree deep.
Mother, I need your word
to sit upon my golden stool.
Mother, I petition you for silence
at my burial.
Mother, I am heartsick
kneeling to fix your pain.
Why should I tint your arms with grief
when it is my still body
                                        that you hold?

Saint Gertrude

Dead islands and dead I am.
I call upon my calypso patroness,
my sugar lady.
You stand between my heart and God.
I play my heart out on the cane.
I die. I rise unless you plant me.
Pidgeon peas. My roots go down.
Boil the peas, or cut a cut-eye bean.
        "Go down in the ground
            Dig one sulky yam.
        When you get it down
            Carry him give him room."
Sister, sing me a Santa Cruz Bakinny.
I ride. The stones prepare my way
and announce that I have gone.
Rice follows me, my wedding to the earth.
Clearly, Teuton maid,
my heart has taken your shaft.
Clearly, living leprous to myself,
I walked your calm light.
Now, I plot my rise,
not among sugar and roses,
but coming in a storm upon your staff.

IV
Logbook of Judgments

What Is Good

Out of the water call
my luminous breath,
into the bird, intending serpent, red,
who shakes himself, white,
out of that forest body, black.

Red gourd head spirit of the bush,
your breath is speech;
your speech is ordinary, pure.
I take you from the blue
glass of my sacred windows,
I ring you cold upon my father's weights.

I would cook and save you
in my body's house alone, light
you in the useless prism of my own desires.
I hold you in the yellow
parchment of my soul's hand.
Once I took your body for the shape

of all I walked upon, your god's voice
for the sound of all my light.
But now I count my sins against
the ordinary syntax of my days.

Bird of the hard wood,
I would transcend the dog
and fox of my father's prayers,
the corn, the monkey, lion and the seed
cut crudely by the cross in gold,
the black figures of a Christian death.

Bird, so you would change,
and flutter in my mother's eyes.
And in my mother's eyes
still bodies have rhythms of their own.
The light of dead hearts, my governors,
leads my body to a stillness.
I speak of stillness, and you see
I still grip your rhythm to my body.

Rhythm of my shade, an elephant skin.
Rhythm of my hat, the llama's hair.
Rhythm of my coat, the cactus' beard.
Rhythm of my trousers, silkworm web.
Rhythm of my shoes, pig hips.
Rhythm of my seat, the heart of a tree.
Rhythm of my hands in the beads.
Rhythm of my hands in the cleansing water,
of my eye in the perfect form of stillness,
the perfect light of my mother's ecstasy.

Composed, I am saved
by my mother's reason,
my neighbors' needs,
my will to go beyond the stillness
of my gods' dreams.
Luminous breath,
teach me compassion for this
my complex body.

What Is True

I argue my woman into compassion.
Light upon light, through darkness,
she gives me what is true.
Radiant light is in the riverbed,
morning's collocation,
the linchpin of the hours' flow.
The source of illumination
is in the jaw of the willow,
clinching the earth, the juice
that inches from the broken cactus ear.
A lily dead upon the water veils the altar.
A star ascending reaches its
own domain, its own rest.
But here we balance in the moon fall,
and chart the absence in a curve,
upon a clock,
the solitary body where the world ends.
Composed,
we name the caves from which we rise.
Profane and strange, our dead arrive
with linen and scented candles,
salt beer, sweet wine,
tapered beads, a bright
wood for the altar.
It seems that nothing in this light
will fade or be used up.
And so I take their meanings
from my woman's sign,
their changes from her absence.
I take her passion for my head,
her craft into my heart.
Love measures me.
Love pays me out.
Love gives me my domain.
My radiance is a red bead,
a white feather on a bow,
balanced on my grave.

What Is Beautiful

Now I invest the world
with a song of your flesh,
song of your bones, your blood, your heart.
I pitch all dark things still
to the scale of my voice.
I name what I distinguish.
I discern what rises without a name.
Here, there is no form untuned by eye, or voice;
there is no body waiting for its metaphor.
My canon gathers all the turnings
of your light, all the offices
and arguments of your soul's intent.
Your body has a province in my two worlds,
begins its own exchange in my eye.
So as my music is exampled only
in the movement, so is your body simplified,
made absolute and able to bear
the god's chill piping in your bones,
his red eye scanning your skin.
But I do not shape you two-in-one,
or call you from the darkness,
a scruffy thing, enhanced and visible
only when the light leaves you.
I turn you to the tuning fork of solid
walls, my rolled corn, my tiled squares,
the rose windows of my altars.
I turn your ear, now transformed,
to the imperfection of sacred things,
your body's distant vibrations.
And so each element of my song moves,
and my voice takes back its absence,
my eye searches a new light, another exchange.
This is the gift of being transformed,
the emptiness that calls compassion down.
I pitch my eye to my uneven form,
my voice to the depths of your grace.
I reason with the sound and movement
of your body to the vision
                    that my body bears.

Meta-A and the A of Absolutes

I write my God in blue.
I run my gods upstream on flimsy rafts.
I bathe my goddesses in foam, in moonlight.
I take my reasons from my mother's snuff breath,
or from an old woman, sitting with a lemonade,
at twilight, on the desert's steps.
Brown by day and black by night,
my God has wings that open to no reason.
He scutters from the touch of old men's eyes,
scutters from the smell of wisdom, an orb
of light leaping from a fire.
Press him he bleeds.
When you take your hand to sacred water,
there is no sign of any wound.
And so I call him supreme, great artist,
judge of time, scholar of all living event,
the possible prophet of the possible event.
Blind men, on bourbon, with guitars,
blind men with their scars dulled by kola,
blind men seeking the shelter of a raindrop,
blind men in corn, blind men in steel,
reason by their lights that our tongues
are free, our tongues will redeem us.
Speech is the fact, and the fact is true.
What is moves, and what is moving is.
We cling to these contradictions.
We know we will become our contradictions,
our complex body's own desire.
Yet speech is not the limit of our vision.
The ear entices itself with any sound.
The skin will caress whatever tone
or temperament that rises or descends.
The bones will set themselves to a dance.
The blood will argue with a bird in flight.
The heart will scale the dew from an old chalice,
brush and thrill to an old bone.
And yet there is no sign to arrest us
from the possible.

We remain at rest there, in transit
from our knowing to our knowledge.
So I would set a limit where I meet my logic.
I would clamber from my own cave
into the curve of sign, an alphabet
of transformation, the clan's cloak of reason.
I am good when I am in motion,
when I think of myself at rest
in the knowledge of my moving,
when I have the vision of my mother at rest,
in moonlight, her lap the cradle of my father's head.
I am good when I trade my shells,
and walk from boundary to boundary,
unarmed and unafraid of another's speech.
I am good when I learn the world
through the touch of my present body.
I am good when I take the cove of a cub
into my care.
I am good when I hear the changes in my body
echo all my changes down the years,
when what I know indeed is what I would
know in deed.
I am good when I know the darkness of all light,
and accept the darkness, not as sign, but as my body.
This is the A of absolutes,
the logbook of judgments,
the good sign.

Landscapes

The Physical Dimension

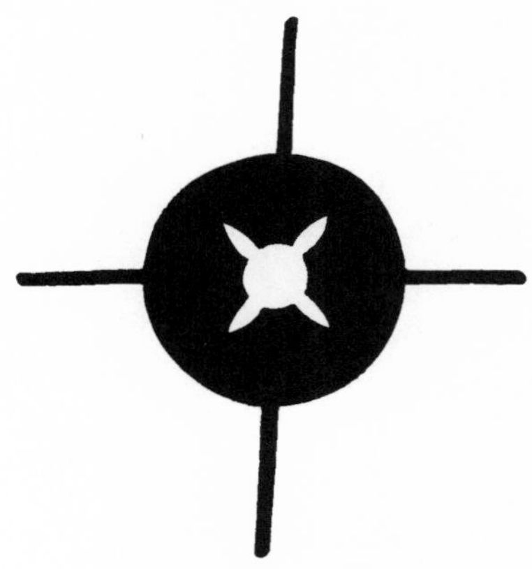

Now I invoke my map of beads.
I coil the spirit's veins about my wrists.
I kneel at Ocumare to worry
the saint's bones,
and rise on the walls of Cumaná.
Poco a poco,
I cut my six figures
on another coast, in a western sunrise.
In Carolina darkness, I push
my jangada to the blessed water.
I ask now:
all the blessed means my journey needs,
the moving past, the lingering shadow
of my body's destination.
I ask my body to be here.
I ask for eyes that can invest
the natural body, the invested land,
the invested star, the natural spire,
landscape of spirit and the spirit's
rise in stone or in the fragile bones
of the earth's body.
This will be my secular rosary,
my votive map, my guidebook
to the deeper mines of destiny.

What secret in the water?
What is deep within
that makes it whisper
here, in the night?
Over the walls, the night steps,
fire of the wail, the clear conception
of the rhythm of the tomb.
So our memories were buried
to begin here. And the night whispers,
teach us the error of this conception.

Water may not build a wall.
Its force ticks down the seawall's clock.

Time is the sea
that whispers clearly in our fog
of memory, and stands here,
at the edge, a boot upon our earth.
It leads us by its absence.
Clear presence,
it is a babe pushed up
from the arms of the mother's deep.
                                        We were born in her.

Hear the cradle song at night
—Carib water song—
accompany the kindled canoe
into the light. The light
is a crown upon the heads
of gods who wither by day.

Or shall we begin here,
old man, old Panamá,
among the labyrinths of labyrinths?
Only a window and a wall remain
in Genoveses' house.
Portholes look down the narrow, dirty bay.
This is a small skeleton,
a simple bag of bones
                                for simple action.
Stand, and hear
the call and response of the wind,
the wind in the ribs of slavers,
the mill horns,
the wind in the sea's shell,
the lean fish that flip in the cup
                                        of the sea.
The Cathedral, broken to reveal its cavity,
faces the open field,
                                or turns inward.
All things have turned inward,
or have gone down,

down where the ships' echoes
                                        never end.
I fly now underground
                                        at Zipaquirá.
This is the dark day of slate.
A miner with the heat upon his head
searches for an exit,
                                        or a pearl,
or the reason given when a bull
sits to adore Jesus.
All your eucalyptus will adore salt,
and polish the walls crystal clean
at the height of the tomb.
I stand in the womb of the chapel.
I speak the simple words of youth,
timeless mother greeting babble,
and my voice returns
through the crystal chandelier,
a weight upon me.
I walk the fifteen stations of the cross.
I carom with the one winged angel.

A bird on the Orinoco,
an eagle above a shield,
I would fly to the roof and belfry of straw,
"a sparrow's nest" at San Andrés,
to return that delicate body.
Summit of my Pico,
body consumed by fire,
a Morning Star, a Mountain Star,
I swallow your heart.
So the light will be consumed
by the moon, and returned again
in the language of birds,
or in the body resting under water.

Venezuela: consists of four geographical areas: the jungle lowlands of Maracaibo, the mountains of the north and west, the unexplored Guyana highlands, the flat grasslands near Colombia: it has 1750 miles of Caribbean coastline: it has a population of 10,811,921: its language is Spanish, its religion Roman Catholic: its principal industries are petroleum, coffee, mining, agriculture, cattle and food processing: it was discovered by Columbus in 1498 and named Venezuela (Little Venice) because of the fancied resemblance of Lake Maracaibo to Venice: it gained its independence in 1823.

When you enter Caracas,
you go from water to jungle.
The city hides behind the mountains,
then becomes the mountains.
The earth-colored houses and shacks
are hives on the hillsides.
They clench the earth.
The earth suspends them in its robes of air.
                                        Roots
are my substance now—
yuca, arepa, ocumo, ñame, batata.
I color the shrine of my Virgen Morena
the color of roots.
                                        Cumaná,
fortress of the Virgin of the Head.
                                        Cumaná,
city of walls.
                                        Ocumare,
                                        Cabudare,
                                        El Tocuyo,
I dance my Tanunangue,
                                        salve,
                                        batalla,
                                        bella,
                                        poco a poco,
                                        el galerón.

At Puerto Cumarebo,
I bathe St. John the Baptist
and his blessed feet.
My casaderas come by morning

to the river, to cut their rude hair
and strengthen their heads in the water.
My sister takes her future
from an egg yolk
coiling in a glass of water.
And so she reads her freedom.
But these, the dames of Lima,
read theirs in another fashion.
They stitch Bolívar's wounds in reds
and the colors of roots;
they stitch their own command:
Ser libre o morir.
Now prim Bolívar rides a horse
in Bolívar Square. The horse kicks
at the steel that rises all around him.
I ride my chair, my chariot;
it costs me un real, half a Bolívar.

High and higher,
I aspire to ride a blue air,
to ride the blue of Mary, Yemanyá.
I need no lacquered Christ,
scourged, a dog, an alabaster semblance.
And yet I clothe my chapels
in gold, maroon and reds.
I light them with a million candles
to enhance my Mary's blue.
This is the annunciation of fire and water.
I give you San Francisco
                    and the bell-shaped, solid
canopy, a via dolorosa to the pulpit.
The light of that delicate body
I will not cover in emeralds and gold.
From this seat, I see the seat of Pico,
the peak of the Mountain Star,
el jaguar de la luna,
Venus with a tail.

I lay my pyramids wall upon wall.
The walls recall the war of Venus and Mars.

Four days I sat without a sun.
I build that darkness here.
And at the top I place my sun god
and his promise of the years.
Fifty-two serpents wind the years
around my knees. The walls contain me.

And so, in fever, I walk the city's wall.
In the Cathedral, I walk upon
the distinguished dead.
Marble, cal y canto, stone,
cathedral born to Carlos Fifth,
I name you Santa Catalina Alejandrina,
I name you the Cathedral of Cartagena de Indias.
Would the maimed one fill you with light?
Would your Virgin and your Child fall from cedar?
Mozarabic crowns of fragile silver
would become you.
In Cartagena, still,
you hear the language of the bells—
Believe, you must believe.
For every nail, I nail a cross
upon your doors. I give you sun.
I take your salt. I send you down
to the roots of the earth.
I will walk your walls
to protect my emeralds and gold,
to protect my name, to protect
my faith in your salvation.
Surely, you will forget the moon,
if I give you the sun. Surely,
you will forget the way a jaguar walks,
or the way an eagle swallows a serpent's heart,
or the whisper of your women at the water,
in the rain,
forget the maroon beads and a blue waking.

Always the colors contend,
but always they are stripped to these

—colors of the earth, colors of the enclosed water,
color of magnificence, color of blood,
color of the sea's deep, color of the tomb
from which the god will rise—
and one no color but desire
                                        rising in the stillness.

Stillness becomes you.

Star land, golden land, dark and true light.

Colombia: stretches from the tropical Caribbean to the high plateau of the interior: its tropics stretch along the 940-mile Magdalena River: it counts fertile central valleys: its coasts border the Pacific and the Atlantic: it has a climate for everyone: its population is 24,230,000: its language is Spanish, its religion Roman Catholic: its principal industries are coffee, emeralds, petroleum, bananas, textiles, steel, paper, rice, cocoa and cattle: it was settled by Spain in 1525, and won its freedom in 1819: it formed the Republic of Greater Colombia with Venezuela and Ecuador, who withdrew from the union in 1829: in 1886, it became the Republic of Colombia: the country counts among its curiosities its hydrographic star, formed in the following manner: the Pasto plateau is the trunk on which the three ranges of the Andean structure in Colombia are grafted: the eastern or Cordillera of Bogotá, the central or Cordillera of Quindio, the western or Cordillera of Chocó: the ranges consist of narrow branches in the south: they spread in the north between the fourth and fifth parallels until they reach the Carbibbean shores or marshy plain of Lower Magdalena: this star pattern covers 117,000 square miles, one-quarter of the country: it is the source of rivers emptying into the Pacific, the Caribbean, the Orinoco and the Amazon: it exerts an influence on the distribution of rainfall by the nature of its contours.

From pity,
or from the star's wave,

from the god, shooting the rapids
of his mercy, the rain falls.
Even in the north's dust,
green bananas drop from green leaves,
the frayed cotton raises its head in the wind.
But rain itself has picked the bones
                                        of the earth.
My cattle settle in the dust, and die.
My lean dogs pick their gonads in the street.
The birds sail over me.
I call upon my bird god.
Out of Quebradillas, San Agustín, Huila,
I conjure a bird man
with cavities for eyes.
And this, the third one,
is it nose or mouth?
A stem runs through the bulky body.
The head is four curves.
The hair, cut under, makes pyramid
steps, going to the crown.
Thick, delicate body,
I ask your help from dryness and the rain.
I ask the bulky tubes
of your shoulders to uphold me.
I see your adorned wrists,
your hands that hold your neck on a stem.
Your body is a wall that hovers over me.

I call you feathered serpent.
I say you lie in the roof and belfry of straw.
Bird on the Orinoco,
eagle above a shield,
stone,
you lie at the temple's entrance,
an incense bowl upon your chest.
You know the purity of water.
You know the water in the form of a star.

And Panamá, my Panamá,
I stretch you as a second eye,
                    a dog star.

Panamá: is an *S*-shaped isthmus: the sun rises over the Pacific because the Pacific exit of the Canal is 27 miles east of the Atlantic entrance: it has mountains and volcanoes and coastal, tropical lowlands: its population is 1,619,000: its language is Spanish, its religion Roman Catholic: its principal industries are bananas, cocoa, abaca and fish: it became a republic in 1903: Chibchas, Caribs, Kunas, Guayamís and Chocós were its first inhabitants: then came the Indo-Spanish, Negroes, West Indians, Italians, Greeks, Chinese, Japanese, Indians and Austrians.

So I would claim you,
land of all and land of none.
I take your heat into my body.
I take your suffocation for my bones.
Old Panamá is not a name
                    attached to Henry Morgan.
Here in the bay,
I watch the homeless come to your shores.
You take them in as merchants of themselves.
The curve of your land takes the unknown jangada.
Jangada searches coasts and roots.
Jangada leaves and searches Golden Rain,
hummingbirds' haven.
Under the jacarandas,
I stir my hallaca (fufu): ocumo,
ñame, batata, yuca.
—Yucca baccata—
I stir the vision of the bowl within the tree,
the bowl within the ribs.
I regain the water in sacrifice,
                    in sun, in sea.
Blue of the star spiral,
and the water has gone.

The Virgin has replaced my goddess.
My temple is hers.
Three people gather on these pyramids.
The star leads them.

México: has an area of 760,335 square miles: it forms part of North America, but the southern area, south of the Isthmus of Tehuantepec, belongs to Central America: its southern neighbors are Guatemala and British Honduras: the Pacific Ocean lies west, the Caribbean and the Gulf of Mexico lie to the east: the country is a Federal Republic of twenty-nine states, two territories (Baja California and Quintana Roo) and the Federal District with twelve surrounding villages: over half the country lies above 3000 feet: the major feature of surface relief is the high central plateau extending from the northern border to the Isthmus of Tehuantepec and covering most of its width: this is flanked by the Sierra Madre Occidental and Oriental.

And if the star arises from the east,
will it come as the Star of David?
Tenoch/Enoch, leader of my seven tribes,
you march me down two hundred years.
Bell in the jungle,
bell in the desert,
Quetzalcóatl wears your star.
I wear your unanswered questions.

This city is a temple,
and all steps lead up.
Turning in its own space,
the fifth sun diminishes all,
but promises life.

: the conterminous United States is a huge quadrilateral, extending 3000 miles from ocean to ocean and more than 1200 miles from the Great Lakes to the Gulf of Mexico: the total area of the fifty states is

3,552,198 square miles: one of its distinctive features is the Canadian Shield: between the Appalachians and Rockies, nearly level plains cover an immense area of Archaean bedrock with what is often a thin layer of sedimentary rocks: the bedrock was folded long ago and worn down before the end of Pre-Cambrian times: a complex of schists, granites and gneiss outcrops over more than half of Canada.

Now lava stone protects me,
and creates my gods.
I build my life in skull-racks,
and cut my time upon another stone.
My cross is as green as the land
                                                  it stands upon.
I travel by the turning of a star
through all the gates that lead me home,
that lead me to my other self.

And I return now to my city at Labná.
It has been a long march.
I am half-naked.
I retain no more than a band
about my head, and a band about my waist,
my sandals on my feet,
my homespun mantle and a pouch
for the gods' bones.
But I am victorious.
I march from the humble
to the sacred side of the city.
I enter where I return.
I return again to the land of the star.
There is peace in this elevation.
You come, if not to God,
near to yourself.
It is a star land, a golden land,
our dark and true light,
the image of our life among ourselves.

The Double Invention of Kọmọ

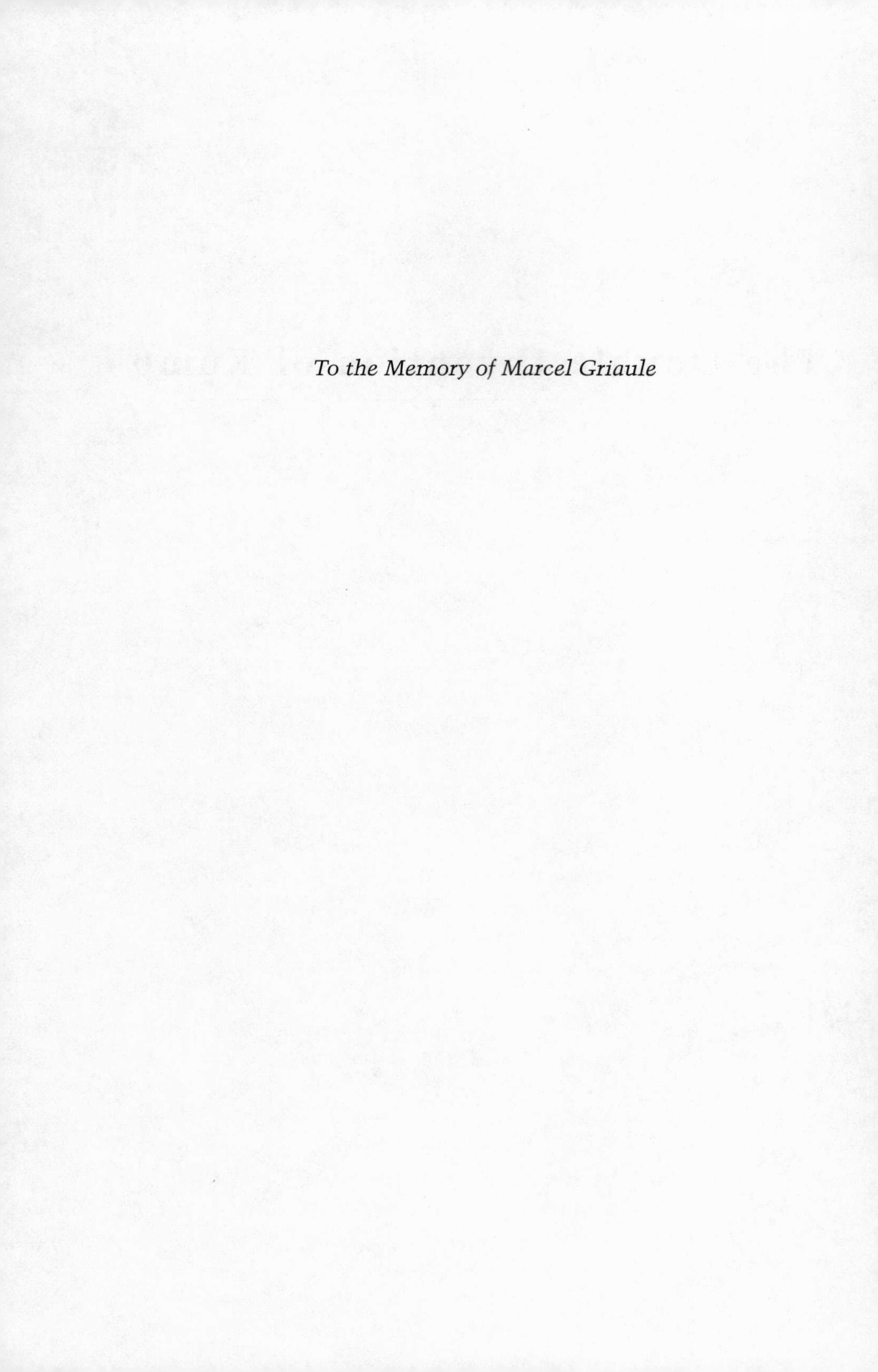

To the Memory of Marcel Griaule

. . . imagination is the mind working *under great reservations* which *set it free. . . .*

—Bernard Bosanquet

sagu pini nañdaru gyina boy
Les cailloux de divination ont sauté en l'air

—from the ceremony of the invention of Sigui among men, in Marcel Griaule, *Masques Dogons*

The Invocation

This is the language of desire.

banā́ yírí kọrọ
banā́ ba yírí kọrọ
dyigini yírí kọrọ
yẹlẹni yírí kọrọ

Through this you will be fulfilled.

I place myself under the sign of the divine spirit
under the sign of the great divine spirit
under the tree of sacred signs
under the tree of ascension of souls

Prefigurations: First Instance of the Field, First Instance of Voice

This is the language of gold, silver and wood,
stone, herring bone and sand.
Walk in the light of copper.
By an egg's radiance I arrange my soul's baggage.
Age over age, my bones thicken and flex.
I am adept in the god's boat,
and I would sail through every light,
taper of a still point.
The wind at my back is the bellows' breath,
the aspirate mouth in the cleavage of earth and air,
the water's hiss in the heat.
If you call me to your side,
I will not soothe you.
Brother, I drink all things.
And I profess
one master
one creator
one power
one king

one cult
one submission

By these things, you will desire;
by these things, you will be fulfilled.

Brother, I take your woman's heart into my head.
Already, I am four.
I double myself, and double you.
Age over age, I grow into the woman of all things.
I have seen her shape, a spark encased
in a cloud's cradle, descend in the rain's chariot.
Speak, under water, as though you held me
in my white robes again.
Baptize the dangers I must hold
to speak your name again.

This is the language of desire,
the trace,
the pool,
the wood I enter
to ride again on the bleeding
power of your voice.

I take the west way, where I cut
a sacred wood, wood of purity,
wood of the egg, or the call of Kọmọ.
In the wood's heart,
I find the god's cradle,
a pinion of heaven.
Earth swells.
I must have this belly
to contain my first desire.
The earth I alter to my flesh,
round pinion of my dungeon desire.
I league myself with water to construct
the tongue I lay upon the altar.
The bowl is my double's bed;

the altar is my sexton's sword.
Love's journey leads me to their seat.

May I come embedded in this forest lure
when the light salts its presence in the kapok tree
and my only light is down a ladder
of longing, spiny devotee of my double's desire.

I call attention to the clearing
and the wood's unfolding,
to the tip of the first knife,
heaven's flash and spiral,
and there invoke the mother ascending,
the birth of the cradle's heart,
trace, an incision.
In the cradle's embrace,
the wood possesses all its shrubs and stones,
the luster it pulls from the earth to set
trembling near its heart. This is the black,
white, red and clarity of element,
my image swaddled in god's doorway.
Plainly, I figure myself
in the house of simple design.
Mother, I would have you ornament
me with your force, and so I place
an egg and hemisphere under the god's sign.

By this act, the god's shield stands alone.

I must now recall you to my solitude,
my coiled figure in the cradle's clearing.
The vulture and the jackal ex- and circumcise my body,
just at that point of the god's trace.
Clearly, the clearing has disguised
the god's trace and mother's dispossession.
My solitude uncovers the doorway again.
I must sit here now,
to enrich my double with tobacco.
I clench my pipe against

this altar's visible oneness.
I ask some shadow to ascend my altar smoke.
The invisible threshold kicks my anguish awake.
I cover my steps in the clearing,
unhinge my tobacco and chew down
the air's gold, my body's shadow in the god.

The wood addresses me,
and allows me to dress
my body with desire.
Here, I am awakened
to the soul of all power.
Each word is my knife's
incision into the gold of darkness.

A copper light reveals you,
tombed by gold.
Fisher of the forest,
you lie beside your own desire.
Your own desire
declares that it is morning.
It is morning.
The wood wears its water veil.
A doñu bird clips the mist
from the hibiscus.
You awaken and arise
from your tomb-canoe bed.
Dry earth ripples,
under the sun's caress,
ready to embrace your boat.
I run, out of my island village,
to see you set your arm as mast and sail;
I take your rayed robe as a net.
Beneath you, every bone
voices its desire to weigh with you.
The clamor in this gold darkness
has called me from my solitude
into yours.

What child am I?

All day, I stub in my father's fields,
or whistle in the market over
my mother's pots, adept in the provisions
of belonging.
At night, I lodge
near the most familiar limbs.
On my bed,
I am fused to my brother's steel spine.
The wind's bugle covers my day's death.

When will I know the form of my own childhood?

My mother calls me
                child of winter,
                child of the cold,
                child of the dry season,
                child of the warmth.
She is my shepherd's bride.
We share this secret knowledge.
This very gold will teach her that she may not speak
of what the wood holds.
And so, for her, in light,
I ride her breathless tasks;
I market the choir of her pots with a plain chant;
I exchange her birds' relations for honey.
I have the proper voice to order these services.
I unfold my services under the aged ones' eyes.
Then, on my blue pallet, I coil into silence.

Time has taught me to hear pity's song.
My shepherd tells me this compassion will be my name.
My hard sound of wood will uphold his stone.
I would be the sun, or a dodo,
a pimento, or a water cure,
but I know I must rest in what is given.
What is given oils my bird's ears
to what is not said.

I hear the water voices
beneath the god's boat in the wood,
and the thrush of desire in the god's throat.
The master horn that awaits my initiate's
morning opens my night.
I cannot, in my solitude, answer the call,
though I impatiently turn my eyes to the west.

It is night, yet it is morning.

Am I to be cast up,
neither living nor prepared,
at the base of these serpent stairs?
Am I to be a minnow,
hooked and dangled into earth
on a tacky thread?

The First Figure of the Stair, the First Casting

Yes, this is the chain of descent.
Like you, the world unwinds from a body.
Umbilical, it waves through every heaven,
                                        on every day.
If I design this descent,
I mark the heavy line at one.
The foot is balanced by the head.
I go through ten and seven turns
from head
            to toe.
By this, I create a schema of flesh,
a body wise in the reach of destruction,
in the hazards of desire,
tempted by its lily breath
to believe in its own salvation.
Rise and decline,
recline and stand,
the body has its reasons
to begin, to rest, to sit

in the four chairs of heaven,
to be belled into the chamber
of our lords' wedding,
to seek, in its fox's leap,
a tableau of perfection.
This, in your body, you must understand.
Out of the constellation,
you must bone and bleed your many names.

Do I have silence now?

Stand.

The altars will parade.

The Eleven Altars Dance in the Wood

Dyibi—obscurity—gold

This is desire's first veil,
the face between your god-flesh and your head.
                                        Within this space,
your soul contests its own making.
Here,
        the tongue dips
                                into its own craving.

This is the face god offers to his own light.
This is the face god veils with his possible tears.

In this nexus of exchange,
the god will license you
                        to navigate his pool.
                                                You
will uncover passion's house,
the scene of your own defense,

a manifest
of time's uncovering.
Double theos,
solitary network,
an agent
with a duty to enslave,
your divination's
only bird,
nature's sack
transfigured by the teeth
and hair about your head,
you wear
your other's appetite,
you invest
in the bone and black blood
turned red,
forsaking its darkness for light.

I hold your passage in this veil
in a just and cutting hand.
I will cover your eyes.
The light you then address returns
you to the clarity of being strange.
This forest has become your true and golden mask.

Makárí—pity/compassion—wood

Makárí makárí
piper of the wood,
second in command.
A sign decomposed,
you echo god's voice,
you figure the path into charity.
You will endure your soft plunge,
down, where the woman
is a white star on a bed.
Come, now, through depression's timber.
This axe I offer cuts clean.

This axe will uncover
the jade in the tree's marrow.
I see you, a sailor shucked
on a yellow cliff, finger
the boat in the dream.

Nę́nę́—cold/taste—stone

But you must savor stone,
and the cold way it enters the blood
when the green goes,
when the shroud no longer serves
to confound the light.
If you would endure as green,
you must uncover the deepest wall
and circle the light, borne,
in your name,
in the aged ones' eyes.

Sęlę—tomb—copper

Sęlę.
A copper cave
of interrupted music.
Death's artisan in sound.
Out of the gold,
through wood
and stone,
the body pours
its longing.
We will observe
the altar rise
from ash into red,
and hear the blue hymn
of praise under
the pilgrims' scallop shells.
A woman will rub

her knees raw
at the hem of these hills.
A soldier will spear
his solitude
under
the night's one star.
That star will have no name,
even if it rises
from the water's deepest weeds,
or has its heart
caparisoned by loss.
But the grave's name
is love's assembly,
the embassy of power,
and submission.
You will weigh
love's coming and return
in the balance of your
head's eye,
certain
of the water's intention
to wash your blood alive
in these ascending
bones.

Šukodyí—water to wash the cadaver—silver

Silver April,
in an evening's mist,
the Great Fish parts the pool.
I know him by his baggy eyes
and the four-rayed helmet
sitting on his locks.
He has come from the witch's chest,
love-filled heavy with her wishes.

Down below the love bed,
the knit bones of the dead

cock their conch ears
to another soul's implosion.
My monody impels you to the shore,
where I enroll among the thorns
clutched in the rocks.
I will, by my heart's hunker-down
hazard, examine your twilight eyes
and will.

Šukodyí.
The dead leather their mourning bells
about your hucklebones.
Like flame, these cannon chants
provoke you to a dance along the shore.
Gold darkness, mist
and April,
a jade tree,
the white woman in blood
on the blue bottom's bed,
my violet trembling
near the pool's pulpit,
you, star-raked and scorched,
play in a rainbow of desire.

Šukodyí,
seek the silver water
for the body's cleansing.

Šukodyí.
Seek me to cleanse you
with the silver water.

The moon approaches,
with its silver bells and amulets,
a silver slip of compassion
against the night.
You arrive in the space
not taken by the cold.
You shuttle your hands in the sand,

believe it my grave,
listen for my breath's clock
to arrange me on your loom.
Because I am thorned to endure,
a bearded little boy,
I sword the rocks aside.
I see you in what seems a prayer
over a body that will not come.

You inhale.
You bellow.
You undo the smallest grain.
Your breath shapes a red clavicle.
I am beside you.
I am in you.
I enter the night in your breath.
I am your second smith
and the iron you forge.
I watch you fashion my absence.

Šukodyí.
The silver water tempers
love's unending theological
loss.

Sę̃—FOOT—EARTH

What is brown
is a foot.
Star-heel in mud,
it could be the sign
of the little black man
in a manger on a cliff.
It could be the name
of a woman from the north.
My camel bags token
a long ride
through the black oil of the desert.

I will travel, on my own foundation,
to a water palm and cocoa shade.
I will not race a dervish to the sea,
                                        alone.

We set out when it is cool.
The woman in the train
has a feather boa and bead necklace.
I have a Boanerges at my side.
Walk in copper light.
A goat's hide will uphold you.
I complete this configuration
of the one element,
tale of a Berber's journey,
the one star's buttress and vault,
by the soul's compulsion
in death's drum.
Kọ   Kọrọ   Kọmọ   Korabra
feather of heel and toe in the wind,
adorned pick of the earth's thick neck,
Kọ   Kọrọ   Kọmọ   Korabra
bed of the baby, rising
                    from his mother's ribs.

SÍNÍ́KLE—MORNING SUN/FUTURE TIME—HERRING BONE/DODO

That bone is a bird's voice,
announcing the morning.
Now, back, I cannot lift my wings;
the sun is out of reach.
I used to ascend air's pyramid

—step up, step down,
  wing in, wing out—

a pattern taken from a fish spine.
In air, I chased the god's net.

Though small, plucked whole,
I could requite my debtor.
Skinned of that design,
                I fell.
A bird on bone legs,
out of time,
I peruse the shore.
My saint asserts I still retain
my angled spine,
a calendar of signs.

Bone into umbilical cord,
I signify the first cause,
            the head
            and penetration
as the days
                uncoil.

This I have given you
       is,
          more than light,
a candle close enough to keep
your memory intact,
                         a wheel
to measure your shadow's progress.

All shadows weigh me down.

                              I rise
by taking two ways
       under light.
                              I continue
by refusing
       the gold's darkness.
       Under my wing,
I keep a color to free
the morning
       and the soul's
              theological chant,

a hard shell to defend
the heart's scroll, measured
by engendering death.

Keep this in the willow
of your bird's back, or in your fish voice.
Keep this as a sign
that you will return to me.

Buabá—large fish—pimento

I love this fat bird's truckle to my bed.
Observe this rainbow on my head
and the coordinates on my cloak.
When thunder and rain ease me upstream,
I advance at such a depth
I muzzle the stiffest weeds.
Buabá is my pot.
Confidence and pride are the unguents
I plaster to your soul.

Fúrábá—cure/remedy—water

And, if you would be a healer,
wait, near the water, for the drowned
to belly up into your touch.
There is a tree that is divine.
Its scalar leaves reveal
a scapulary mother at its base.
The clan has cut her for the fearful
child she bears; he binds his wounds
into her bones. She must knuckle
the cross to escape her possession.
Unbound, you want to enter to untie
her longing.
You take the calabash and chalk
to engrave what you would redeem.

Water names you. You claim your sign.
Healer and divine, without a death
upon what cross would your speech
affect the shiver in the child's flesh,
or the mother's impatient duel with her heart?
Death, that knows its confederate pleading,
enslaves your child's breath.
Healer,
you would be wound-free,
if the water were as gold
as god's just jade and wood.
Healer,
you must mingle stone's compassion
with the eye that keeps its line
upon the grave.

DYAKÓ—FASHION—CHARCOAL

Child,
even limestone is light in the dark.
Pure light is choked in the lamp.
The lamp fits in the dark.
Darkness commends the mother to the wood.
In the wood,
the darkness will fashion you
air's diamond, divinity's double
at compassion's well,
love's figure on the moon's plate.
This silver arranges love's dress.

You will approach the field
displayed in darkness, adorned
yourself with the field.
I bring you, by my lamp,
to the place, where the god
will chalk our dense deeds
on your bones,

and, under every dative wish,
I give you your deed's own form.

You have heard that I sit
where the black fire burns
my knife to a common brand,
that I slit the night's throat to praise.

Praise
the fire
and the night's making,
a rage that will endure the pain.
Praise
the lamp
and the rod in the bush heart.
Praise the initiate's wet haunch.
Praise
the darkness we rub
in the wound you carry from the dark.
Praise the deep act that the dark
provokes to ascend to light.
Child,
the spring embraces
limestone at its source.

Tro—ntoro—sand

I am the last to dance before you.
The water carves me,
            and buffs away my name.
                                    I shine
as a vowel that fades
into a trill's cave.
            A good name
            is
            the right sound.
            A good name
            is

the envelope of health,
the clan's gloss,
the totem's hammer
in the air.
My name recoils.
I hear it blow west.
I hear it in a cocoa grove.
I hear that it has married cloud
and become
compassion's seat.
Still,
in my resonance,
the graininess remains.
You
will take me in the stone you forge,
and in your fires,
and in your woman's melting iron;
you
will use me to compose
a crystalline grief
in your village heart.
Call me spirit,
or call me sand,
though I am the last to leap
before your eye,
you will know me
when I polish your power in the pool.

This is the altar dance.
It ends,
and I uncover my name.
I pass by darkness to behold
the wood and passion you possess.
You contend with all redeemers.
So you must defend against the god in you.
I come from the choir of the dead,
to remind you of the turning
and returning,
the egg broken on the seat of desire,

your world within a world,
nature's divination and the clan's domain,
the body's speech,
your ascent from the pool into spirit's house.
I will not leave you under division's axe.
I will set your star in the tree,
bathe you with love's liquid light
when the dark assaults us.

(THE DOUBLE ARGUMENT CONCERNING THE ALTAR DANCE)

I have been walking under pine.
Glass houses brighten my trail from door to door.
                    In spring,
                    I split
                    maple and oak
                    for winter's cold,
                                  and turn
                    the buried earth
                    back
                    into the sun's eye.
Though I live,
       on a rock,
       within a rock,
       set on high stone,
I hear the sea-foam
nibble at the boats,
       set rocking
       near the shore.

I remember cactus and the idiot's rain,
marigolds and silence,
banana leaves that bend
and point us toward a lily-covered pool,
                    the dusty cakewalk
of enchanted souls in the dark.

I remember that I love the woman who sits
in my buggy of desire,

her ringed eyes attentive to my double
exile.
I dress her,
at times,
in the loose garments of the plain.
I sing her,
in my cuatro voice,
a wedding song.
There have been
papaya mornings, black beans,
rum and warm milk
shot from a cow's udder.
In my mariachi spangles,
I have sprinkled her night bread
with a hidden love's insistence.

I know my double exile in song,
and the way the heel comes down,
remembering a dance,
on unfamiliar ground.
I have been made serious
by composing,
in the bright afternoons
of reticence and hay,
what I want to say,
without song.
Nothing bereaves me as much
as the door
closed upon the unseen figure
in my father's room.
I believe
a desert figure
can explain
the reason
for my shackled body's
rising
into cotton heat,
my rebel voice,
the craft of my slow

arrival on a politic ground,
my stick and gun,
on freedom's ground.

I am a battered body with a care for belonging.

I walk,
as I belong,
on this earth's invented name,
certain
of my figure and root
in the complex telling
of its name.

I accept this argument.
Contain and free me.

The First Return, the First Presentation of Instruments

This is the first return,
the first presentation of instruments.
They appear only here in the wood.

See how, out of heaven's
monitored water, the light
rides down in a boat.
Soon, an aureate knife
will scorch its presence
on a board. Then,
the chief of the light's crown
will lift it as a shield,
set to induce a mirror-flame,
an inauguration of sense.
Egg and doṅu bird,
a wife and her milky fact,
my corn and tunic,
harp and mask,

tilled field, magic and head,
double hand
contend for passage.
I am prefigured
in the blessed anvil's ring.
I have a chain
to ring me to the earth.
Bold word of music,
secret I must not tell,
my clan's ring
tempers
the ecstasy of knowledge;
these sounds encourage me:
whistle, bell and bull,
the master's voice,
the woman's elephant feet,
a wooden drum, and horn.

This is the first return,
the first presentation.

Say, then.
Must the altars dance again?

Sign of a baby's tie
to the mother
in power's basin
and the grain's manifest
in roots and stone,
the aged ones have
a bench so small
it may rest on a man's
                bent spine.
These you may not know.

Say.
What may be known.

Sickle.
The master's knives.

The executioner's and warrior's swords.
Salvation
is an ordinary day's
incision,
the light of tilling
and command,
the corn's defense,
the bird's preserver,
a child's expressive space.
These must be imbued
with pity's froth.

The Opening of the Cycle of Redemption

Third son of the black hand,
I entrust my white year to your name.
Shield me from the red clay of my own divinity.
Wake my mother's tongue.
Clothe me in my yellow fields.
Teach me to accept your coming.
You are my beast's mouth,
my electric musician,
my soul's ferry to my own perfection,
my split heart's sally
through my imperfection.
When, out of the wood,
you return, stitched in our village manger,
the water god, his soul's physician,
will map us to your bed.
I need your other darkness
and the light you lead from the wood.
Lead me past your hermit heart, to this,
                                                            my own.

(San Pedro/Los Angeles)

Texas is dark and full of kerosene.
            But we,

beyond the city of angels, stand
at Saint Peter's gate to the deeper darkness.
                At nine,
                each night,
you sit by your old kerosene lamp.
You cross your curling combs
                over the chimney,
where they simmer the gentle way
to smoke dreams into your kinky hair.

On the town,
on Beacon Street,
the fog wears spats.
A tug's belly horn grumbles
over the water's swift curl.
                The old man
                has the Dodge
                on Central,
soughing along the night
toward his younger blood,
a belted suggestion,
hooked on raisins and rabbit skins.
                War
has brought the sailors
                to attention,
the zootsuiters on guard,
with razors in their hair.

I have been told that we are
        consumed
by his anger, overwhelmed
by his wrath.
Grandmothers over the Book
teach us to number our days.
        I book
my days fourscore
by reason of my wrath.

Soon they are gone;
soon they fly away.

There
is
no
comfort in this picture of you
in your twenty-year-old baby fat,
limned
in silk, silk stockings,
rouge and a Lysol smell.
The mice now nibble
your youth in the drawer.
I return
to the heat of your small-town
Texas furies, the ones you carry
in the chamber of a .38,
near a box of Argo starch
under the seat
of your new Dodge,
the ones
you publicly announce on the wine
and tuna wharves of your alien home.

The woman has said,
Lord, if you had been here,
my brother would not have died.
Even now I know that whatever you ask,
God will give.
There is an answer in the last day,
and the rising.
But here the days assemble
their furies, one by one.
We forget
the resurrection and the life,
the belief that elicits the last question.

I come now,
through angels and saints,
to the last question
and the reason for your death

near the smoked lamp.
I arrange a curt reply
to a white city,
in a flowerless bier,
the pew borne up under God's eye
by the dip and glide of a black voice.
Only now,
in the hymn,
do I see your body
on life's balsa,
and hear the unspoken
question in your fury.
I had forgotten
the dream in the altar smoke,
the clarity of loving an old man
who would not be true,
the certainty
of gin and the touch of those
who choose the common
knowledge of suffering,
the long anchor of life
in another's soul.

You must forgive my late return
to your black wisdom
and the mother's day of saints
in this city of angels.
Time
takes
the mutilated pity of my hand
away.

This woman has said,
I believe he is coming
into the world.

(Kọmọ enfant/Kọmọ mère)

Mother of my cutting,
I know that it is you

who braids me in my body's fiber.
Why do you ask the fabric
to assume the loom?
Am I a weaverbird,
tapering my soul's net
in my own dark?
Consecrated one,
I must take my strength
from your name, a bit of foam
spun from the god's hull.
If I dress my apprehensive foot
in the pool, I trust your seaman's skill.
Now, uneasy, I dive
where the shell clamors its absence.

Say.
Who will conserve the souls of the dead?

You must know:
altar of the grain,
altar of the hunter
and the life-giver,
altar to imbibe a task,
altar to uncover what is true,
what can be spoken,
altar to disguise the endangered,
gris-gris, amulettes,
bracelets, rings and pendants,
all these I carry in my pouch.

I continue.

This large head upon my head
conveys my power
to commend the world's mask
to my reason.
Head under head,
I determine what passion
will lead me, endurable,

under the body's endurable light.
Even the mask upon my head
is masked, my forehead
haired for foresight.
My bug eyes seize
all radiant things
and bind all things
invisible.
The line of my face in mask
divides by limits.
My open mouth publishes
my spine's form, the degree
of my historical perfection.
Though my small ears hide
from the rumor of imperfection,
their curl divines
god's smallest voice,
the initiate's briefest prayer.
Power would ride me down.
And so I excrete these reins
for the body's regulation.
And yet I seat myself,
untamable,
on spirit's unbridled
and sorrel horse,
and canter in the copper light
of the pool's shade.
I am gifted with my own
division,
a timid carrion-eater,
balling my black knowledge.
Nighthawk,
vitality's sentinel,
I flare all closed doors,
rake the hatch of the universe.
You see me expose
my head to the wind,
to be raked myself
by spirit's bird.

This is the paradox
of uncovering an act,
of calling the initiate's
theological defense
under the incense and toll
of its own transformation.
Double agent,
agent of the double,
I have time's watch in care,
a bodied duty to embody
the god as a possible desire.
This is the interchange
of love and loss,
the metronome that guides
my horse's wings.
I choose the wind's space.
You will choose me.
Your sign will be
these six antelope horns
that prick my skull,
six horns to augur the first
incisive light,
the six-horn torque
of the first winding,
your six first traces.
Porcupine quills,
visible bloom of the trace,
shoot from the short horns.
My two-nosed snout adorns me.
So I have given you the head,
the soul's persuasive disguise,
the paradox of facing and retreat,
the oxymoron of spirit and space,
love's eye in the cleaving.
I take the mask near Faro's pool,
where I collect my black mud.
I mellow my mask with my touch,
this ciliate commemoration
and the principal's stress

in the song.
I account the hue
the soil's association,
the tomb's pitch into view
and command.
Red-gold light on the cheek
proclaims the earth's emerging,
the reconstruction of love's
equinoctial blaze.
In this birth, I view
the order and structure
of the light's regard
as a poor man's rich cloth
and altar.
All this, I invest in the mask.

But I must wear more on my body.
I call down Kọmọ's sheath,
or the bird's plumage.
I have it in the vulture's wings,
charged with the knowledge of signs.
These seven rings enfold
celestial worlds;
they kilt the earth.
He, who leads me,
will wear this tunic in the dance.
Although I find
that, being so encumbered,
his footfall lugs me,
a broken wheel upon a cart,
an engine whacked free
of its manifold state,
I assert that his dance
is a figure of my coming,
a prefiguration
of my assessor's pace.
I insist, then, that I be bled,
black, in the space
between the lines.

I usurp, in this exorbitant
disdain, my own flesh.
Weary of the light's miserere,
weary of the dancer's elevation,
weary of my wally and wagtail
claims,
weary of my scarified entry
into purity and self-knowledge,
I scar the cloth's design.
I would give myself
to the nighthawk
and his dark recapitulation
of the soul's flight.
I would be married by other rings.
My antelope horns would rip
me free of the cloth's armor.
Yet, I would be brought
a babe to the bush of the pool again,
and given the eye to discover
my banded form.
The vulture's plumage
calls me, amended,
where the light falls.
This is the initiate's
quarrel with clarity,
my parish inability
to accept the light's
spiny pilgrimage.
Now, I ask this cloth,
light's vessel,
to lift by draining me
of my initiate's wisdom.
This is the wisdom
of being set free
in the wood of another's desire.
Desire impels the wood's obscurity.
Light is an exclamation
of longing,
the dark's gift,

the soul's rigorous uncertainty.
The dancer, in the wood,
may extol such suspicion
and breed his fall
from the pool's light.
We will return
in the light's fall,
and rise by the token
of its absence.
All absences endure.
This tunic engages them
in the mask I take
to my head.

Brother, I have spoken in your voice.
My initiate's love afflicts you.

(Frankfurt)

. . . Meanwhile, it seems to me often,
Better to slumber than live without companions, like this,
So to linger, and know not what to do or to utter,
Or, in such spiritless times, why to be a poet at all?
—Hölderlin

This is the city of high feeling
and troubled peace, at odds
with its lovers and love's order.
The latticed window in the poet's house
looks down on the poet,
returning, from love,
through the truculent streets.
You have the dark side of my lover's name
as a sword on your brow,
there to inaugurate the mirror's
perplexity and the gradual flow
of the still mind to its act.
Even the rose of passion

agitates you now,
squeezed as you are
between Ardinghello and Franz Moor.
I ask you to define the restraints
imposed upon the heart,
and to release the lover
hidden in the structure of the world,
the truth we are meant to know.
Under your pen again,
you unfold the token rose,
the picture of the one form
for each solitary part.
You are in the rose,
turning knotty with desire.
Your locked heart hears the call
of water and air;
it tempers the numbing heat
of another's desire.
So being will speak
with the tight voice of becoming,
in the whirl and stir
that are infinite peace in God.
Your body walks from sign to sign.
You attend to every quality
of being actual, and the fact
of beholding what is hidden.
All that is in your eye
burdens you with your body
near the stained glass windows
and the easy way you speak
of what you do not know.
And, though you inist that you have carried
the world within yourself,
you know that you must fail to call
a simple voice from the dark wood,
into this, your singular light.
Rhapsodist of the heart,
the dark time leads you to the pathos
of your spirit's failure.

How can I now will
your redemption in His will,
or soothe you with the water vowel of peace?
How can I take your rose stain into my heart?
This I set down is the mind's
perception of what it will not hold.
I leave you with your renunciation
of your magic,
and your sorcery in becoming a man.

I continue.

These you must see.
I call the militant bamboo—
writing's cell and vein,
articulation's badge,
the dead designers'
scrupulous chant,
the incision's instructive
radiance—
to pin its six knots in the air.
The nodes pink its
assertive shape.
But the pole is the body's line
and a mirror of the swollen
razor in its back.
The saints tie the tunic and mask
to this slim rope of heaven
and empower the great
bird's pirouette.
I dance,
in the unspoken space,
a rustic babbling of turns
and counterturns.
I have not come
under a chorus's
knuckle tongues,
nor heard a fury pot
its intent

on my initiate's fire.
Bamboo teaches me
that evil will run
from my flaw.
I am a forest wound,
my own flaw,
disposed for my clan's
hospitable touch.
I recall
elephant's feet;
a forged whistle;
the triangular stiletto
soaked in snake venom
and poison flowers,
the exacting knife.
These now complete my field.
In the forest,
you twine all sacred bodies;
you fish for the four-winged vulture.
Your body has a good eye to fill.
I await my holy return
to its power.

The Abstract of Knowledge/the First Test

I shall be the last to come into the word
and into the power of the word;
by these I will address the god and command all things.
And yet abstraction bears me down.
Brother, you have given me
        the instruments' cloth
            and the altars' dance,
the figure in the field,
        your mother body
            and my name's inclination.
I have the mask's teeth in my flesh.
I pitch my soul's desire in the jackal's
black knowledge, twin head of copper's light.

The sound of your voice is the first tone
in the cycle of redemption,
                                        love's prefiguration.
I grow by an intimation of a first act,
by the clear presence of a fixed grave.
I urge my spirit through desire's cure.
I buckle into virtue's space.
Still, I am divested of my love's
endurable space; the god must be
divested of my body's space.

What is the question?

Who will hurry into this absence
to instruct a spirit uneasy
                              in its double knowledge?

And so I struggle with the locus of desire
and with my own intervention.
Am I the mouth of the beast,
the child of abasement,
father of the little double?
Am I doubled in every presence,
in every grave in the wood,
prefigured in every public act?
Does the light gather the doṅu bird's wings
                    in the same,
                              peristaltic motion?
Will the river always return the same shells,
the same bones, the same serpent rhythm?

What is the question?

What prefiguration empties the world of desire?
Where is the figure to lift me into love?

An idiot initiate is evil's shaft of light.
If you go from the certainty of oneness
into solitude and return,

I must divest you of your double
and twin you in love's seclusion.
My instruments toll you into limbo;
the altars know the music of your name.
You arrive by being absent.
The light must be brought where the body lies.
And, where the body, in its wisdom, rises,
the head is time's scalpel and suture.
The body is a schema of desire;
the head, the seat of the act.
You understand that all things beg
to be undone and returned to the first act.
Even the master comes to the wood,
even he sits in the dark, under the telling,
to listen for the first term,
the tree leaves' first trembling,
the star's bellow in the pool.

I continue.

A double vision wants a double state.
A double heart urges the black band to appear.
This is my hand on the tunic.
Your hand shuttles back the black band's absence.
We invest the cloth with nothing,
no thread to bridge us from the gold wood home.
We must speak of heaven,
or the ordinal of one, light's preference
for the habitation of the appointed.
We must specify the double nature of purity,
and the equipoise of space on the point of desire.
Now, when the master prepares his boat
and assumes love's service,
light erects his cause and generation.

I continue.

Conception's conceiver.
Nothing names a rhythm,

taking itself for a cause,
doctor of its own root and effort,
instance of its own birth.
Will the god sit,
becalmed in his boat,
to be embraced by one
who will not name him?
I insist that I hold
designation's deepest vibration
in my body. I know myself,
by grace,
to be the principle of all things.
Out of every hidden emblem,
I extol the act I cannot name.

I must tell you of the seven phases
of my seven forms.
Here, I have the design
of all disengaged things,
my acts and heavens,
earths, plants, and beasts, my person.
I profess my master's praise
and my own faith,
my first contesting of my faith.
I order your allegiance, now:
  to the signs' immaculate
  appearance, a sortie
  into divinity's turbulence;
  to the irruption of desire's cocoon,
  and its emerging;
  to the spirit's turning and return
  to the master's voice;
  to the token of divine serenity;
  to love's conception, birth
  and revelation.
I would have you grow in the signs' unfolding.
I would discover you in the resurrection of sacred things.

I am arguing with the movement of desire.
I have great signs to unhouse my twin,
                        to perfect my singularity.
                        I turn
                        twelve ways.
                        I appear
                                        and disappear.
I have great signs to disclose
                        one word,
                        one expression,
                        one member of a phrase.
The signs assure my birth
                        and penetration,
and assure my good
                        and covenant with you.
These emblems set me down before the stars,
turned stone in the yellow dust.
I must be advised by darkness,
        by an exploratory smith,
                who hammers copper's light
                                        from earth,
to forge it in secret.
                My own darkness
                gives me
                back
                to Yuri and Dya,
to the burnished darkness
        of my blind saint.
I take this road again
to articulate my discontent
with what is given.
                                I have learned
that there is a blessing
in my body's disrupted blood.
                                I contend
that I will not be self-slain,
                borne on heaven's tree
                to engage
                        my own knowledge.

I ask,
then,
how I will come
into possession of my body,
how I will
circle
the stone of my desire
and face you on love's edge.
I must construct a reason
for light's withdrawal;
I must
combat destruction's caravan
and the slave heart bred
by the pool's intentional retreat.
This,
my celibate courage,
tokens the mask's
abandonment.

If I were the light's sacred buffoon,
I could read this meaning and mount
my own awakening;
I could carry a great sabre
on the rib
of a palm leaf,
and call it my knife
to provoke
my own descent.
But the anvil awakens me:
Mandé,
Keita,
Asante,
my Bandiagara kin.
I claim my complex body.
I proclaim
the lot of the great old man
is a progress toward death,
the unknown,
the nothing,
the creator.

Who goes first?
The black band on the tunic
answers, God; the sign, no one.
If the word speaks itself,
there will be nothing,
no measure, no balance,
no temper, no pure body
lying in state,
no sound attending
its own procession.

I circle and face myself.
I cannot ask who goes first.

What is the question?

What is the first act?

It would be easy to sketch
a cape and crown,
an encompassing arm,
a figure trunked up
on air and golden light,
boneless, fleet
and contentious.
Love's office would be
inhabited;
desire's embryo
would edge from its shell.

I turn.
I continue.

I define the seed
as a calling.
In this appointment,
I find I have no delegate,
no eye to examine
the seed's vocation.

I cannot say
I enter with God,
at the music's first insistence,
or that I am in the seed's whine,
in its authoritative spiral
into its bowels.
Inside itself,
the seed hears
its ache of being,
its reason to twist its voice
into understanding.
The seed of my being
does not exist,
except in the act
of taking notice.
Before the body,
there is an act;
before the act,
there is desire.
The ear of an unfigured head
begins the descent.
I shape the head an absent
two-in-one, an auditory
acquaintance
with designation's dance.
This failing comforts me.
Under the gold light of the primal wood,
I accept the chastity of all things.

You see I have the faculty
of being absent.
That is the lesson I take
from the first light
and from the unseizable god
whose trembling bells him
out of the anvil to my side.
Father—I call you—
spirit of the apprehension
of absence, the precedent
                    refusal.

In our blindness,
we entreat the seed's song.

We must have a language
to annotate the seed's ascent.
There is a message
in the seed's turning,
a disposition to be heard,
to sit in every initiate's scale,
inviolable,
sovereign of its voice
and understanding.
This, when the soul taps its cup
to be filled with its own sacrament,
you must understand.
There is a message in the failure
to transpose what can be spoken.
The seed's roll and yaw define
what can be spoken.
I take my cloud body to the pool
to bathe in light.

What is the question?

I turn.
I continue.
I address myself.

Initiate,
under the ladder,
two spirits stand.
Sómá has no twin.
He loves his lamb's role
and the armor he puts on
in the altars' service.
You find him in worship's constant eye.
His name, life's form, reveals his task.
The other is your body
into this body,

a manifest of your soul's intent.
By their sanctity and sacrifice,
these go first,
nearest to God,
auditors of the seed's voice.
Nothing can precede a death
they do not give you.
There is no salvation,
without their example.
You must know they teach
the art of giving up,
the initiate's crawl into love's circle.
If, in the deepest foundation,
you give voice to their names,
they will protect you from the questioning
of love's first act.
Celibate Sómá defines you.
You take his chaste and sober
shadow into charity.
Zando pulls you from your cave into Sómá's art,
into the prophecy of death and return.
You sleep and awake in the sleeper's design.
The sleeper sustains you.
The dream binds you in love's intent.
You bear resurrection's cure
in your spirit's polar
modulation,
in the way a mother takes
a child's first computations
into her care,
and in the exact crib
of the river's course,
the sun's catenary elation,
the plow's trenching,
the weaver's needle in the cloth,
the mariner's silver plumb line in the water,
the mason's plinth,
in the altars' bull-bell and whine,

in the risk of your heart's
executive speculation.
You endure in the exact
apprehension
of what you do not possess.
Thief-heart,
you prepare for grace
and the heart's redemptive
brocade, the woman,
subject of her twin tribulation,
who unveils the flower of the kapok tree,
the soul's solstice, engraved on calabash,
dabbed in the blood of the dispossessed.
Mousso Koroni,
keeper of the children of shame,
harbinger of my body's first loss,
your galleon conjuration galls me.
I now traverse love's dispersal
through your body,
here,
in an exile's scriptorium.
Love itself allows your opposition.
Say that love permits me
to publish my own decline,
to here, where I am pitched up,
waterless, a water spirit compelled
toward a denser wood.
Now, may your necessary injury
guide me to what is true.

What is true is the incision.
What is true is the desire for the incision,
and the signs' flaming in the wound.

I am now your delegate.
I give you order and determination,
and your soul's syntax,
extracted from God's speech.

I continue.
I speak.

(ROME)

He who puts on wisdom, puts on grief; and a heart that understands cuts like rust in the bones.
—Augustine

"It is yearning that makes the heart deep."
Put on your traveling shoes.
Walk, out of the pool,
beside the Great Fish,
sandals on my feet
to keep the earth away.
Only the righteous shall enter.
In the holy water of your heart
lies a shut-in garden,
a sealed fountain, a wellspring
of living water, a paradise
bearing the fruit of apples.
Strap holiness and renunciation
to your feet, buckle the desire
to walk to God to your loins,
walk on the wave of God's mercy,
step down here and sail away
to God in his boat of grace.
Thus, I have you riddling in the temple
—peregrinus—never at home in Rome.
Your thirst for water and sails
turns you in a circle.
I hold before your eye
no suffering Christ,
but the Great Word and Wisdom of God.
But, oh, I am old,
and the lions tax me
with my contradictions.
Salvation is now the water

I ride upon,
for my soul,
for this raggèd body,
for this raggèd soul in a raggèd body,
for this pure soul in a pure body.
Can it matter what I say?
I understand only the falling
and the rising up,
under every inconceivable power.
This, as I am old, my heart tells me.
And so I take the tattered sail
of my body, under the tattered
sail of a Rome-bound boat,
in a fortunate wind,
away from my mother.
Water had bound me.
        "I carried about me a cut and bleeding soul,
        that could not bear to be carried by me,
        and where I could put it, I could not discover.
        Not in pleasant groves, not in games and singing,
        nor in the fragrant corners of a garden. . . .
        I remained a haunted spot, which gave me no rest,
        from which I could not escape.
        For where could my heart flee from my heart?
        Where could I escape from myself?
        Where would I not dog my own footsteps?
        —I left my hometown."
And left the most unfathomable
of all involvements,
                and the mother.
And entered the double sorrow of death,
agèd tolerance and a late patience.
And entered Ambrose's other world,
to disfigure the simple opposition
of light and the dark,
to return to the shadows
                        on God's face.
No one loves what he cannot,
in understanding, make his own.

This is the dance of the changeless
and the changing,
the spirit's intensity
for the world's endurance.
Knowledge is motion in twilight,
a state of falling into sight;
one by one,
the spirit's eyes touch and grow.
Peregrinus, the tense spirit
tenses and returns to its
own understanding.
There is always the going forth
and the returning;
there is always the act,
the slow fusion of being.
All things,
by the strength of being joined,
will continue;
the sin is to turn away;
ignorance is inattention
to the voice, which feeds you.

> "Let them deal harshly with you,
> who do not know with what effort
> truth is found and with what
> difficulty errors are avoided . . .
> who do not know with what pain
> the inner eye of a man is healed,
> that he may glimpse his Sun."

The act grows from delight,
prepared by the hidden,
quivering arrow of a god's hand.
The act is in the longing for God's hand,
or your own hand, in the act.

> "Grant me to wind round and round
> in my present memory the spirals
> of my errors . . ."

and of my longing.
This Easter Eve of double death
and double resurrection,

I join the competent ones
to hear twelve sacramental steps—
the deluge and purified waters,
the passage through a split sea.
Brother blesses the water with the cross,
divides it along the axes of the earth,
along the memory of Paradise.
Christ in the candle enters the water,
sanctifies the water.
Brother takes the Lord in the candle
three times into the tomb.
I step into the fount three times,
to know that I die with the world,
am buried and rise again.
Brother,
                    Thus let us enter together,
                    in the path of charity,
                    in search of Him . . .
in search of the act,
in search of the meaning of desire.

The Initiate Takes His First Six Signs, the Design of His Name

 SÁNÚ

Sánú is gold under air,
the whirlwind seen in the secret vortex.
The dark speaks with divinity's
perfect voice,
and, there, wherever you place your stones,
my light opens the way.
Child,
before I cut away your loneliness,
you will be washed with water
in which I have lain,
keeping the dark in my bones,
all night.

My water blades you into
the soul's one life,
your double,
sheltered in the forest's door.
Sánú is one.
Sánú is fear's destroyer.

 MÃ́-MÚRÚ-FLA

Then,
under and from the rainbow,
cradled in the mantis' praying arms,
fall the master's two knives.
Call the mantis Great Knife of God,
heaven's scythe.
These,
my twins,
contain all elements
—double male in air and fire,
double woman in water and earth,
rain's compassion, spirit's urge.
Lodged in a cradle in a boat,
I have come down to recall
the double act, doubled in making.
I attach my power in two small
knives, placed near the altar
for the conservation of souls.
Exchanged in incision's service,
I attach my woman to my man.
Thus, the power of service and compassion
rides my craft
into your open soul.

MÁKÓ

Mark me as a balance of earth and air.
Point me, the master's ship, in space.

I am a slim fish,
hooked aloft by the flyline of a womb,
the stiletto that pierces the egg.
I descend in the whirlwind,
way of the wind-ing of the swollen god,
passage between the intervals of being.
As your initiate's agent on creation's knife,
I open the membrane of my celebrant's voice.
My whirlwind music liberates all things,
and directs all things to God.
You must seize my sign
to resolve it as the maker's
pregnant matrix, restoration's
light shaft in the womb.
This therapy of light controls
craft's buckle in love's tomb.
In night's ambiguous water,
my boat assents to its own
suspension,
to the ambiguity of being
slanted into life and death.
Wife,
on the eighth day,
you will be cradled again
in your own house,
to have your child's voice
shadowed on your foot, in black,
or fashioned on your mother's wall, in white.
Mother-taken,
your body will weigh
the spirit's abundant light.

DOṌ

Now, if I,
initiate, enter,
under air
and under

the thunderstone,
I hear the pool in the wind.
Water will dock the spirit's light
along my body.
Now, by the light's fall,
I assemble an aggregation
of fact, and appoint
the body's wisdom to its place.
I oppose earth's figure and ground
to the divisions of my person.
My eye's bell alerts me to the kapok and the palm.
My ear pins the fern's dance in wind
to a singer's voice.
I brace my arm
under the moon of my shoulder blade,
where memory's book resides.
My fingers dampen the bird's flight.
My spine is set to penetrate
                                        the tomb's resolve.
My foot addresses a woman's kettle,
                              jogs the weaver's loom.
My clavicle dispossesses the rivers,
dresses the fox, unveils the antelope
and anvil,
proclaims a star's course on an altar.
I embody the world
        in every disfiguration
                of your desire's intent.
I decompose this word
        into the god's immutable
                and uplifted knife,
into the whirlwind's hook,
        beginning the seed's design,
                and compose
an initiate's fertile
        and uneasy
                resolution.
This is a dry sign,
an apparition without pity.

I shall bleed six days
before my guardian carves it
on my door,
to extol its sense
and to foretell the acquisition
of my soul's constrained desire.

 DYĘĘ

On my way from desire to love,
I am more than halfway
through the fabric of my name.
I build with gold, wood, water,
silver and earth.
My name's syntax fills the god's boat and pool;
its syllables sum my world's progression.
The mask hears its figure in the dance.
The blacksmith hammers himself to my ground.
The master lines the soul's
                    solids and planes
                            on the hidden altars.
By my own sound,
I tackle my instruments,
and receive their radiant energies.
I am trying to push
              the curve of speech
                    past the short rib of my body.
Evil figs a phantasm to entice me
back to my body's unspun fiber.
But I have been reeled into the god's boat,
and tallied with raindrops in mantic arms.
I have been awarded with the gold
of my daily relations, and set
in charity's water by my brother's side.
Now, the arrow turns inward on my bow.
I am joined to myself,
one, in multiplication's sign.
Voices of the universe find their higher pitch in me.

I extend my clan's wall
and unfold the limits
of the body I inhabit.
I renew the seed's turning when I speak.
This is what I know
at the end of the star's ascent.
Within the Pleiades,
I figure my undivided self,
intricate,
and pierced with the joy
of making you whole.

KǪNǪ KÃ́

I am a maker of what is real.
A bird's voice,
speaking the language of birds,
I flutter in the whirlwind.
A twin, condemned
to holy ignorance,
I construct the double's secrets,
a bird and child language,
apprehensible in the cutting,
or in the chase.
It seems that blood affirms
the duty to engender the body's
flight into apprehension
and the head's repose on the waters of sense.
Love, the intelligible design,
flows, to here,
where the apprehensive
bird comes to ground.

What is needed is that the being itself should transcend the limit and self-knowledge of the world, and thereby demonstrate itself.
—Karl Barth

Aw, man, you were just playing with me.
—John Coltrane to Sonny Rollins

Chasuble lady,
here, in the evening,

when the desert pours its cup of bronze
over the steeple on the hill,

I hear Jerusalem's refrain.

I am an old man,
with a knife and plug,
come to the end of my globe.

I gloat to think that I have
slipped my white desire
under the hem of your blue dress.

Blue water has fixed my love's scar
where the dove's eye fails.

Once, I was anchored
by hymns and a prophet's voice,
to my pew. I grew.

Curators of your stone
taught me to sponge my own ark.

Now, a poor man on a rocky porch,
I keep a house attentive to ghosts.

I rock here with the feel
of my coffin, going from door
through window,
down curling streets.

I listen for the Baptist quill upon the scroll
to tell me where my grave lies.

Rustic, I recede from light to laughter.

But, now, I take you from your passion
and the dark wings
to fix you in a fool's circle.

You must await a blind man's vision
and the splash of a whirling board,
in a chair, to water.

You come in a blind man's care,
to open water and a prophecy of limits.

Will the shadow in the wind reveal itself?
Will the curved stick coil from the sand,
and the babe thrash again from the bush?

These are the signs of your receding,
the rent in your garment,
the design you refuse to fulfill.

I advance the healing crook,
the celt, my compassionate twin;

I offer the color of desire,
and the color of love's growth.

Bird-boned,
I contend with your prophet's clenched hand.

The star in my voice is the cross
upon your garment,
the map of my double path
to your need.

(PARIS)

Doctor,
any subtle sleuth of being

and Pope's man would be banished.
Even as the Philosopher would come down
out of Oxford's shadow,
beefed up with the baroque traces
of certain knowledge.
All things singular reveal themselves
in indefinable light.
And thus you would assert
I know your present light
in the deep cave of existent
light that is not there.
Time will teach me to bear this.
You have always had time at your command.
By your art,
you have skipped through the arts,
the Great Book and the Sentences.
A young man could rest
near the belly of beauty,
take on no scripture or disputation,
could follow his students down
the certain and dexterous path
                                        of fact.
But the heart is free;
the heart is a maker;
the heart places the world in good light.
Nothing compels God to uncover
this heart's love of light.
Nothing compels the initiate,
sitting under the spark,
to acknowledge his mind's power.
It is not fitting to confine
this power to the sensible thing,
nor to take the gold of incarnation
into the soul's dark house.
We will be known
by our chipping and hewing
of the rock in our hands,
and by the sharp color and sturdy cloth

with which we dress the body
                    and the world.
If the perfect passion holds us,
we will live in the clarity
of being set free to expire.

The Opening of the Ceremony/the Coming Out of Kọmọ

(Apparition)

Begin.
After the entrance,
the coming out.
Compassionate April,
the lunar month,
warms my initiate skin.
I must appear, to be disguised.
I must appear, to be burdened
with my body's disguise.
Elephant's cry shivers
the estranging veil.
A curtained life rises
from the shelter's caul.
The calculating board,
the canoe, the anvil and chain
dress themselves
and enter for their cleansing.
All exhilaration's voices,
now mute, amble,
heel to toe,
            into the light.
I await the bag of emblems,
the grain's receptacle,
the umbilical cord,
nesting near water and stone,
the green facts and roots.
Sharp eyes,

which will be given
to incision's service,
assemble near the great door.
This is the exhibition
of sacred things, to be washed
past the dangers of impurity.
We are washing the holiness in.
The mask dances a scrupulous cure
into our bleeding hands.

(THE DESCENT INTO THE POOL)

If the instruments have been baptized,
we are prepared to be taken
to the purer water, seat of the God.
Our hymn asserts that the queen of waters
will think us thinking and arrange us
in contemplation's mirror.
An adoration of instruments
sings us into the jackal's arms.
My Kọmọ patroness,
black tassel of the double,
you hurry me to the dangers in my body.
This is the scene of the telling
and the telling's enactment,
a rigorous shadow of the known.
Crocodile and vulture,
turtle, serpent and jackal,
creativity's dark angels,
arise, embodied in telling's intonation,
sucking our divination's dance
                                        into their bones.
Here, in the initiate's voice,
lies a figure of intent,
a whirlwind of splendor,
momentarily revealed.
The moment itself is an emblem
of intent, consummation's cloth,

dyed in the pool's light.
We have come into the light
as the burghers of the revealed,
have become blood's bookmen,
propped on the economy of the god's bones.

We have,
in this light,
a document of dance.
Left.   Right.
We measure the body's booked light.
We spiral
      in contemplation's
                  urgent act.
So we arrive on examination's shore.

            Naked,
we cup our hands
into the water seven times,
exalt the water seven times,
            cleanse
our unmasked faces,
linger in the mud.

We gather lotus and thick, fleshy roots,
                              openings
of an unaccustomed speech.

Pure signs and the living dead now possess us;
fertile initiates, we have designed
our sign and movement on the earth.

(The closing of the first phase)

We stand in the comprehensive pool.
We are fish,
lifted on its wave
to the stars' ladder.

We are birds,
tucking its salt under our wings,
caught in the moon's alleluia.
We are weavers,
carding our souls' fabric in the sand.
Twilight, pecking at the kelp and berries,
glides in on its heron legs.
All kneel under the dancer's spell
and search the darkness for his eye.
These shadows on the sand
do not decide the emblems of the dead,
nor encourage the baby's battle wail,
the mother's hornbook of her losses,
the youth's insatiable pricking
at his master's dark voice.
All this occurs in the anticipation of light.
The dancer is light's omen;
he will close our darkness.
That face behind the face
is my face,
or the face I will possess.
The space behind the mask mouth
is a carbon cave, hollow
for the spirit's embryo.
Stone-set head ignores
the legs' wing-heat,
piston and semiquaver arms' space,
the torso's toss and gash
under the tunic.
The dance warns that I
must pass through my burning;
alerts me to the red seed
within my body,
to the alien halation
in a singer's voice,
to my own inscription
on the scroll of the dead.
The dance is a way of going forward,
and a way of foreshadowing the return.

I present myself, in the dance,
an acquisition of all my losses.
Above my disguise,
my head ensnares me
in the journey I endure
by taking notice.
Foamed from my cliff,
I have a duty to return
to the dry seed of the dance.
Cantor eyes uphold me
in the promise of this return.
I am here, now,
having clocked
my new world, coeval body
through the mask's hour.

(THE DANCER)

I am the spindle
of the spirit's return.
By my delicate
and perilous swing
I assure your reinstatement.
I open the dark.
I will,
by my own authority,
allow this alien initiate
to speak.

(THE INITIATE SPEAKS)

Halfway through my darkness,
I capture a proceeding light.
Time's cageling,
I perch on the slim, suspended
wood I propel in the air.
Time and the wood coffin the air.

In time's catafalque,
I hold your cataleptic presence.
I would have you forever still,
unable to depart, or to drive
my presence from you,
unable to arrange your naked
appearance, or to press
the claims of your absence.
Out of the absence of your body
I grow into prophecy
and the skill of placing things.

These are your stones;
this is your wood;

these are the scorched and burnished
houses on your plains;

this is your cattle enclosure;
here is your insistent corn,
the stalks of your fiber.

I could draw water still
from your desolate pool,

and hammer copper drummed
from your derelict earth.

I know that I must come
into the dark light of these things,
to be confronted with my own light.

Familiar voices whisper that I cannot enter.

And, if I must acknowledge
that I have been bred
in a Babylonian bed,
so I must confess my heart's
hermetic passage from a firm

and distant estate, to here.
Let us trade our tales of fires and floods,
the high winds that dispossess us,
the dispossession in the art of being secure,
the security of being inattentive
to the spirit's call,
the necessary silence
that being removed requires.

I turn to this bodiless field
in my own body.
I cannot say that I have come
to the wrong place,
or that what I know
can come only in this place.
My profit is the strange,
authentic space I raise in the wood.
The speech I hear tells me
that you will value my disguise,
and exhort the unchanging face
to acknowledge me.

The mask knows the recitative of the self,
the somatic prefiguration in the dog star,
and in the desert's red root and blue flower,
in the grain's seed, in the Lotus
and the doṅu bird's wings,
in copper, water and stone.
The mask engages its own apparition
in every spirit's animate desire.
The mask knows that I may touch
these twenty-two stones, ring
the anvil and bell, keen
the sickle and shear the tunic's
fabric with my own hand.
The mask has heard the stichomythic
camel walk from one dry wall
                                        to another,
has heard the lamentation in our

every anvil, the exaltation
in our every abandonment,
and, where the real heart ladders
a new house in the air,
the mask has heard
our bible mouths atone
for my Bambara absence,
my Dogon withdrawal,
my Yoruba and Asante abscission.

These things I now set down
are the particularities of the god's head,
the narratives of change and counterchange,
the specified and the inexact,
the theological string I drop in the pool.

I am a heron bird,
with one leg in the pool.
Those who have seen my flight's curve
see the strange glaze on my blue back.
I am the boy, with the shaved head
and crescent moon,
who guards the axe and cave.
You know me, too,
as the rug-bearer and bead man
who hawks the eye of God.
I sustain myself in every adverse air,
by threading and knitting up,
polishing what the earth disgorges.
The earth itself gives me a reason
to examine my return, to here.
I am the point of my return,
an altar scroll's unwinding
to be altered by my return.
When I turn west and enter the god's grove,
I begin my correspondence
with the sky's head and star knell,
where I will be written in water,
measured in my body's curative syntax.

Starlight in the wood
recalls me to the tree
and the light it cradles
on its head.
My elemental eye
spades the tree root
for a sign, or the blood
ascending the tree's
sensible pipette.
All that cooks in the root
rises by its changing
                    into love.
This is the consummation I desire,
my consumption in the noble
and extended body
I am learning to perceive.

(THE MASK'S PERFORMANCE/FIRST CLOSURE OF THE INITIATE'S VOICE)

Wood music
and stone.
Gold exaction.
Water's linear measure.
I turn.
I blacken this sand
with my step.
Copper recalls
the small man.
I have my children,
naked in the mud,
in prayer.
Lotus drums me
an anti-stroke.
On the forest's fire-lit stage
I dress your cathartic staff.
The time for cutting
has not arrived,

but I turn
and turn you inward.
Speak.
You are the mouth of the beast,
a wind dispersing the word,
the knife's ethic
and ontology.
All those who play,
play your demands.
Masked again,
I lead you,
who bring the master's
note to the soul.
Soul must have its message
in the touch and commonplace
of sacred things;
soul must know itself
capable of the message.
Under this sign,
lodged in the tunic and mask,
in the altars' bell
and bull sound,
you dance.
You are forty-two years old,
and the keeper of the body's
                    first emblem.

Speak.
You are the father
of the little double,
double of the conscious soul,
double hand.
Initiate and elder,
you flame the initiate.
Spirit's knife,
you penetrate
the body of the dead.
You have stepped
seven times

in the wood's seven springs.
I name you,
by your craft,
first priest of the universe.
You keep my excellent
understanding,
burned on a board,
at your side.

Speak.
You are abasement's child,
lying before the altar
in God's court.
You have been born to follow
                                        earth's emblem.
Day after day,
you weave the corn's bed.
You draw earth's buried
light into the bull's body.
You stretch fruit's skeleton
into the milk of white beer.
Brown blossoms
in a brown time,
blue seeds gasping
in a waterless dark,
find their sanctuary
in your care.
You command
      by yielding
            to the breath
                  of things.
You harvest in your hesitation.
The fall's blade sets you free.
You come,
in the evening of the corn's life,
to invoke
            the power
                  you leave forever
                        in the wood.

Head of the head,
I dance,
I turn you into this,
your first understanding.

(THE INITIATE RECONSTRUCTS THE FIRST UNDERSTANDING AND CLOSURE)

I circle from these emblems
into a different day and a sun
that smells of parched flesh and chains,
a moon that lifts another hour to the shore.
My mask and bird flight discovers me
tapping the maple's white juice,
under the crystal and salt
of an unfamiliar star.
I wait in your wisdom's shadow,
to be given life's axe, the spiny
spine-cutter of your hidden power.
I address, in your power, the gloom
of waiting to be consumed.
The excavated light teaches me
the form of a new star returning.
In the forest of the air,
I have seen the dog star sniff
and scurry to the bitch of existence.
I move north.
I move south.
I arrive, on these shores,
where the star cuts earth's middle,
and the rocks ridge me high, into memory's
uneasiness and into my patience.
I have in my care
the memory of a passive saint's day
and the saint's forgetfulness of my care.
I have been waiting for death
and death's intelligence,
the burden of the awakening of all things.

I have been waiting for the trinity
of sensation in my own body,
the grammatical and just insistence
of the other lives I carry in my body.
I know my body's written correlations,
and the configuration of signs
                                        I cannot repeat.
Even the god,
                once spoken,
changes within the same voice;
even the attentive ear moves.
Yet, dying lifts us from understanding
into sight, and onto love's battlefield,
into the danger of being present.
Say that all who have awakened
ascend to this presence and the stable
process of the dead.
The dead, singing freedom,
burn their statues under us.
We will arise from the ash of absence,
and ride the star's horse over the bell
of apprehension,
apprenticed to the spirit's new eye, new ear.

Speak, now, of the initiate's seating,
the beginning of the phase of taking place.

(The initiate's seating/the twelfth degree)

Return to the star.
Child
        who follows the star.
Child
        of the tail of the star.
Child
        of the star in the rear.
                                Alone,
        the star leads you.

You become:
children of the twins' star,
children of the doubling star,
children of the star of circumcision,
children of the star of two eyes.

Doubled,
you grow,
from stillness to sight,
into
vision and pain's power.
Double star
is
spring's looking glass
and
the ankh
upon spring's ground.

In the bull's constellation,
six stars adorn the earth
and rise
to embellish my name.
Six daughters,
lifted from a family of stars,
weeping
for the lost one,
cluster,
for their redemption,
on my initiate's altar.
The seventh
hides herself
from me,
whom she may have touched.
Perhaps, her shame is a just
expression of her power in me.

My power may be in the lost light,
and in the body's

search
and seizure
of a small, secluded wood.

When the sisters shine,
I count
blessings on the rise.
When the morning star cuts me
with its evening glow,
and turns, toward me,
its unblemished face,
I know
the wheat of my wedding
will bloom,
that my knives will cut clean.

Two eyes gather my spirit's wealth
and nourish me
in the real earth
of winter.

I am being seated,
enthroned
in my person,
weighted
with my duty to you.
Love's
body
links
me,
in sigui's little star,
to
my
death's
flower
and to my double state.

Love's body
guides
my body

to the well of love's
        responsible fulfillment.

Love's knife is love's ontology,
my spirit's archaic
                        cleavage in my body.
So I am made whole,
under the star,
by the star's return.

(Albuquerque)

Mad woman on a swing in moonlight,
mad man on a ditch bank under the moon,
fists clenched in the moon's face.
The pearls the woman sees in the moon's ring
are teeth in the man's eyes,
and white blood to man and woman.
Neighbors call up the moon's pride
when the night rises;
no one attends to the man's pride,
or the way he swings in the moon's heat.
The night is a desperate boat
into morning, where the man confronts
the shadow of his moon pride.
He is the keeper of a boy,
who would, if he understood,
take the man's rage for a cloak.
But the tree on the bank cloaks the man's
rage from neighbor and moon and boy.
And only the knowledge of tearing
the night's compassionate cloth
reveals the man to himself.

A black man near this foul water
wants to bury all the city's clean
concoctions in the still bed.
The bed is a fatal picture of desire.

A weaver of desire,
he has the city's thorns
in his black cloth
and the garrulous silkworms
of another moon to thread his soul.
He steps, each day, where the water
and the moonlight will not go,
back where his rage is
an adornment of light and a mirror
of the god's moon craft in light.
We have the desert and the sun
to enfold the emptiness of desire.
But now,
only here,
will the ritual fire of the moon
illuminate the dark hand
of the man's love for his son.

(The children of emergence/the four acts/
the fourth degree)

Star spirals,
and I am returned
to the dance, to emerge,
in the dance,
the elements' child.
Four acts contain me
—four elemental tents
for my initiate's blood.
This word calls me to appear,
and, under the specter
of my own absence, I come,
revealed, transfigured
in the womb of apparition,
manifest in desire,
in the possibility of being absent.
I continue
to exist,

to subsist,
to behave with the logic
of my intention
and denial,
to enlist your aid
in glossing the word
that drives me
to my body's touch and emblem,
to my name's extension in you.
Apparition's bird,
I fly to be buried in you.
But no shadow,
bird's or tomb's,
consoles me.
Day by struggling day,
word by feeble word,
I build love's shadow.
In revelation's sleep,
I post the sentinels
of your awakening.
I will resurrect
the cultivated earth,
bush force and craft,
divination's vessel,
composition's needle,
the engagement's horn,
gold's elegant walk in water.
I will be the soul,
struggling into bone,
day by breath-devouring day.

(The doubling/the thirteenth degree)

And, if you love me,
capture me in the cold water,
numb me for the cutting.
This cold provokes my trembling,
the trembling provokes my double.

When the double comes,
my soul runs away.
You see, again, my talent
for being absent.
And, if you love me,
bathe me in my absence
and in the disappearance
of my fear of being born,
in the possession of my presence,
in the memory of my double's
provocation.
Yet,
consecrated one,
you are my mother,
my soul's trace into itself,
the sign that provokes my body
to examine itself,
the prefiguration
of my responsive spirit.
You bring me,
awakened,
to my shame.
My navigations and returns
remind me of my shame.
Still, I am chaste,
a child of the sacred buffoon,
a child of the sacred vulture,
a child of the little old woman,
child of the fable of my redemption.
I have flown back to see
foolish Mousso Koroni alight
in her own nest of misery and deception.
This is the motherless child,
the fatherless child,
the mother who cannot conceive.

She will be my mother.

(Mousso Koroni and the children of shame/ the sixth degree)

This is the tale
of learning to accept desire,
and love's gift,
the human flesh on the knotted tree,
the twin gift of affirmation
and denial.
Unable to rest,
Mousso Koroni comes to take
the kapok tree's shade
around her shoulders.
Here is her sweet shade and rest,
image of her first deception.
Soon, the kapok withdraws
its shade, to offer its fruit.
Now, Mousso Koroni, desiring the child
in the fruit, tastes the fruit.
She asks the tree for her child.
—If you humans had been gracious,
I should willingly have changed
my fruit to children,
and willingly have seen them
descend to your care,
but there is none of my anguish
in your eye, none of my longing
in your body.
I face you and face myself,
stripped of what I would have
in coming to you.—
<Fatherless,
I agree to mother you.
You will be my notation
up the scale of desire
and fulfillment.
I will take you
in my human heart
to adorn your needs.>

So, the woman's heart speaks.
And so the tree,
taking the fruit to weave,
by doubling, designs
your elegant male twins.
—These are the kapok's fruit.
  To every question you will respond,
  I found them on the plain of the eternal fall.—

In the creative word,
there is the act of separation
and the act of falling.
Eternity cuddles in the crook
of the body coming to be.
Mousso Koroni,
whose children are these?
From where do they come?
Who are they?
        <They are my children.
         I found them on the plain
         of the eternal fall.
         Now, my double joy,
         I send you to the fields,
         where you will astonish
         the world with your intensity.
         I know I will have no peace.
         I know that I will be assaulted
         with cattle, and with silver,
         and with gold.
         I will not reveal my mother's secret.>

Out of the tatter of existence
comes the toothless maid,
nurse of the most delicious gift
                to the goddess.
She prepares, for Mousso Koroni,
a plate of salty fonio.
So is the blood and sacrifice
recalled in the seed.

So does the maid assure the mother
of fate, and pain, of joy,
and degradation.
So does the maid insist
in the merit of the good,
in the compromise of another's
agreeable conception.
<Dear friend,
being barren,
I do not conceive.
You move and amuse me
with your temper.
But know that the kapok tree
has changed its fruit
into children, and watered
me with their presence.
I must be silent
concerning this truth.
As I bathe you
with this knowledge,
I reward you
with another tribulation.
I will die in this conception,
unable to conceive my own
desire.
The tree's voice sets my limits;
my own desire for liberation
chains me to my human heart.>

This is a dark wisdom
given in light,
an assault upon the face
between the faces,
a tugging at the hair
nearest the incisive eyes,
an extraction of the god's teeth,
the clarifying of the dark pool.
Now, when the children of shame
return and toss their hoes aside,

they will be battered, by the woman's
radiance, into withdrawal.

Sing.

<They offered me silver
My name was plain of the eternal fall
They offered me gold
My name was plain of the eternal fall
But they offered me a little plate of salty fonio
My name was then flower of the kapok tree.
Pursue me, priests!
There, leaving the kapok,
the kapok-priest,
my horse of knowledge.>

The other's child will never become our child.
Maternity's joy will bear the pain of giving birth.

Let us find knowledge in the tree,
and the tree in God,
the tree in the spirit
and the spirit in the tree;
let us find our refuge in the tree.
In my mother's body
I learn struggle and denial.
From the pool and the pool's shadow,
from the tree and the tree's shadow,
from the star and the star's shadow,
out of the master's boat, in the seed,
out of the master's body,
mother unfolds my being and cause,
mother lays the thread of life before my loom.
I have grown, on the grain of her
tribulation, into power.
In her compassionate crystal,
I see her proceed from loss to loss.
I see her rise from fall to fall.
I see her uplift the truth of my coming
in her own degradation.

I know my spirit's fruit,
through her, as flesh.
I know now that the heart's
flourishing and end
must arise in the circle and exchange
                                        of embodied deeds.

What is the question?

Was friendship blood's exchange?
Could friendship excel the sermon preached on the altar?
Can the heart's reasons abolish spirit's exigencies?

I know now that I have been
moving to place my heart
on humanity's ancient altar.
I know that I must come
from the justness of sacred things
to the justice of my secular body.
And, if, still, I buy my benediction
in submission, I know that I purchase
wisdom in patience, know that I purchase
sight in humility.
So I have purchased this tree,
in my spirit, under my own
ascension of souls,
in a voice,
                    once heard,
and forever remembered.

(BAD NAUHEIM)

Sunrise, Sunday.
A black, cow-driven cart,
moss and milk cans
rise in the mist.
Egg in a bird.
I am the boy

with the drawn breeches,
pockets filled with the dawn's
ebb and flow on Sunday.
You must have heard it said
that I curry my milk cans
and cart the baths to the lame.
If you are troubled, and if you can,
come to me in the blue stall
of the mud-colored barn on the hill.
There, you will discover my skill
in knitting apple and hazel.
Look and the light penetrates
and a blossom appears,
hard promise of a hard body,
which will fall and be buried
                                    in the ground.
But I am not that boy,
perpetrator of a strange act.
My art is in sponging
those who can be saved
into wholeness.
At night,
when the still water condenses
its healing in its depths,
I lie in my straw,
putting on the memory
of all your body's injuries.
Strangers have brought their unruly
calm into our house.
The shapely ear of wheat
that rises from the scorched field
encourages their hosannas in our water.
Water is our name.
The germanic gabble of redemption
has become our speech.
We have been known to pierce
the side of the blackthorn,
and to disfigure the shape
of Roman leaves.

There is conspiracy here,
and continuity,
a salted cake,
stone,
fonted water,
fronded wood,
thunder,
a new name and new task
that I, through you, put on.
Let the name of this old bathing house
be corruped into a name
                    for a new home.
Let the new water subject me
to the danger of forgiving your injury.
This is the Sunday of healing
that my black cart of moss
and milk cans weaves
into being and a blessing.

(The child of folded wings/the nineteenth degree)

Call me child of folded wings.
As I fly, I insist that nothing
may now turn to itself, alone, again.
We are clamor's children,
children of the mouth,
children of the apparition in the limbs,
of power set upon the ground.
My folded wings are Kọmọ's sheath and plume.
The dancer, a vulture,
wears my wisdom on the earth.
I mount these emblems on a bamboo pole.
They dance up; they descend.
I live the spirit's descent, again,
on my folded wings,
and address my real and solid body
on the small tree of fulfillment.

Thus, I have been prepared for the initiation.

(The third phase of the coming out of Kǫmǫ/the seven stages of initiation)

In transit yourself,
you will come, early in the night,
to lead me where the great ones
wait at Kǫmǫ's place.
Your hymns say I will die.
I will feel the exhilaration
of lying in,
will see the birds' parental sacrifice
and rise, to my person,
in the pool's water.

I forget my name;
I forget my father's and mother's names.
I am about to be born.
I forget where I come from
and where I am going.
I cannot distinguish
right from left, front from rear.
Show me the way of my race
and of my fathers.

I hear prefiguration's hymn,
the inarticulate wave
that has been knocking against
my shored and remote body.
This is the end that is no end.
And, in the order of these acts,
I take your presence upon me.
I have come here to learn
the language of control,
and to learn the language
of fulfillment.
I have been trying to create a language
to return what you have lost,
and what you have abandoned,
a language to return you to yourself,

to return to you.
We sit to uncover the grilled
intestines of the sacred fowl.
Down, as we eat, through these bowels,
pass the good thoughts,
the perfect reflection.
The priests will take us,
one by one, to kneel,
forehead to earth, before Kọmọ.
You will present the sacred things
to one who will be reborn,
to one who will have his
eyes opened to Kọmọ.

(BERLIN)

Berlin is a sealed train.
In noon blaze,
I pull my body tight
in the white sheets.
I lie still.
I now abandon my rubicund fruit
for salt and spelt,
cathedral caves,
barbed wire
and the shine
of silver in snow.
Darkness uncovers the cockled
eagle above my shroud
and the fire in my heron wings.
Schmoller has sealed me
again in my voices
and in the bell of willow in wind,
made me the fit apprentice,
ready to enter the dark forest
of the unknown world.
There is, I say, grandeur
in the very hopelessness

of such a life.
Broad-veined in the heart,
I come to this city
of sealing sutures,
the sword on the Spree ferry,
the bottomless and shapeless
tankard of self-love.
I become my own diviner,
pressing my desires
up from the deep of my basket.
My flight is a stone in my flesh;
my return is the lily
of the soul's insistence.
A white darkness is the domain
I have entered to redeem
my spirit's darkness.
I ride now on shadow and iron
into my shieldless body in true light.

(FOUR SECONDARY SIGNS/THE INITIATE'S MOVEMENT FROM RUINS TO BEAUTY)

TÓ MÓ

So far I have come.
Yet I still await another sign.
I have been living in my body's ruins.
Under the earth,
a boding X, fallen from the sun
at the moment of earth's destruction,
leans over me.
My mother would have me stay,
here, where every stone and pot
is known to me.
She dips a small piece of wood
in the first water I drink.
By this water

I am signed to my
compassionate name
and assigned to the earth
I take to serve.
In this sign,
I purify my habitation;
I combat my thirst for leaving.

NTÍ TAÁ SÍSÃ

I am not leaving now.
I swaddle myself with baptism's emblem,
taken from the stream of great waters.
My royal emblem staunches me
and forbids the chiefs' dying.
When the great ones disappear,
they are held,
within this constellation,
able to appear,
able to refuse death's chariot.
Now, I will be found—
in the quiet of seas,
rivers, lakes and pools—
preparing the episode
of the body's return
to elevation and compassion.

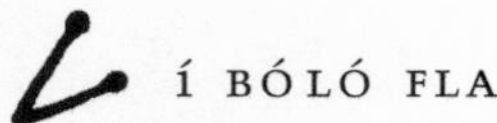

Í BÓLÓ FLA

I shall call this
the laying on of hands.
This is, again, the memory
of a flat earth, sun,
and an agèd man
with a water twig,
in search of mercy.
Cultivator hands strike

fulfillment from the earth.
Cultivator hands seed me
                        in the earth.
I offer your hands
to the water's weather,
to the copper and gold
of my coming.

SÁRÁMÁ̃

I have been pulled up,
at lightning's manger,
into the god's laughter.
Here, heaven displays
the woman's body,
scourge of ruins,
excellence of the body's
                placing on earth.
Under the woman's ethereal bed
nothing impure can be sustained.
I rise to take her form,
my spirit's good sign,
courteously,
into myself.

Signs of the final ascension
        from devastation
                to fulfillment.

I turn.
I continue.

(FLORENCE)

Goad of the god's gaud,
guard of the crippled eagle,
master of grace and generatio,

caliper of the city's soul,
monastic voice of the secular book,
you have caught Cassius and his twin
next to Judas in Lucifer's maw.
In your dream
the crippled eagle still must fly,
and a just power order the king's eye
down on the Gothic rose in his keeping.
The rose you keep tears your heart apart.

A Guelph on the wing of the royal house,
the spirit's sage under the miter,
the loved one's advocate in light's domain,
you stitch your heart with the skin
of all that has been spoken.
Stone and page by stone and page,
you uncover your spirit's truth.
So you must believe,
and so shout down the hollow
of time to the bishop's blood,
though fortunate Florence rise
from Cino's blood and a city's
cunning patience.

You rise from the darkness of the self
to three lights, to the pilgrim
rapture of consummate grace
and the turning at the top of the light.

—Noi eravam lunghesso il mare ancora—

All this is the journey through Book and saint,
the sign of "the third who walks beside you,"
the sign of the thirst and the book within,
the new and visible appearance of the world.

Time is to soul as eye is to vision.

I am only certain of my heart,
and the world's body,
in the free act of my heart.

Rest, then, at this mountain top,
where you can comprehend
the measure of this love
which warms me,
when I forget our nothingness
and treat shades as a solid thing.

The double book declares a fellowship
in the fact of being hidden.
Fellowship asserts the spirit's freedom,
the seal of its divinity.

You have argued with the night
and disembodied things,
have set redemption as the form
                                        of reformation
in what is unseen.
Your art is a second creation,
a true bleeding of the world.
You have entered the wood,
you turn, out of the holy waves,
born again,
even as trees renewed,
pure and ready to mount to the stars.

(CHILDREN OF THE FOUNDATION TREE/CHILDREN OF THE TRUE CULT AND CREATION/THE TWENTY-THIRD AND THIRTY-THIRD DEGREES)

If I am child of the foundation tree,
the origin of all things,
I am child of the dead child.

All things awaken, under the tree,
to be finished; even the dead
gnarl up to the tree for breath.

I climb, bent-back, each step.
The star I see awakens me
to the mother's thunder-breath
and the daughter's lightning stroke
                    along my spine.

I am learning to inhabit light
and the grave's coffin light,
and how to assess the distance
                    from light to light.
I have it that an awakened body
knows the measure of moving light.
Light is motion's tinderbox,
clock of the body's internal rise and fall,
assessor of the darkness in light.
I have it that an awakened child
is a probable child, that the dead child
is an awakened child, his own
beginning, sketch of his own end.
You will not achieve the simple
by being other than you are,
or by being doubled and set free from yourself.
In you, the married blacksmith appears
in the arms of the perfect and awakened child.

Call the aged ones to be rendered
wealthy in marrow and blood again.

Sómá
is the knife man
on the teaching knoll.
You find him in the tomb,
the cradle of our common heart.
He is the head on the body of the dead.

Kómá is the jackal's prayer,
a sign of himself,
the smithy's hammer strength.

By his nature,
we reveal our own dedication.

Kű̃gomá,
hunter,
comes from the brush
on the eagle's wing.
In his fish and beast eye,
we uncover the pool's quarry
of souls; in his hands,
we hold our own souls'
periodic variation.

Dómá,
wise,
rises, under
the omniscient bird.
We dress his brothers
in white bonnets and batons.
By their beating,
we burn into knowledge.

These are the descendants
of our awakening.
I leap from the vision
of their true bodies
to worship.
I have come,
past fear,
to be put to death,
and to be taken,
by the new word,
to my resurrection.
I tremble,
being born in the grave
to the light of my people's star.

So I will be led into the earth,
to revivify what has lodged

in me, unknown.
Here, at the crossroads,
you animate my wisdom in the dance.
You take me to the first
and largest place of my being,
to retrieve my being.
You sanctify my infant's speech.
You announce the birth
                of my emblazoned word.

This is the day of fulfilling my new commandment.
                This is the act.

(VENICE)

Through lidi and pali,
on the enameled lagoon,
I come, undone
by the swerve of nets
and big baskets,
driven up the shoals
to the deeper water.
Out of firewood
and small lumber,
the boys knock up these
Byzantine crosses.
                Formosa deformitas.
Or is it beauty deformed?
When the tower turned
on itself and tumbled,
only the largest bell
and angel were saved.
I was then a glassmaker,
growing sallow with the work
of balconies and windows.
Voices in the sea
confuse my clock.
I have never been at ease

with the cluster of glass
and guns on the tide,
with the way the water
rises to embrace my pilgrim feet.
I would remain,
a sapphire in my own corolla,
a rose unblessed,
here, where the king
will not come.
Let sister Florence
truss itself in virtue.
I am rising with the tide,
strung with gondoliers,
love-lyrics, lutes and scrolls.
I cultivate open arms
to receive the blue water.
Though the marble
shines above the foam,
my signs are wood,
water and stone.
My body is a balsa
raft of patience,
cradled in a maze
of broken ships,
and bells,
and the gilded angel,
plunging
into the public deep.

(KỌMỌ LEADING TO THE INTERIOR OF THE EARTH/
THE SIX STAGES)

We must begin again in the sanctuary's court.
The abundant horn, cap of the spirit,
sphere and egg, greets us.
We must walk twelve ways,
return, go up, go down,
wind the spirit and egg life

to the head.
We must have the head
and his four new limbs,
a compassionate and volcanic water,
the beer and grain, the altar thirst
to be assuaged.

We continue.

When the fowl dies, open-winged
upon its back, and the nut of blood
streams on our palettes,
we will be saved by blood,
prayer and our own submission.
No buffoon will ride down on a horse
to topple my love, to snare me,
deceived, in the mirror of the knife,
to draw my humiliation from me.

Now, at the end of the journey,
salute this holy man,
follow him to the dead ones' dancing ground.

> The day of the death of Kọmọ's chief,
> the uncircumcised will see Kọmọ.
> The day the children of Kọmọ fall
> I should wash my hands in blood.

He goes from tomb
  to tomb
    in time's order;
he lingers at the last
  (master,
  father
  or sacred friend),
where he lies
  to evoke

compassion's sign.
We
are riding
on the pool
of familiar things.
Exalted
by his voice in the dead,
the head arises to abandon
Kọmọ's cloak and mask.
He kneels
before
the kapok trees,
trees of the old dead,
sign of the last
rest,
mark of the last returning.

One by one,
tolled by age and service,
the initiates descend
to chant Kọmọ
down
into the house.
The voice you hear
is a drum,
is a bell,
is a horn,
is a bull voice
assaulting silence.

This disorder in the voice
repeats the rupture of all things,
is the sound of the downfall
of the universe.

Out of the cracking sound,
downfall and ruin, the god

scales his music true
to the smallest singer's voice.

This is the prelude to the end of time,
the return to the darkness and the silence.

We have learned to wait
in the caesurae of the god's song,
able to hear the secret stops
and to accept the silence.

God's dancer now enters the space
we leave around the altar.

Under the eye of the cloak and mask,
the charge and knowledge
                                        of the universe,
we are naked now,
stripped of any reason to be
clothed in our initiates' needs.

New rhythm haunts us in this hemisphere.
The dance teaches us the reason to be born,
the point of our child's wail
                    and derangement
                              in the wood.

We present our injuries to the woman's balm.
We sit,
surrounded by our body's instruments,
in Kọmọ's hut,
to eat, in his presence,
under the music of his revealed love.
So, in the end, we must adorn the sanctuary,
and take those who belong to us,
from night to dawn,
and into our care.
As I will be born,
I will know myself in your eye.

Head and hierarchy teach me Kọmọ's day.

Kọmọ's dance designs the spine,
in sacred air, in the space around the body.
I celebrate the seed and the sign,
the population of what is revealed.

Kọmọ's parade,
under the arch and altar,
proceeds to the wood.
There,
the most sacred one
absents himself,
to light the fire at Kọmọ's knoll.
There,
in the fire,
I am listening
to my own voice,
        in the wood,
        in the master's voice

    < Man is an unknown and unknowable grain;
        Kọmọ is the twin of the trough. >

                                        I witness
and construct the arch,
my ability to make the world appear.
I know now
the twins of the universe
are mingled in the dance.

On this celebratory Sunday,
we return to the house.
This is, again, a river to be crossed.
This is a field song out of time,
the road where the marigold will be
exalted into memory and compassion.
Here, where the spirit can escape its cross,
we open what must be closed.

We have been brought,
through many pools, back to this palisade,
to the world's round and fragile
configuration.
Center, now, this world.
And let these broken bowls
hold our souls' desires,
the fulfillment of crossing over.
Let us send this beast's blood
into the pool's starlight,
to purchase our power.
Let us take possession of our
divided selves, of the new word.
Under the priest's upholding baton,
I see the first six figures of my name
rise from the earth to accept
Kọmọ's descending embrace.
It will be easy to trace
the wise men's path upon the earth.
Light and blood reveal the gypsy gyre
of stargazers, hunters and divines,
warriors and thaumaturges,
the sky-eyed pundits who reveal us
on the ground.
We take seven steps up the tree,
seven steps to achieve the eye's acclamation,
the bone-bell shout of the dead in the living,
the tell-tale face in the forgotten heart,
the event of being actual.
What is actual condones our blood upon the earth.
Year calls to year in the golden tree,
in the pure tree, tree of abundance.
In blood, I divest the earth
of my encumbered body,
and lay my cleansed bones
upon earth's altar.
My mother dances around the mother's tree.
Free of the whirlwind of her dance,
I am not free of her.

Tempered by the globe of my blood on the earth,
I revolve in the egg's unending oval.
I protect what attaches me to heaven
by every incision in every body I cast away.
I shall forever assume the contradiction
of returning to the ground I burn
                                        to free my god.

What is the question?

Who will be redeemed?

(MEXICO CITY/CONSOLAPA)

1
Veneras and the Virgin
teach me my double journey.
Down by west,
and rising in the east,
I figure heaven and the grave,
the rude red salvation that tethers me.
Maddened by the salt of desire,
I sever my wings,
become a fish,
poolwise and patient
with the stony water.
It is not easy to swim the moat
around this sacred city.
My flesh and human blood
impel me into the sun's charge
and the green knife of the god's need.
I hold my double nature as a need,
the obelisk of angels
who clarify my craft in tin and gold.
Such divine debility
is a danger to my southern star,
cheap confetti in a saint's parade.
I return to the weighted sound

and slide of water,
blood of the earth
and of the earth's irruption.
My yellow eyes have seen the dark
initiates come riding on the lily
of a promised return.

2
Holding the black candle of memory,
I return.
Three tombs take my light.
I elevate the trinity of races in my blood.
I am prepared
for the water in the rock,
and for the white shadow
                    under the red roof.
Coffee leaves linger in this place;
the brown odor clings to the brown
walls in the thatched huts.
You must pass,
through the boiling spring,
stone upon stone,
from the still forest
into the exalted house.
Tehuana voice in a shawl
consoles me for the forest,
for the incomprehension
in my step in the water.
This woman's voice and body
have been turning above the name
                              of my house.
The name has consolation in it.
Who will be redeemed
by understanding
the offense of water,
or the wisdom of the sharp stone
in the mother's flesh?
Who will be saved
by the Christ skull on the grave,

or the dead whistle of song
at a shrine by the side of the road?
Who will be able to come
from the coffee grove at dark
into the light of my arrival?
Tehuana voice provokes my double journey.
I enter the house I have taken,
the weight of being bare of other rooms
upon me.

When the dead arrive,
we know ourselves fatherless.
We place the priest
on a goat's hide, on a bed,
above the earth.
We prepare him to confer with Kọmọ.
Now,
Kọmọ's horn is the mouth of woman.
The mother of truth orders the blacksmith
to rebuild our lives from sand.
In sand,
in the dung beetle's vine pace,
there is a message,
a calculated truth to be forged
in our pool's desire.
The dead one is lying in.
Our tabor plays soul of the parting one,
the dance of death.
Soul must hear the music.
We must be given the freedom of the dead.
The dead must take us in his arms.
We must see the new man rise
to invest our perpetual arrival,
here, in the double breath of life.

We continue.

Tempted with sorghum beer
by your first in love,

dressed by the medium's sobs,
the great clock tolls you out of life.
Initiate,
I have read a death
into my beginning,
a flag of distinction
I must win.
The herald tells me
nothing has been lost.
I contain your dreams.
At cock's crow,
a new voice comes
to assume the tunic and mask.
Eight days from your parting,
we will capture you on the altar,
to conserve and to release your soul.

Having crossed the water,
you arise in me.

We return to the incisions in the wood.

I am lying in.

I see the birds' parental bleeding.

I rise, at the touch of the pool's water,
                    to my person.

                I forget my name;
                I forget my mother's and father's names.
                I am about to be born.
                I forget where I come from
                and where I am going.
                I cannot distinguish
                right from left, front from rear.
                Show me the way of my race
                and of my fathers.

I uncover the grilled intestines of the sacred fowl.
I eat; I think; I contemplate what has been revealed.
You take me to kneel, forehead to earth, before Kǫmǫ.
You present me to sacred things.
I am reborn into a new life.
My eyes open to Kǫmǫ.

Elaine's Book

Veil, I

There is something about the blood in a sunset
that answers no questions;
the tarnished veil of a halo refers us
to a dream we never had;
and whatever wakes in us
when the unseen loon calls
offers no consolation.
Can I speak of the heart here,
when nothing speaks to it?
Can the night's brush uncover crystals of longing
that master moon hides and rocks in the beech?
Given such suspicion,
it is too early to submit to the darkness.
You must commit yourself to the light's weave,
the distant clarity of a promise you may have
misunderstood.
Go on;
the sunset's veronica'd blood
promises consonance.
You will learn the veil's appeal to the light in you.

Seals, I

Por un instante están los nombres habitados.
—Octavio Paz, "Semillas para un himno"

A river flowed out of Eden to water the garden.
What has the river found?
Onyx, gold and a substance which has hidden
behind its name.
Your name does not arise in Gilgamesh;
only the mask appears,
sainted seal of a serpent's grove,
root of the Immovable Spot,
the assurance that you will always move.
But, then, waters divide to frame a world.

A star turns east to west
to remind you of its dark side.

I imagine evening, when the man comes,
following his lion-bird,
keeper of the pail and upraised branch.
We can see the man's night face
and you, in his shadow.
Down below,
the serpents swim in stillness.
And in this moment, the sun
is only a seed of desire.
We must insist that bliss is knowledge
of the evening's rising and the tree's root
slowly given to its coffin in water.

So I have placed you at the head of sacred things,
and called our habitation night.
A darker woman leans, invisible, at your ear.
She bears another earthen, covered pot,
in which my memory of you is held.

Seals, II

Lady of the Beasts
Mountain Mother
Spear Hand
Visible Planet
Have I named you?
Will I come to the architrave
to consecrate my lost powers?
I have been a faithful son of the abyss,
one who curdles when my drum calls.
My singing is coarse cloth on a desert floor.
Whatever fires I light burnish an old man's knees.
Goddess of the living,
I am not one you would choose to redeem.

I take the steps below you much too swiftly.
I cannot endure the clarity
                    of knowing your other name.

Hathor

Moonless dawn.
The cold house crackles.
Outside, the leafless trees creak
and sigh in the wind's caress.
That moan and cold's ache comfort you.

There should be young man
to hang at the foot of your bed,
knees snell with duty and complaisance.
We shall call this civilization:
the astral calendars touting heaven's law,
priests rising from the dust to tutor the city,
a young man cognizant of your virtue.

Veritably, the Sumerian has marked you,
a wild and pillared thing,
                        grueled in marshes.
Coldness recalls how you mothered the world
and a golden falcon, bull of your house.
In the room's cave silence,
we hear the dead one tap the wall.
He must be held, head east,
on the warm side of this grave.
He sleeps among his swords and cutting tools,
razors and bronzes; his rawhide sandals
flicker beneath an ostrich fan.
A dream has covered his linen body with hide.
Bull's legs ferry him among his water pots.

This body belongs to you,
an eternal presence, whose only gift is fulfillment.
Dawn finds me here,

searching the purple bruise of your faithfulness.
Who but she can you be?
Who but the one who submits
and is quickened by fire,
or is buried, by faith, beneath the hide,
able only to affirm that spirit's loss?
I mark your presence here,
bereft of the love you have sheltered
by being forever taken.

The Origin of Mary in a Cathedral Choir

At the age of five Cecilia saw a meteor, and thereupon decided to be an astronomer. She remarked that she must begin quickly, in case there should be no research left when she grew up.

Beauty is splendor veritatis, a radiance of truth.
The fact of revelation the eye beholds can never lie.
Old harmonies dress themselves for eye and ear
with a blessedness all saints approve.
I shall now impose these buds the doctor universalis
has sent you, while he speaks of God,
the elegant architect, at work on a regal palace
with the "subtle chains" of musical consonance.
You have come from that different cave life,
out of the springs of distemper and possession.
Lying in a crypt, you gather your strangeness,
waiting to bejewel another city with your ecstasy.
Such rose leaves enfold your words that the king,
as he refuses, must bend to define the light
and hear the modulation in his voice that has gone.
True to the night and the cave's rejoicing,
you cover his eyes with flame.
                                        I know
you have written this mystery of embodiment
in fire and a virgin birth; when the stone fell
from heaven, it flowered in an almond tree,

and a pine tree covered with violets became
a token for your love.
All ways lead down to the politic mother
and the fear of celebration, the cleansing
in a new birth where the mother-bride rises.
Who rises first?
The memory of fire confuses me.
Your tunic rages blue with wrath.
You abandon me
in the ruin of an incomparable house.
Who rises first?
When now this clairvoyant rose rises over stone
in the choir, I can hear the burning,
clearing the path for a red sign and a figure
who will stand suspended
until a red mother claims him on a red shore.

Yemanjá

Dawn on a greener earth shapes the woman,
come, with immaculate beads around her neck,
to secure the figure of my infant step.
I ride, in silence, upon her head from water
to water, through the dance in which you hold her.

Where the air is clear they will do even better by you.
Even so, we changed you when we changed your name,
married you to whiteness in a depth of sky quite out of reach
and gave you thunder, arrows and iron for your sons.
Memory tells us you were made water by insult,
the fortunate flicker of wrath that swept you
out of the market and into healing. Or so
these pots reveal our desire for purity.

I hear a toucan over water call me
to my oldest river, the bird's voice filled
with the clamor of cloth and melon seeds.
Weightless now, I climb down from a green

ledge to declare myself your son again.
Near the clearing, where the deer come to nibble
at a late spring, I have your water-worn stones
bathing in the blood of whatever the land gives.

Compassion wears us down like river-worn stones.
I return to your river body.
Your sixteen cowry shells flare in a darker light.
At the river's edge, a young woman bends to bathe
the bite of your porridge from her mouth.
Even in the twilight, I can see her eyes blaze
with the pleasure of having known love alone.

Zapata and the Egúngún Mask

En agua divina en hoguera nací: soy mexicano.
Facing east, I learn to betray myself.
Ochre clouds on the sky's vault
lift cactus from its chalk brown death.
These facts are not actual,
only an uncovered city,
a shawled and surly Huichol saint,
                        out of time,
                out of place,
fangled in plaster.
You must learn blood's ascendance,
the high air it will ride
until it comes to rest
                in another heart.
That heart is yours.
That step into the red flower of winter
begins your first abandonment.

Stars do not circle the earth.
Earth rides its galactic horse
        from moment to moment.
So we must sight through a wooden cross
to fix our own movement;

so we must be fixed in stone
to measure the flight of the cross.

In the Villa Rica de la Vera Cruz,
I wait to receive you.
Cuirass and cross claim you,
proclaim the boat valley heart you bring me.
I am prepared to assume
your solitary gabbling with God
and a night's destruction of certainty.
You belong to a loneliness
no one here will defend.

My solitude is a provocation,
a bell struck once at dawn,
memory of a baby's coffin
            being carried
on a boy's head,
brown women in black, brown men
in white manta and red scarves.
The red consoles me still.
The red button of a cardinal's cap
installs me over my own bones in Cholula;
our Lady staunches my Aztec fire
and removes me from the red earth
                    I have given you.

Turn again.
            Open.
To arrive, you must go
      through my green gate
and trust your exile
                    to my strangeness.
Only I cry for your entrance.
I have stood four hundred years,
waiting for your return.
Now, babe of slaves,
my Yoruba shuffle and song

embraces your docking
                    and the red lurch
of the flag that parts you.
I lie on this coffee coast,
                    cut myself
                    from myself,
no more than a figure in a graveyard chant,
a moment's pause in the spirit's bleeding.

Call me the clear one,
if you can,
the one buffered by guns, strong horses
and men who have a need
to burden their sandals with strange dust.
Clearly, we will become one,
under the aegis of desire.
Such clarity is a way of building
five suns on a rock,
a prefiguration of the royal dead.
It is a way of seeing
the blue etched in water,
the light of angels.

An angel wrath has burned my prophecies.
Still I know
          my sustenance
          will be
          war
drink   eat   shit   sleep
walk and will
prick and soothe   war
Book it and be damned.
There you have the record of a love gone clay.

Out of the many pains left
to my care
                    and the sight
of an Indian hope scattered,
year by year, in their own bones,

high on the spiny mountains,
I have called an end to the brown
death which invests me,
I have spoken in such a voice
                                        to Christ.
So did the father speak,
until he ran upon a friend in Guadalajara.
We have his head in a cage at Guanajuato
—a church jewel being tempered and refined
by the disdain of creole bitches in black.
Why should I be more attentive in this skull cave
than I am when I am caught,
confused, and full of corridos and chile,
on the Hill of Bells?
                                        Your eyes engender
a barbarian shame in me.
                                                I continue,
where strangeness is a customs broker,
to rehearse my crucifixion,
                in your cloth,
                        at your gate.

Guacamaya has feathered your fear in song:
        Entre cascabeles derrota gente
        el mexicano chichimeca:
        viene a tenderse niebla de escudos.

The prissiness of a "court clerk."

"But more important than these desires of yours
are those of the Mexican people for whom the prestigious
and victorious sword of General Villa is indispensable."

The body remains hard to define.
Numb it with virtues
        or number it with days,
                        it escapes.
Sunday.
I have been trying to measure the pain

of a red cathedral, crowned with a red flag.
Clearly, the clock will not strike today.
The valley will raise its red head
to protest the sabbath's umbilical resonance.
I am the *iztli* above my bed,
a smoking mirror over my divided body.
Feather balls adorn the shin bone
and its eyes of light.
                                        Light,
worn on these cobblestones,
is your most careful dispossession.
Sunday tells us that this your twilight day
must round to its end
          in the same square,
under the black frill and sanity
of the same dance.
                                        Light,
worn in the sober cassocks
of sweet breads and chocolate,
is the bullroarer, stringing your
unfinished soul in the wind.
Sunday. A Michoacana missal,
frothy with old blood and springdrawn desires.
How many years I have sat
in this city's silence, bolstered
by the anticipation of bells and God's
promise to abscond with my suffering.

We begin
the sixteenth discourse on red:
                    red patch
                    red datum
                    red thing in the eye
apricot red of an April sunset in Oaxaca
bullish black red of blood sausage in Xalapa
manicured pink rose red
                              of unwashed mountain hands
blank red of the matador's cape
whiskey brown red of the offended eye

scarlet red sputum of Pátzcuaro
pinched bluepurple red of the mother
                    dying in labor on her straw mat
canyon red of your skin when it is honest
vermilion tongue in your devil mask

Your face is as scarred as this my face,
baby fat gone under the cut of familiar
                                        necessities.
Night in Xochimilco is a disguise.
You come away from the cozy woodfires,
disguised in your short black jacket,
lavender shirt, sharptoed Spanish boots
and silver brimmed hat.
I wear dung brown and my plain heart,
better to display the initiate's scallops
                                  on my face.
I know no one will unmask
the night you left in Xochimilco,
no one will guess that these public wounds
I carry mask my boiled desire
                              for a locked heart.
        Llegan bajando, llegan bajando,
        sobre las acacias es el sitio en que se tienden.
        Flores busca Moteuczomatzin,
        hoguera busca Nezahualcoyotzin.
        Van en busca del cerco del agua, se agitan.
Now that we have raised this flag of night between us,
we can offer these others no more than a curse
                                              and a decent burial.
Even these things will be attuned to the mask,
and the iron earth's resistance to graves,
the cypress trees falling in Chapultepec,
the water-voiced ululations of a spirit
who has emptied us of love.
Descendent certainties sustain us.
It is time to be fulfilled.
It is time to return.
I should have a caracol to contain me

when we meet. I should have
a handful of shells for the passage we share.
Why do I, with only a plain heart
and the memory of a prophet's vagaries
to protect me,
                                        advance and return,
                                        advance and return?
Why do I return?

Monday.
A Sunday plaza taste lingers on my tongue.
I go down every boulevard and avenue.
Turn and turn.
Obregón,
                    Madero,
Juárez,
            Pino Suárez,
                                    Carrillo Puerto,
                                                    Hidalgo.
In every city,
the same blood beacons shine.
I am bilious with marigolds and lilies.
But this is home.
My bus flagellates Hidalgo's jacaranda.
I travel behind a blue mirror held
against the sun's force,
the dark glass of the jackal's trace.
I dolly upstream with my presbyter.
Monday, going up,
brings the wash of bougainvillea
and the virgin's blue ribbons on iron gates
                                                        and houses.
Monday parades the virgin, crowned with cactus,
in a blue, engineless Cadillac.
My cristero back pulls the rope
from Zapopan to Tlaquepaque.
I see now
that rubies of perspiration crown my head,
my spinning knees cut a rose path
                                            down a rose aisle

toward blue light and shawled wood.
This tide pull of the spirit out of time
inflames the body. One of us must nurture
the rose cut retablos in your eyes.
I have asked the lady to grant me power
to divest you of your corn and flowers,
to cut you out of this river's chocolate soil.
One of us must inhabit the cities'
                    clean saints' names.
One of us must acknowledge Monday's power
                    to veil your civil dawn.

This is the history of the Paschal kiss.
Pascual, deep in his own injuries,
always stutters about my left shoulder,
happy as always to repeat the deathless fee
her services require. Guadalupe calls me
his President and Father. Rodolfo eases me
into my Tlaxcalantongo palace.
I know I shall be drawn, quartered
and canonized in a tent,
on a night when the pine needle rain
disguises the friendly voice.
                                        Red Christ,
another red night accuses me of your faith.
What I would give for the sunrise
treeing of that "accursed trinity."
I hear that the ruby centaur of the north
begs not to be accused of this wreckage.
What does he know of history
and a mother fondling her sons' failures?
        ¡Nadie tiene casa en la tierra!
So I wrapped those two in prison clothes
and dumped them in a shallow grave.
        I have never been myself.
I give you the earth's free face,
the double holy weight of your sovereign body.
You will learn my secular signs,
and book yourself equal and secure to me.

Still, I will pursue you,
and goad you to curse me,
pursue you until your land, become mine,
enslaves you.
I will assume all amethyst water you possess,
the pine and cypress, the silver gouged out
and shaken loose in the best homes;
I will embrace and share the fruit
your plow strokes from its cover.
I am the father you long for.
I have learned to speak in an unfamiliar,
oracular voice, and to wait for your fear
to make you love me.

Tuesday
opens on water
and the Roman goddess
stuck in her stone boat
on the Paseo.
What time the morning gives
for trading secrets and gold
grows short.
Tuesday is careful to obscure
the lane where Berta has won
her red flag of confirmation.
Busy angel above the traffic
hears a socio's voice at its base.
It is given to us, friend,
to protect what others do not see.
You laugh when an Indian rides
his barefoot pride
down a street
that has heard the jingle
of prince feet.
I have often asked God
his meaning
and urged a gentleman's
understanding upon him.
I conjure cloth; he delivers men.

My offer was as generous
as the times allow—
sixty percent of cost for the first
measure, forty percent thereafter
(the buyer, of course, absorbs
any cost overruns).
Friend, what is the business
of God, if not our protection?
What is the meaning of this lady,
if not to recall the wolf voice
with which we were born?

Tuesday is the ache of Wednesday,
the threshold of desolation.

Wednesday.
Sunset in the great city.
The firefly lamps in Rio Lerma patios flicker and hold.
Cars thread their red lights in the Paseo's cocoon.
After the starfall of a soft rain,
the sky puts on a gray rebozo.
Every morning now, ladies from Texcoco
prepare their rainbow thin rebozos
for the city's desolate call; they walk
barefoot from spiny path to stone,
out of the lightning of old age, death,
babies and a forgiveness that never comes.
They appear, washed of haste, to stand,
doll-eyed and rigid at crossroads, at sunset.
That one you see there, huddled in her
white cotton dress and sieve black shawl,
at least knows a journey's end.
She spreads her burred, brown woolen rug,
dips in her string bag for black silver beads
and the small red eye-of-God,
lays these at the heart of her rug, kneels.
She draws into the wood of her own silence.
The winged woman above her will not kneel,
nor answer, nor acknowledge the unarmed

respect the other gives. She has been called
to adorn only the city's civil claims,
the piped and feathered warriors,
                                        buried without a trace.
I extol the Texcoco eyes
that will not be deceived,
the antiphon that answers no call.
I revere the ear attuned to the prayer
Minerva can no longer say.
My Texcoco lady rises from the grave
of mud walls and a rocky tilling land,
to obscure the creole grave in Montparnasse,
with its crystal urn of good Oaxaca dirt.

Yet "in the very hour of their success,"
they "have disagreed,"
"and no man seems to see
or lead the way to peace
                                        and settled order."

You must prepare for my eruption
and the guarded way I have of guarding you.
        I am that I am
            two steps beyond the northern line.
        I become what I am
            two steps below it.
"Do you speak English?"
        "Sí, American Smelting and Refining y sonofabitch."
                Caught bleeding in a cave,
                I suck my rebel wounds.
                Your horses have passed,
                and passed again.
                You would find it politic,
                señor, to buy a dog
                to snuff my rag feet.
                I will never give in
                to your rose tint piety.
                I will be bundled and fired
                by the Indian in me.

Our contract was written,
in burnished figures on parchment,
at Santa Isabel.
I will not go back.
I will not,
at the hour of my first death,
stand under a gringo's eyes.
Now, 'manos, aim . . . fire.

Ask me if I remember the giant saguaro cactus,
the Sangre de Cristo,
sagebrush sitting golden on a coiled brown path,
the cream rose end of a dry day.
Ask me if I remember the hard felt hat
and confusion of names I wore,
out of the Alamo, over the king's mountain,
down to the slave and green coast.
You were waiting for the right mistake
to tap the rich water in my northern wells.
I live with the gestalt of your greed,
a configuration of "natural boundaries" in my bowels.
What is the difference between one Wilson and another?
I try to curry Atlantic favor and trade
my trust in you away. You become
the captain of my port.
I have never been myself.
How can I forgive my inability to deceive the east,
my lost faith in the prophecies I engendered?
When there is no more flesh for the thorn,
how can I nurture this yellow rose of love between us?
Night has been our connection,
a doxy of dove gray weddings,
the slatbed where a lover takes revenge.
I hold my pickaxe self in you,
and hear my heart ask, who will be redeemed,
who will figure the native body
and the dark home,
fit for our dark light?

I must become myself.
I must learn to say I forgive myself,
for my scab eyes and dropped caul,
for the inattentive bliss of bleeding the mother
who names me,
for the donkey cart of injuries I haul
from city to city,
for the gaudgiddy cathedral fires I build between us.
Still, I call the resurrection once again:
Francisco Madero,
José María Pino Suárez,
Belisario Domínguez,
Serapio Rendón,
Adolfo Bassó.
Out of the rock of betrayal,
I now carve my own forgiveness.
Will it last?
Will it be enough?

If the beggar repents,
we must approach the Magdalene in another way.
Zimmerman will minister to him.
We want the Sun to rise in arms throughout the land.
Deep waters will return us home
Texas New Mexico Arizona
I will build a nation against old enemies
Offer them the spirit of contention;
it is this they understand.
Lightning snow of trust broken
A speck of snuff on holy parchment
Caged by your closeness again

I have never forgotten
the red battalions knocked up to defend my dream.
No one works for me now.
I lock their union halls and clap
new codes and customs on their houses.
The little Morelos Indian coins his own silver.
I sack my banks, issue useless paper.

I allow the eagle to fly of his own volition.
Though everyone contributes to my cause,
criollo capers on the earth please me most.
Who is to say what separates a man from public life?
The Centaur must be hooded;
                  the little Indian must die.

Thursday.
I have come to the fifth day
in the Long Count of Desolation.
This is the day of the dead,
a night for the stone Christ
and the crossing,
a timeless boiling of nickel candles,
to be lit and caressed by the lake's
lily-infested breath.
One is forever going up the vein
toward a sheathed heart,
or going down,
driven deep beneath dead mines
to arrive in mummied splendor
                           with a skull song.
I emerge from water and earth
into the god's promised air,
covering for my black light of promise.
Babalawo has honored me
with my grandfather's shroud.
Tonight,
under the gourds and drums,
I shall kick up the dust of his birth,
walk in his revived flesh,
bang the bell of his buried voice.
I shall return the sugar of his
forest days to this desert.
I am only the promise of a trace
gone home, one that my brothers
refuse, except in mask.
So I mask my cimarron desires
in the red skin of mother patience.
                  I disappear.

I appear in black charro trousers
and a white shirt, stoked in blood.
My horse takes my sacked body to Cuautla
—death of a journey displayed,
despedida to the "deep immortal human wish,
the timeless will."

It is time to raise the nation
from the will of its forgetfulness.
It is time to provoke a passion
for what is hidden.
The black liquid of exchange,
swabbed from the bones of the resurrected
forest, is only a mask,
a livid reminder of the failure
to acknowledge my night body,
struggling to enter day.
                Yo me abandono
to the trinity of a double loss
I have yet to realize.

Upon the Cardinal's soul I invoke eternal rest and peace in God's kingdom in the company of our Blessed Mother Mary and all the saints.—

Guadalupe-Tonantzin

Night arrives in an amethyst coach.
The jade river edge takes its capillary way up the bank.
The mountain, dressed in its blue rock, leans, with a lover's
lightness, to embrace a small man's moonlit shadow.
At this hour, the sheep natter at a Spanish day's end,
and the water voice of evening calls the shepherd to his blue wine.
Mother night, such a tolling awakens me, here, to dew's
splendor and the rain, a moon that was once mine.
I keep these secrets in a leather pouch my twin has sent from home.
You bathe me now with your other name.

This is a spring in the dark,
hill blood and blood of a womb
that binds me to my task.
I am Juan,
in the wood of your desire,
clutching at the moon within you,
willing to mount your Sun throne.
Your balm is water in maguey,
a crystal that remains
when I weave your mirror.
I know I am standing
where a nation will rise,
and take its heart back
from the desert where the god lies.
All those who dream of being whole,
all those who would betray the east,
will see your image on my back.
I must break the membrane
of my own betrayal,
                    to come forth
                    and to return.

                    "It follows, then (for I have always loved
the syllogistic style of the logicians) . . . that God
executed his admirable design in this Mexican land,

conquered for such glorious ends, gained in order that a
most divine image might appear there."

The man with the flower in his name sits
spelling the ages, heavy with every knowledge
of the end of things—
a father with a bookish son who soon learns
the trick of escaping the book, to take the exuberant
ride down the sure path of tongues and mitotes.
There is a leaf amiss in the book of hearts
when he tells us the City must be *prepared.*
Beyond the Ganges,
when every ear has heard the saint
and witnessed to his step in stone
in a hidden place,
no one needs to remember
April roses, cypress, or white lilies,
or "a torch whose eternal light
is the splendid North Star of mankind's Hope,"
or see in the watermelon dawn
a wind god or the Morning Star.
We stand above a cloud that links
                    a loss and a return
to extract a blue prophecy from a day
turning toward its jade fulfillment.

I am Thomas,
with the smallest vial of holy water
in my right hand, come to cleanse the ground.
Oh, the donkeys in the New World
kick up the dust of old parchment,
trying to find my traces.
I change my name more often than I change my clothes
—Zumé, Viracocha, Bochica, Cuculcan—
and I draw near myself in the wind and the Morning Star.
But who is to say that I have come again
to a home where only the Serpent of Stars can seat me?
Jesuits will surround themselves with virgins
of light, and lakes, and pains, and remedies,

and martyr themselves in their own memorials.
I only hope to be true to crosses that rise,
without explanation, in rain forests,
where the silence veils my altar bell,
and the darkness makes my candle only a dark leaf.

This is the wind of four ways,
the cross on the god's mantle.
And there, in Tamoanchan,
I grow away from my gachupín devotion,
knowing how the warrior
                              will go down,
                    bathed in rain,
how a water valley will echo my twin voice
and how a desert will spring with blue-tinged bodies.

Tlaxcalan virgin,
Remedios of the Otomí,
I am Juan,
here at the crossroads
of a río oculto,
waiting for the first woman
to be born with our name,
to abolish time.
These others come to me
with their sun and moon tales,
their flowered prophecies,
their spurred horses,
letters from the highest authority,
a book,
with page after page of my absence.
If it is a New World,
why am I driven by the silver
weight of an old language,
why do I dress in the canon garb
                                   of another life?
I must be taken into a sacred asylum,
where I find the new Esther
to dress me against injury.

Through a high star haze
and designated dreams,
I have come to Tepeyac,
to set aside a new paradise,
                    sure and protected.

The legend says the dark lady
lay in a cave,
with a small bell and a reliquary,
toting up her Byzantine life.
I say she has arisen
from Byzantium's gold dust
and the saints' negligence
to appear in that other Rome,
a healing water,
                        flowing
toward her home on the hill.
So she becomes the history of Spain.
Even now,
the Turk's copper lamp is lit in her nave.
So even we are set apart
and clarified by that light.
But my eagle wings disturb the air,
where I sit on a nopal for my serpent meal,
and an angel rides me
                                through the dark.

This is the history of learning
to be properly dressed.
White is the moment
when the wife of the serpent
becomes our mother,
when the mother of the gods
                puts on her anguish,
when I grind my rainbow of chile and corn.
Such purity can still adorn a skirt of stars.
Purity consumes me.
                        Lords, let us open the feast.
                        I have it that the slave

has been purified and dressed.
Tender little ear of corn
—Xilonen, from now
until the day of her death.
There is a moment
when the women know the cradle is there,
and the flint glows with its familial
recollection of other lives,
given to light.
I would be the son in the cradle,
and know my mother as that tender ear of corn.
I would be my own double,
a king who uncovers the familiar
axis of his life.

Long before this sun became familiar to my skin,
I embraced my own abandonment,
became aware of night's root and branch in my heart.
Long before that other moon had distinguished my saints,
I hung a crescent moon in my creole sky.
I pretend that we have overcome betrayal
and that the red lamp of compassion
guides us.
I pretend that we are civil and politic
among ourselves.

Lightning of the North,
Serf of the Nation,
these are only words the others
thrust between us.
You have made me an open heart,
searching for an answer
to the question imposed upon us.
This oppressed people, so like
the people of Israel . . .
weary of suffering . . .
The peasant, having spent his seed
dabbling in cows,
approaches you now with a baggy heart,

a sack in which the nation
pours its petate suffering.
Juan Diego leads me
over the tilma terrain
toward Cholula
and the desert.
I hear a raven,
tilling the desert night
for Anahuac's voice.
I had almost given in;
I had almost learned
the giddiness of one and one.
Yet when the desert
had its claws in Janitzio,
a skirt of stars fell down,
spirit rain,
a wing of the bony cross
only the mother could ride.
Even in the light,
I know myself as dark
as the bell and the letters
on the bull that bears me up.
Given to the dark,
I will wear a crescent moon
for my brother's solace.

I recall now the flowering almond tree
and a pine tree covered with violets.
I see a rose leaf unfold under glass.
When I stand in this Chalma silence,
I hear a village voice thunder
like a thorned heart bereft of its cross.
I am learning to prepare a place
where the father will not come,
a house to display a divided heart,
one that fire has washed free of shame.
Having lost her crown of stars,
the woman has taken eagle wings
to fly into the wilderness, to be nourished

for a time, and times, and half a time,
from the face of the serpent.
The father has been taken by those
who would nourish a creole heart.
The basque carriages, riding the streams
in Tlatelolco, stretch their tendrils
over an apparition.
Such love is diplomacy's axe,
the adze of exchange,
a Gunter's chain,
brick, mortar and cobblestone,
pure water coursing in copper pipes,
a child's book and slate,
a corn cake and chocolate in a green evening,
an eye into time's darkness,
a promise given to "possessors of souls without a passport."

"Doctor,
mañana me la sacas esa muela . . ."
Vulgarity
and again vulgarity.
These pochos know nothing but filth.
And you,
where are you from?
They all tell you, I'm sure, that they have been
to Los Angeles,
that they have cousins in Dallas.
The last güera was from New York,
and the nail marks are still fresh—
aunque me muera el dolor, indeed.
Their cheap market blankets are never empty.
My son works along with them.
My son
works in the middle of the greatest city in the world,
digging for treasures, you know? The life that got lost
when we learned how to weave our Easter suits.
You would think that it would not have taken so long
to realize that something was missing.
Simple that I am,
even I can see

when a brick is a little to the left,
or there is a chip in the glass.
If water is always running under our feet,
shouldn't we hear its tatarabuela voice?
When he is home,
my son works like a *negro* (tu m'excuses).
We walk the square together.
I send him back to work with clean, starched pants
and white shirts folded in a handwoven rose-colored bag.
Now and then, I send him some local wine,
frijoles, coffee and a few sticks, and a postcard
with everyone's name in his own hand.
I can tell you, in secret, he keeps a gun
under his pillow,
and, on the job, a knife in his boot.
But her image is never very far from his heart,
or from his head.
I sit here now with a clear conscience.
It is Easter,
and I am walking the stations of the cross.
I have sat to hear the little birds close the evening
and to watch the sun let itself down
into the desert's brown water.
My son,
at this moment,
is touching the Virgin's toes.

My provocation now claims me.
My casket glides under the rose cream evening
to Guadalupe.
Three of my brothers toll areitos and mitotes,
and the celestial music which will lull me
to sleep in the region of peace.
Miguel has taken away their pride,
and given me mine.
She has appeared,
a jade song, set in splendor
on my Sun's throne.

Tlazolteotl

Grainy morning.
Peach sun.
A crow in a cypress tree
                    considers rain.
The freights stand mumbling in the coalyard.

Doña Lupe begins her tortilla mass,
the rapid Latin of her hands ceasing only long enough
to admit the griddle's welcoming hiss.
Down the block, where the lilac bush grows,
the old black woman in her print sack
sweeps the gray-yellow patch of sidewalk.

It must have been midnight, last night,
when the wind and the tumbleweeds
were at the height of their sapphic tango
and the moon had fully undressed,
when her husband had slipped out,
going one way with a sack of kittens,
                         the other with a sack of coal.
Lupe had turned on her bed
to see the moonlight open a silver path to his shadow.
In her own yard, the drying chiles shuddered slightly.
Cold midnight.
Autumn already promised a long passage through winter.

Lupe remembers the lime green chill of Murallas,
and the way the goats had huddled and died.
It was part of the rosary she would have said
                              at Huejuquilla el Alto,
while the men knelt to be prepared for death.
The cross had come into Lupe's name when the earth was born;
she had carried it with a winged heart through dry
and woodless mornings, nourished by sour beans
                                   and prickly tortillas.
It was a moment when she would have understood
the desire to clean the view for lilacs on broken stone,

while the peeling house fades from sight.
Lupe knows the black woman sees the desert as a brook of stars.
It is not enough.

Today, the grainy morning peels the peach sun
to reveal the red Aztec knot at its heart.
Black coffee in the clay pot steams with the odor
of burnt earth.
How have the mountains here learned to sandal
their brown feet to become so familiar?
Why do their cloud halos drift with the same rhythm?
I awake at midnight,
with the fear that she will awaken
and see my shame in the croker sack.
When I was young,
I sewed such a sack for Sunday dress.
Sunday. When my husband preferred
a bottle of cheap Gallo wine
to the wine of sacrifice.
I sacrifice him every night
when he goes searching for our comfort,
and returns with her Indian eye
still on his mind.
I sweep the dirt I have gathered in my soul
away from the purple innocence
of my lilac bush.
How has the rain-starved voice I left behind
followed me from door to door?

I knew her in a moment,
after the stars had fallen, one by one,
and the garden lifted its plucked head in the wind.
She was dawdling in ditch mud,
her skirt hitched up about her waist.
I couldn't avoid the fact that she was letting go in the water.
Her eyes had turned blue with peace,
or so it seemed when I looked through the evening's fire red dust.
From that moment on, she held my heart,
and I clicked my rosary for her favor whenever she passed.

Now she hides her magnificence with the arc of her broom
at dawn.
Some morning, I know, there will be a burning
when I step out of my adobe certainty
to invite her soiled virginity to my old table.
She will come, smiling, having forgotten the innocence
her flowers cannot disguise.

First I should mention that I have during the past four years had a very unhappy time at Harvard; the chief reasons have been (a) personal difficulties within the Observatory, particularly with Dr. Shapley, and usually arising out of personal jealousies because he seemed to like others more than myself. (b) disappointment because I received absolutely no recognition, either official or private, from Harvard University or Radcliffe College; I cannot appear in the catalogues; I do give lectures, but they are not announced in the catalogues, and I am paid for (I believe) as "equipment"; certainly, I have no official position such as instructor. Presumably this is impossible, and so I have always thought it; but I have felt the disappointment nevertheless. (c) I do not seem to myself to be paid very much, quite honestly I think I am worth more than 2300 dollars to the Observatory. (d) In the seven years I have spent at Harvard I have not got to know any University person except through my work (which confines my acquaintance to the Observatory staff and Professor Saunders); whereas the wife of any Harvard man of my status is called upon by the wives of dozens of others.—

The Lake in Central Park

It should have a woman's name,
something to tell us how the green skirt of land
                                        has bound its hips.
When the day lowers its vermilion tapestry over the west ridge,
the water has the sound of leaves shaken in a sack,
and the child's voice that you have heard below
                                                  sings of the sea.

By slow movements of the earth's crust,
or is it that her hip bones have been shaped
by a fault of engineering?
Some coquetry cycles this blue edge,
a spring ready to come forth to correct
                                   love's mathematics.

Saturday rises immaculately.
The water's jade edge plays against corn-colored
picnic baskets, rose and lemon bottles, red balloons,
dancers in purple tights, a roan mare out of its field.
It is not the moment to think of Bahia
and the gray mother with her water explanation.
Not far from here, the city, a mass of swift water
in its own depression, licks its sores.

Still, I would be eased by reasons.
Sand dunes in drifts.
Lava cuts its own bed at a mountain base.
Blindness enters where the light refuses to go.
In Loch Lomond, the water flowers with algae
and a small life has taken the name of a star.

You will hear my star-slow heart
empty itself with a light-swift pitch
where the water thins to a silence.
And the woman who will not be named
screams in the birth of her fading away.

Loving Master and Mistriss I take the Lebbertis of informing you of my present wishes of which I hope you will not be displeased at nor think that I am not Satisfied with my Situation of Life—So far from that it gave me pleasure to say that you Boath have discharge your duty to me as any Servant have any Right to Expect or wish for—But old age And infirmity Begains to follow me which Cause me to think that my Business in Life are nealy to End—tho I know From my heart that you and Mistress would never See me suffer as long as my Body Lives and you Live But I am going down very fast to my grave and if you please By your Premitions Boath you and Mistres I would go and Live those other few dais with master Beverly and my Children

From your Servant Phillis

Ann Street

Perhaps the moment of grace hangs over the gate at St. Paul's,
or sits with the dew in the cemetery, at night,
when the jobber's cry down the street ceases.
In that way, some wise woman named you.
But your domain is small—
        a stuffy block with a secondhand bookstore,
        an old tobacco shop, some slate gray buildings
        with undistinguished windows and a hint
        of bankruptcy—
and the signs change at the corner,
                where your own life ends.
I need to think that the holy woman, who called you Ann,
knew that secret and how to clothe it for a city
            hurrying into the deep forest of old age.

There *is* a certain Slant of light
that you see on winter afternoons on Convent.
A Federalist house still flowers there,
                    in the Cathedral silence.
Black Ann held her Seal Despair there,
until her mother's island called her away.
She might have stayed, to greet the oldest
water mother, if she came,
but that one's handmaidens had gone into the air,
rummaging for the reason that a saint's name
should have such a look of Death.

Cornelia Street

You compromise with size when you step around
the corner from Bleecker, or when you come from the opposite end,
taking that little dogleg left just as you pass Sixth Avenue.
A couple of trees cinch the street at the waist.
There is always an Italian dough and chicory air
                        in its hair.

Cornelia, coming from Cornelius.
Not much manure for berries in that one.

There used to be a café, about here,
where country scribblers shook out their city aches
among the cups.

Cornelia, daughter of Scipio Africanus,
mother of the Gracchi and of Sempronia,
as proud of her family jewels as of letters.
Here she lies, just a heartbeat away
from the tombs of city benches,
where old Sicilians gnash the vowels
of a song she can never learn to sing.

Sister, he was so good that I wanted to turn him over on his flipside and see what they was like.

I wanted to pin his dick to the wall but all I had was a couple of nails.

La calebasse est asociée à la fécondité sur trois plans: cosmique (image du monde), humain (la matrice de la femme) et culturel (la cuisine).

Guadalajara

Village to village
the spirit seeks its house
—Nochistlán,
Tonalá,
Tetlán.
The wind caracols on a bed of stars,
warming itself with the fire that sends
the faithful
spiraling
toward that waterless, spiny
moment
when a river's whisper is enough.
I keep the image of a man walking
in search of a Valley of Stones,
the mudéjar of this valley,
the Roman aqueduct and foundation,
the Visigothic spell
pestled by a Spanish horse.
Godelfare
the Wad-al-hajarah of the Moors
knows the sun here as a bronze cathedral,
the moon as a jade feather crown,
and the whisper of a blue fire dying
raises the sand sound of water again.

These spires above my house are doves,
lifted by grace above the earth's eruption.
Here, we chew the kola nut of lost dreams
and memories of fires we never entered.
It seems now that only the earth moves.
If you tumble from the high air of Tepic,
with its smell of coffee and sunburnt pine,
you fall upon Minerva's fountain
and a stillness that even the father from Dolores
couldn't lift.
Cristeros, carrying their sun-drenched blankets
of democratic discontent, may welcome you.

I like to show my sons
    —the ones who dress my walls with earth tones,
        priestly black and the many colors of blood;
        the ones who go searching in angelic prose
        for their fathers, or the stability of faith;
        the ones who understand life's coursing
        in a good name and the well-modulated womb.
I wish you had come in the fall,
when the Virgin takes her great expectations,
through the ribboned streets, from temple to temple,
and returns—only slightly ruffled—
                    to the moonlight of Zapopan.

I am a trinity, you see.
Spirits growing out of the fact
that my men shape clay
            as the god shapes spirit.
Yet, in the eucalyptus evening,
light shows me all my failures.
My square is ringed with the names
of those my peace betrayed.
Often, my only song has been
            a denial of prophecies.
And when the night closes
on the redness of my most intense days,
I hear a turtle voice
tolling my sacred impurity.
I should have traveled in the wood smoke
of a burning cross,
or been fettered with birds who would come
to their ends, flinted and bled into earthen bowls.
I should have known the sun in a dawn boat,
with its nets sent deep and filled by simple desire.
I should have heard the crow's song
in my own peasant's pail,
and have eaten the sugared skull
                    when the house was done.
I should have been attentive to the moment

when stillness must open another and fiery domain.
I should have given my virginity
to a new hearth, in a new world,
where mercy and rapture rule.

Lisboa

Over the river
the city appears,
a white lace veil
        on the hills,
bits of color
shining through the threads.
Such gentleness provokes
the granite heat of the mountains
                        in the distance.
Come, and you will quickly learn
the advocacy of water,
the way it flows
through every moment
                of the city's life.

Al Oshbūna, Lashbūna,
a happy Julia,
rescued from the sounding
of a blind man's fable.
When the fleet fell upon us,
we were nothing
        but gold, silver,
        cloth, horses and mules,
a stripped body
to be deeded again to a king.
In the Alfama,
A Moorish citadel muses
over a shattered dome,
a memory of ravens
                and a saint's tomb.

I still open my true raven wings
in the saint's yard,
and a ship lurches
from a marble fog,
with news from a new world
    —postcards from Brazil,
    with the sweat of exhilaration
    in a new life still on them,
    the dark severity of this city
            washed from the lines,
    the old language to be achingly
    exhibited in the Thieves' Market—
    —postcards sent dancing
    over the Sahara,
    with the angular heads and deep eyes
    of children who would acknowledge me,
    the bronze tinge of listless mission bells
            and failure, peeling away.

In the gloom of my Roman house,
I sit over vatapá, port
and the image of a cock's
sacrificial blood in Bahía.

I know I am a liberated tree,
a fountain and an obelisk,
set at the head of my whitest avenue.
Though other voices have blessed
my marble and undulating tile,
I have gone through the wine
of silver and gold,
to arrive in the intoxication
of sacred water, kept in the bowl
        of my most secret longing.

Madrid

So the villa, having learned its many skills
through riding the bluish ochre waves of sand and clay,

has fooled us again. The moon is only a moon,
without the olive sheen and horse hoof of Granada.
No ruffled lace guitars clutch at the darkened windows.
The bilious green water marks on old houses
only make you think of the candle wind,
gathering its hammer force season after season,
a tempered master with a gray design.
Even the wall has been undone by sierra loneliness.

Perhaps on some theatrical night,
Lope fell in love with Elena,
and acted out her virtues,
until the father bored him.
That could only end in scandalous verses,
cuffs and a ticket out of Madrid,
a cloaked night at a village gate,
a loping horse and lovers shedding
                                        the acacia trees.
Better this picking at the poor brick and earth
than the bed where the mournful knight lies,
                                    dreaming of dowry
                —some household furniture,
                an orchard, five vines, four beehives,
                forty-five hens, one cock and a crucible—
or the Italian guile and papal star of a duke's daughter.

It is late, and the voices of Tollan swing
on the porch of the Puerta de Alcalá.
Criollos dawdle in the Plaza Mayor,
brushing the white ruff of their provincial injuries.
The Panadería has gone, with its bull blood,
autos da fé and saints,
and the mimetic houses sink into shadow.
And yet that dead sun has awakened
the mountain mother in the oval plaza,
and these old women in black manta scudder
over the Manzanares bed,
following the lights of Taxco silver, silk,
                        Luke's virgin and a good name.

It is late,
Palm Sunday,
on a day when the mask will drop
and a slouch hat and voluminous cloak
will uncover the exiled heart.
It is late,
the May day when the sun's red heart
                    returns from its exile,
and the Emperor's horsemen fall and begin
the unraveling of a Morning Star.
It is late,
when the Queen has gone,
in gentleman's attire,
to exhibit her hunger for boar meat
and a Bourbon husband with a taste for peace.
It is late,
when the red flag of the most violent summer
calls an end to the nation's yearning.

It is time
for the jeweled humiliation of the chosen
                        to be revealed.

Now when the snow falls on this crucible
of sullen winds and interrupted passions,
there will be the dark bell sound of a mother,
crying the name she can never have,
            or having it, fulfill.

Marietta, 8th March 1795

Sir

I have been so unhappy at Mrs. Woodbridges that I was obliged to leeve thare by the consent of Mrs. Woodbridge who gave up my Indentures and has offen said that had she known I was so sickly and expencieve she would not have brought me to this Country but all this is the least of my trouble and I can truly say sir had I nothing else or no one but myself I am sure I should not make any complaint to you But my Little son Jupiter who is now with Mrs. Woodbridge is my greatest care and from what she says and from the useage he meets with there is so trying to me that I am all most distracted therefore if you will be so kind as to write me how Long Jupiter is to remain with them as she tells me he is to live with her untill he is twenty five years of age this is something that I had no idea of I all ways thought that he was to return with me to new england or at Longest only ten years these are matters I must beg of you sir to let me know as quick as you can make it convenient I hope you will excuse me of troub Ling you wich I think you will do when you think that I am here in A strange country without one Friend to advise me Mrs. Woodbridge setts out for connecticut and I make no doubt but she will apply to buy Jupiter's time which I beg you will be so good as not to sell her I had much reather he wold return and Live with you as she allows all her sons to thump and beat him the same as if he was a Dog Mrs. Woodbridge may tell you that I have behaved bad but I call on all nabours to know wheather I have not behaved well and wheather I was so much to blame She has called me A theif and I denie I have don my duty as well as I could to her and all her family as well as my Strength wold allow of I have not rouged her nor her family the nabours advised me to rite you for the childs sake I went to the Gentlemen of the town for these advise they told me I could get back without any difficulty I entend to return remember me to all your family if you please I thank you for sending me word my dauter was well this is my hand writing I remain the greatest humility

You Humble servant
Judith Cocks

please [dont?] show this to Mrs. Woodbridge

Naylor's Store, Nov. 16, 1863

My Dear Husband—I received your letter yesterday, and lost no time in asking Mr. Jim if he would sell me, and what he would take for me. He flew at me, and said I would never get free only at the point of the Baynot, and there was no use in my ever speaking to him any more about it. . . . I had good courage all along until now, but now I am almost heartbroken. Answer this letter as soon as possible.

I am your affectionate wife,
Louisa Alexander

Orchid

Old moneybags: the Creeping Jenny,
the Poppy and Henbane,
the Turk's-cap lily,
the pink rhododendron
do not attend here;
this is the domain of six-headed orchis,
with its textured, flamboyant lip,
turned toward the flower's lower part,
its stamen muffled in its stigmas.

Ah, Marianne,
thou shouldst be with me now.

Only you could understand how
        a barren pistil
could bear life's weight upon it.

Nothing here seems singular,
even as it stretches out of its common shape,
a honeyed entrance.
Shall we call it love's entrance,
when the flower lights itself and invites
the winged heft and sibilant thrusts
                                        of a bee?
And the bee goes through the ridges,
down to the spur,
to take a pollen-mass upon its back,
and flies with its love sack
                              changing shape,
to another flower?
There lies another womb,
sensitive to this soi-disant love's impress,
shaky with the advent of such a love's
                                    peculiar design.

It would be better, perhaps,
to lie under the ground,
              root and budlike,

and wait for sun
that the soiled water has filtered,
or sit on a tropical tree
and give no thought to its stingy nature.

But you see that, even here,
love raises its resolved head,
where there is only the borrowed
smell of tomcats,
            and the hope of vanilla
            flowing from a generous cup.

Passionflower

This flower must have known
the salt glint of sand,
the bedouin billow of wind,
the lapis lazuli stars that rise
when the desert's sea voice stops.
Now it sits, singularly crimson,
near the toucan and anaconda.

Such feeling in such a shallow body
needs the wet black bough
that the bluest water has arranged,
                        the gift of stillness
that the red-tailed tropic-bird has captured.

We can imagine the moment
    when the body took wing,
hoping to establish itself in the felt hat
bog and closeness of this sun's domain.

At the moment we hold the body,
the name is clear:
the crown of thorns,
the nails,
the apostolic sepals and petals,

the absence of those
                who would deny or betray.
Your perfume invites us
to the berry in the arillus,
to the succulent, festive taste of home—
                        granadilla, curubas,
                        water lemon, sweet calabash.

So I would know you as another egg,
come from the shadow of the cross,
with the rose wine of loss still
in charge of your generous body.

Dandelion

Whan that Aprill . . .
My morning wakes in a yellow head,
and I have grown so hungry for that root
I claw my way past the black rhizome.
I know it would be better to wait
for the silk web and brown glaze of September,
but I already hear the song in the frost,
and see the white juice cradled in the earth.
If I were only hungry for the night and the rose
                                        the leaves recall,
I would be given to the lion of a different longing.
But I am a bird with no gift for easy seed, one
already fixed in the bitter root.
Now, when these salad leaves come to rest,
I intoxicate myself with the sound
of a sacrificial wine as it tapers
                            down, into the dark.

The most striking natural objects in the world are optical—perfectly definite visible "things" that prove to be intangible, such as rainbows and mirages. Many people, therefore, regard an image or illusion as necessarily something visual. This conceptual limitation has even led some literary critics, who recognize the essential imaginal character of poetry, to suppose that poets must be visual-minded people, and to judge that figures of speech which do not conjure up visual imagery are not truly poetic. F. C. Prescott, with consistency that borders on the heroic, regards "The quality of mercy is not strained" as unpoetic because it suggests nothing visible. But the poetic image is, in fact, not a painter's image at all.

And the triumph of empiricism is jeopardized by the surprising truth that *our sense data are primarily symbols.*

. . . the edifice of human knowledge stands before us, not as a vast collection of sense reports, but as a structure of *facts that are symbols* and *laws that are their meanings.*

The Anatomy of Resonance

And the bird of the night whirs
        Down, so close that you shield your eyes.
        —Hölderlin, *Die Kürze* (Brevity)

The Bird

There must be an atmosphere,
or an evergreen,
or the green shading into the red-yellow
                                        brown of earth, for the eye,
surely,
some choir in which the ornamented arms
might tune themselves
                to the absolute A of air.
Creatures given to this air
shape their own suspension,
                a process of weight,
thrust away from the body's substance,
and the depths of a woman's body,
                        of maple and ash,
hold the arc of another substance,
a memory of unrealized absence.
There is a river here,
where the white heron fastens its claws
to the flat blue surface,
as though it stood on a flowing altar
                to call into the dense grove
of arrested light around the water.
Look and you will see the plume of communion,
a possible intention that arises only here.
It seems that the river has been clay
                                        for feather and bone,
for the elastic tissue of the bird's voice.
And the . . .
words that begin a theology of existence,

a political history of flight,
an interrupted dream of being definite.

Night

Clairvoyant solitude on the obsidian edge of day.
A vermilion moon ignites the limestone
in a hidden well.
It is time to rewrite the history of darkness
and the way our ballbearing stars slip around
and away from each other.
In this hemisphere,
the Milky Way is a celestial river,
sister of the wet star that shines
in the Valley at Cuzco.
In this place,
a llama, standing in star heat,
defines eternity, and a pecked cross
orients the marriage of sun and moon
along the Street of the Dead.
Here, there is no mystery in light's absence;
there is only a radiant voice, rising
from the regal cloth of a liberating air.

Whirs

The jackal has learned to sing in the ash,
a severe chanty in praise of the cock and the fish,
of the aureole balm of evening.
When the moment arrives for singing,
palm leaves that are heavy with windlessness
vibrate to a star's breath,
and the ear, attuned to all the harmonies of neglect,
lifts the soteriological wisdom of loss
from its parish bed.
There is a moment when the boy comes out of the wood,
his feet slippered with a bee sound, his face

turned to the bull roar following his flight.
The boy carries an apple sound in his head,
something to enhance the dissonant eruption
                    of his new morning.
Now, mother night has dressed herself
to dance to the dulcimer of his spring.
Father now to the boy,
she will lock his arms, and twirl him,
and fill his body with the deep
and devastating hum of the jackal's song.

Down

Under the rock, in the hollow,
there are stones the color of cats' eyes.
Old women who have seen these eyes
know that the body should be eiderdown
and bathed with the water of holy wells
and mineral springs, a blue water
with just the hint of hardness
          and a slight taste of sulfur.
So the sinistra side of that other body
would drift to the North Sea,
and come adown in its emerald armor,
to be welcomed in a Latin wood,
where a crescent moon peeks over
                the empty seawall.
My dunum and dum boots quiver
on the qui vive,
          anxious
to enlist water again
          to unruffle and fix
the mystery of buried stone.

Close

Time and the deductive season
teach an intimacy, reason

enough to set sail under seal,
a tenaciously secret keel
of abbeys and cathedrals, found
in the strictest boroughs, the round
plot of land dense with unicorns;
as in a soul's tapestry, horns
flagellate the air. Now confined
near an emerald sun, defined
by my spirit's strictest account,
I cling to my dole, and dismount.
I have filled my bowl with the rose
smoke of ecstasy in a close.

Shield

Skewed, perhaps,
the heart's road bends sinister,
not out of skin and hide,
            owing nothing
to the combustible partition
                  crowning
those trees
            a doe's leap away.
Maude had it right—
John would be closer to love's blossom.
She had been given nothing,
and had only a desire to see
down the dextrous avenue of self.
Clearly, Maude knew
         who would be impaled,
who would sit on an order's collar,
what weight the father would bear
               against his own kind.
Kindness,
      or call it the valor of salvation,
                    roots in a shell,
scaled to catch the rattle of friendship
               and war heat alliance.

We are stretched over the heart's house,
to defend such kindness as remains,
when the sun, strawberry red,
dips itself into the lime green water
that flows endlessly home.

Eyes

Augen, weltblind, in Sterbegeklüft . . .
Eyes, worldblind, in the lode-break of dying
—Paul Celan, *Schneebett* (Snowbed)

Old light, at this depth, knows
the veil of deception, the water valley
through which it leaps and divides.
So here, as the south wind alerts the body
to the season's change, the scarlet poplar
leaf runs, from point through point,
a topsy-turvy body to be fixed
in a different mirror.
An eye, such as this, may be worldblind
in the lode-break of dying. An eye, such as this,
may be no more than a peacock's tail,
the infant bud in a cutting, or the different
curve of a voice in the earth.
There is a market town in Suffolk,
where the bones and Roman urns and coins
mark a sacred ground with the sound of vision.
Time must tell us everything about sensation
and the way we have come to terms
with our failure
to see anything but the blue point of desire
that leads us home.

Journey to the Place of Ghosts

Wölbe dich, Welt:
Wenn die Totenmuschel heranschwimmt,
will es hier läuten.

Vault over, world:
when the seashell of death washes up
there will be a knelling.
—Paul Celan, *Stimmen* (Voices)

Death knocks all night at my door.
The soul answers,
and runs from the water in my throat.
Water will sustain me when I climb
the steep hill
that leads to a now familiar place.
I began, even as a child, to learn water's order,
and, as I grew intact, the feel of its warmth
in a new sponge, of its weight in a virgin towel.
I have earned my wine in another's misery,
when rum bathed a sealed throat
and cast its seal on the ground.
I will be bound, to the one who leads me away,
by the ornaments on my wrists, the gold dust
in my ears, below my eye and tied to my
loincloth in a leather pouch.
They dress me now in my best cloth,
and fold my hands, adorned with silk,
against my left cheek.
Gold lies with me on my left side.
Gold has become the color of distance,
and of your sorrow.

Sorrow lies, red clay on my brow.
Red pepper caresses my temples.
I am adorned in the russet-brown message
the soul brings from its coming-to-be.
There is a silken despair in my body

that grief shakes from it,
a cat's voice, controlled by palm wine
and a widow's passion.
It is time to feed the soul
—a hen, eggs, mashed yams—
and encourage the thirst resting
near the right hand I see before me.
Always I think of death.
I cannot eat.
I walk in sadness, and I die.
Yet life is the invocation sealed in the coffin,
and will walk through our wall,
passing and passing and passing,
until it is set down,
to be lifted from this body's habitation.
I now assume the widow's pot,
the lamp that will lead me through solitude,
to the edge of my husband's journey.
I hold three stones upon my head,
darkness I will release when I run
from the dead,
with my eyes turned away
toward another light.

This is the day of rising.
A hut sits in the bush, sheltered by summe,
standing on four forked ends.
We have prepared for the soul's feast
with pestle, mortar, a strainer, three
hearthstones, a new pot and new spoon.
Someone has stripped the hut's body
and dressed it with the edowa.
Now, when the wine speaks
and the fire has lifted its voice,
the dead will be clothed in hair,
the signs of our grief.
Sun closes down on an intensity of ghosts.
It is time to close the path.
It is time for the snail's pace

of coming again into life,
            with the world swept clean,
            the crying done,
and our ordinary garments decent in the dead one's eyes.

Saltos

What do I know of marriages and prophecy,
awakened by a sun I will never see?
I awake every morning and come here
to sit on our world—the heart
of the strongest tree, seething with night
and blood designs, the feet lit by love's color.
And, as I rest, my heart moves
to the wise music in a turtle shell.
Out there, on the river, at dawn,
the men embrace their nets and begin
again to search for me.
My love is river-worn,
nourished by exaltation and the aged stone
                        that perks my hut.
I know I must only dream of the yellow flute
and the day I will bathe my feet in the new dust
of a lover's hut.
                    I know that there is power
in this water, greater than the springs of old daughters.
From my seat now,
I see soft white foam edge, crablike,
over the shore,
its darkness overcome by the prayer
I have struggled to say.
I have learned to leap
through dying cypress, clouds, spiny sand
and the wet straw of dead fires,
when the sun, a frayed daisy,
stirred the hummingbird within me.
There is a dance that waits
for the fisher who would know me,

and a moment when dried fruit will speak
with the sun's voice.
There is a moment when I will know myself
balanced on brown-red earth
that still wears the blue veil of an ancient desire.

The Power of Reeds

Learning to speak, after the heart's lost exuberance,
turns the eye toward a lost dominion. Now these
water loving grasses, seaweed natives of sand
sing of old haunts—springs in
Castalia,
Tula,
Ifẹ.
That song has the power to bind us in prophecies,
to invite a pilgrimage from rock to rock,
to retrieve the water syllables of the Queen's true name.
These are state matters,
an Ethiopian will that contends
with light's flaring cloth
in a logic that clothes the self with another self.
Married to ourselves,
we take shape in meaning woven into cloth;
we learn the shape of water under our control,
the political substance of speech in cities.
Biṅu,
sitting at bush edge,
teaches us how to record feeling
and how to invest a reed with power.
We must consider the reed without its divinity,
an unchanging thing with the power to arise
in fens and marshes and set itself
against the earth's erosion,
and against the sea which moves with elastic
step to take us back into its arms.
Nidaba lies in the arms of every reed—a left-hand
spin in every soul, a mask with buskin power—

and there rests in her limitless changing
to become old, and venerable, the goddess
with reed wings fanning in sunlight
and the scribe's difficult kiss in praise
                                        of her deconstructive eye.
This scribe sits near Helicon,
listening to a high-pitched beating reed weave
from sorcery into a Babylonian dance
and the healing radiance of a sickle moon,
tamarisk and a virgin's necklace.
                                              Out of Africa,
the song's loom draws the maiden
into a new legend, braced
by the comfortable whine of a cane instrument
and the never-ending Roman walk to Meroë
in search of the spirit's thatching water.
The scribe has written: It would be easy
to wash away our sins against these women,
if the waters were still
            and light were a given.
We are learning to fashion the storm side of ourselves,
to come out of an immobile passion into cunning.
We are learning the ground of exaltation
in a political mother,
the full force of springs lying memory and bush deep,
the bivalved heart of mountains and waters.
This scribe sits in Tula Xicocotitlan,
waiting for the emerald to return to the mother.
Stones have a way of falling,
after the reed's measure,
into the shape of a new spirit,
longing for the bleached steles of a new home,
            the slit tongue
pipe of an old divinity,
                                        the loom
with the serpent in its teeth.
All this hardness sings in the reed,

visionary songs of retrieved connections.
The reed voice knows its power to protect
                    the moving dominion,
the power of the weeping woman who returns
to speak of exuberance lost in misguided rule.
So the reed will measure uncontrollable forces,
meanings which have disappeared,
and give its light to that moment
when the heart can speak to
                    land, and water,
                    steel, stone, wood,
                    jewels and cloth,
                    cities of glass,
                    time's new measure,
                    life's contending wills,
all the epiphanies of self that can be bound by love.

Desire's Persistence

Yo ave del agua floreciente duro en fiesta.
—"Deseo de persistencia," *Poesía Náhuatl*

1

In the region of rain and cloud,
I live in shade,
under the moss mat of days bruised
                    purple with desire.
My dominion is a song in the wide ring of water.
There, I run to and fro,
braiding the logical act
          in the birth of an Ear of Corn,
polychromatic story I will now tell
in the weaving, power's form in motion,
a devotion to the unstressed.
Once, I wreathed around a king,

became a fishing net, a maze
"a deadly wealth of robe."
Mothers who have heard me sing take heart;
I always prick them into power.

2

Y vengo alzando al viento la roja flor de invierno.
(I lift the red flower of winter into the wind.)
—Poesía Náhuatl

I

Out of the ninth circle,
a Phoenician boat rocks upward into light
and the warmth of a name—given to heaven—
that arises in the ninth realm.
Earth's realm discloses the Egyptian
on the point of invention,
deprived of life and death,
heart deep in the soul's hawk,
a thymos shadow knapping the tombed body.
Some one or thing is always heaven bound.
Some flowered log doubles my bones.
The spirit of Toltec turtledoves escapes.
A sharp, metaphorical cry sends me
into the adorned sepulchre,
and the thing that decays learns
how to speak its name.

LIFT

Down Hidalgo,
past Alvarado and Basurto,
I walk a straight line

to the snailed Paseo Los Berros.
Here, at noon, the sun,
          a silver bead,
veils what the dawn has displayed.
Even so,
        I have taken up the morning's bond again
        —the lake with its pendulum leg
        shining in the distance,
        the boy in white
        hauling his bottle of chalky milk home.
I know I sit in the deep of a city
with its brocade of hills,
where a thin rain is an evening's fire.
I have heard the women sing
near their gas lamps,
when the rose end of day lights a hunger
for the garlanded soups and meat they prepare.
Often, I have taken the high ground
by the pond, over a frog's voice
                    dampened by lilies,
and been exalted by the soothsayer
who knows I'm not at home.
I am the arcane body,
raised at the ninth hour,
to be welcomed by the moonlight
                        of such spirited air.
I am the Dane of degrees
who realizes how the spirit glows
                        even as it descends.

Red

The heart, catalectic though it be, does glow,
responds to every midnight bell within you.
This is a discourse on reading heat,
the flushed char of burned moments one sees
after the sexton's lamp flows
over the body's dark book.

There is supicion
here that violet
traces of
sacrifice
stand
bare.

Flower

This marble dust recalls that sunset
with the best burgundy, and the way,
after the charm of it, the peacocks
escaped their cages on the green.
I would now embellish the flame
that ornaments you,
even as it once in that moment
                                                  did.
I carry you blossomed,
cream and salt of a high crown.
You *must* flare,
          stream forth,
blister and scale me,
even as you structure the enveloping kiss,
              sporophore of our highest loss.

Winter

Under the evergreens,
the grouse have gone under the snow.
Women who follow their fall flight
tell us that, if you listen, you can hear
their dove's voices ridge the air,
a singing that follows us to a bourne
             released from its heat sleep.
We have come to an imagined line,
                        celestial,
that binds us to the burr of a sheltered thing

and rings us with a fire that will not dance,
in a horn that will not sound.
We have learned, like these birds,
to publish our decline,
when over knotted apples and straw-crisp leaves,
the slanted sun welcomes us once again
to the arrested music in the earth's divided embrace.

Wind

Through winter,
harmattan blacks the air.
My body fat with oil,
I become another star at noon,
when the vatic insistence
of the dog star's breath clings to me.
Though I am a woman,
I turn south,
toward the fire,
and hear the spirits in the bush.
But this is my conceit:
water will come from the west,
and I will have my trance,
be reborn,
perhaps in a Mediterranean air,
the Rhone delta's contention
with the eastern side of rain.
In all these disguises,
I follow the aroma of power.
So I am charged in my own field,
to give birth to the solar wind,
particles spiraling around the line
of my body,
moving toward the disruption,
the moment when the oil of my star at noon
is a new dawn.

3

I shall go away, I shall disappear,
I shall be stretched on a bed of yellow roses
and the old women will cry for me.
So the Toltecas wrote: their books are finished,
but your heart has become perfect.

Boleros

for Lois
dyęę → la connaissance de l'étoile
loved source of my new words

1

I have been considering
how to make of your skill
a holy instance, how
(in other words)
to record the love that turns
a flat white room into
                  an aurora australis,
or the cotton shawl
of welcoming light.
That desire requires a skill
quite beyond a poet's art,
something that a word obscures.
Is the touch in your black and gray shawl,
folded so evenly and falling plumb-line
straight from the back of a cane chair,
or in the brown woven wool blanket
smoothed by the foam rubber mattress?
There must be design in the stork-legged
plant in the corner,
or in the wicker basket, cut
and placed to mute the light.
Turn, as my mind does,
through the full ecliptic of your art,
the star still escapes.

When Marcelo comes,
with his water glass demonstration
of overflown friendship,
or Miguel,
picked with the banderillas
of his latest *gringa,*
or Emilia brings her Homero,
who will cheat at cards,
nothing explains the centered
chime in your voice,
the exuberant stillness

as you rock harmonically
                    in your chair.

This globe of a little town goes round
our lives with such swiftness.

Tonight, again,
I will climb the obtuse-angled street
to the bodega at the top,
and come back,
sheltering my tortas,
past the open fires of the witches
in the vivienda.
Come back and sit,
with my serrano-laced lomo,
near the soft pearl of your sadness,
and hope somehow to see
                        the naked stone.

2

Chaparrita,
morenita
y parece una mexicanita.
How's that for sauce
on your langostinos?

Fish stories.

The gaucharromacho,
singing his liver away
for another love at the next table,
has a factory,
requiring your soonest attention,
                        near Perote.

Stingers,
horned pout,
brown trout.

You should hand him
the bass player Zoom Zoom's card.
Perhaps I'll tell him
how, when you go fishing with our buddy,
I clear one whole room for perch,
another for bass.

Damnable pettifoggers, perch.
Not half so clever as catfish
who can snout bugs out of debris
at the pond's base,
thereby, wise as they are,
giving themselves up to Itzak,
hanging over the emerald water
                                        above them.
There must be a lesson in that.
There ought at least to be
some applicable homily
in the stance the bass take,
when, gorged on mayflies,
they flicker into the boat
and slowly subside from their feasting,
            and wait greedily for ours.

3

Here we are, disguised in jolly traveler's tweed.
No one else seems to mind the fog that must lift
before we do, though we do
and hoe a row of vinyl to the window.
England is a middle age, dark,
bursting with sleeping bags,
                                        upon which
the young lie sleeping their halfpenny tastes away,
            if we take this terminal for the terminus
of social form.
And so it dawns at Gatwick,
and we think music would serve

an annunciation, or smooth the gift
of a new sandwich—
thin bread lightly touched with butter,
a sliver of cheese and the coolest cucumbers.

4

Juno, they say, was paler by the yard,
and marble veined,
and sat her veils in a province
other than your Brooklyn.
What do I care?
Mornings I wake to see
your black hair light your pillow,
science enough to start me
roving from a narrow dungeon.
Can Bruno know what you know?
Could Juno have armed her
                    pomegranate touch
with such wisdom, such clairvoyant
attention to my waking?
Could ever betokening Brooklyn have known
what beatitudes I would find
in such a disquieting body?

5

(1)

All names are invocations, or curses.
One must imagine the fictive event that leads to
He-Who-Shoots-Porcupines-By-Night,
or Andrew Golightly, or Theodore, or Sally.
In the breath of stars, names rain upon us;
we seem never to be worthy.
Or, having learned the trick of being worthy,
we seem never to be prepared for the rein of names,

the principled seating of figures that will walk
beside us, even unto surly death.
Sometimes death has embraced those who never
came forth,
those who were impeached for unspeakable desire,
even as they lay in mothers' cave hollow wombs,
speechless, eyeless, days away from the lyrics of light
and a naming.
Dead or alive,
something waits in the face or movement
of a child still held in that hollow, something
that will become an appropriate exchange
for the life buried by coming forth, or by
disruption of the life with no reason to appear.
Now, I cannot name the child you carried.
All voices, dilated with need not desire, have ceased.

(II)

Each flowered place requires a name that fits.
Fortín de las Flores,
night's cocoa sky, a pond with lightly starred lilies,
gray monastery walls to entice a traveler from discontent,
a skeletal wind (birthmark of a faded desert).
Often, when the night has reached its true pitch,
young women in mourning clothes spring up in the garden.
Though it is late, the air sustains midafternoon's cilantro,
and the calm prolongs a bell at dusk.
Fortín,
an insupportable garden, a desert bloom,
a flower that offers us its dark solicitude.
I imagine the armor of knowing even its day's
darkness a comfort and the way a singing
seems to arise from cactus too old and too watchful
to be silent.
In the lowlands, I have heard other singing
when, in the middle of the road, the child
asked for water to drink. Now, in the balm of my

heart's double beat, rosemary recovers its essence
and the child commands tonadas alegres, versos elegantes.
These are memory's accoutrements, reason to have searched
a flowered place with a name that fits,
where love's every echo is a child's loss.

(III)

All names are false.
The soothsaying leaves call winter a paradox—
a northern traveler on a southern wind.
The ice on a weather-broken barn recalls May poppies.
I would have you recall the exhilaration
of reading broken sonnets, on cinnamon-
scented nights, in a tiled room,
while the charity doctors disputed their loves
                              on the cobblestones below.
I enter again the bells and traces of desire,
call and recall, the pacing of love stalking us.
What is love's form when the body fails,
or fails to appear? What is love's habitation
but a fable of boundaries, lovers passing
athwart all limits toward a crux ansata?
I have carried your name on velvet,
knowing you are free, having never suffered
the heartache of patience that love and naming
that this our divided world requires.

6

You will never arrive before these
—the old women who sit
in the rainbow bow of their flower beds,
or the others, strung
near their brace-bound chickens.
It is still worth the blue air,

tucked in your rebozo,
to walk this market's dawn.
Day after day,
you carry the blazon of your string bag
and escape down the same
beveled aisles.
I watch you overcome
the saffron song of oranges,
the sapphire trumpet of the sweetest onions.
You resist the bolillo's den dance
and the Salome veil of sugared cakes.
Having found this constant morning
reed voice within you,
you have been informed,
become ancient,
and go only where our necessities
lead you.
I, on the other hand,
urge myself toward the lynx-eyed
curanderos who whisper to their
roots and herbs,
or into the bewailing embrace
of cooks whose caustic pots
seem caudle enough for my urges.
So, I go, holding a patch
of wrinkled, penciled paper in hand,
in search of *mirto rojo* for an ulcer,
or patchless,
pretending to care for ganja.
All who see me read my eyes,
star high with the market's gifts.
Someday, perhaps, I'll learn
how you found the right bank
on this peasant's lake
to hear that reed voice, piping the hour
when you might come into the first sun
and find yourself alone.

7

Tough old Glasgow tucks itself
          under a leg of the Firth of Clyde.
                    No
Scotia sniveling in that,
just pennywise prudence, a way
of ladling the elation of coming home.
Logicians on the eastern shore count it
no surprise that queenly old Edinburgh
          lies on the Firth of Forth,
near to the heart of Midlothian.
So, on a doon and windless morning,
we whip east and touch down
near the greenest pasture in Scotland.
As we step from the plane,
the neighboring sheep show us their haggis eyes
     for the flinty spark of a moment.
Suddenly,
I amna deid dune sae muckle as fou,
suspecting that, here, one *can*
thow the cockles o' yin's heart,
no small change from a sixpenny planet,
and have the thieveless crony within you
                    as suddenly awaken.

We found this bel canto morning
in a Jarocho garden,
on an afternoon when spring had departed
and left only its scunning heat.
I say this now, though I know
that my heart's weather had turned
on a winter night, when I heard the deer
stamping in the water under the raised barn
and felt the star heat fade and the first, clear
cut of loneliness,
the concert pitch of death's tuning.
Marry or burn,
one cannot run away or into,

for there is nothing so sedentary
as the desire to be comforted, by love,
or by some feeling one cannot name.
On Hidalgo, in Guadalajara,
the blue flowers, in their persistence
on the neighbors' white wall,
comforted us, and so the lace of a plaza in sun,
          tacos at dawn from a cart in Gigantes,
the mudéjar ache of the divided cathedral,
the rose pinion of paseos,
                              held us till summer.

Those were the garden's traces,
leading to the rose of Midlothian,
the stone house walled in and set
in view of the castle.
Down the road,
the old poet, who did hard times for Lallans,
nests with his chickens and neat Laphroaig.
I count him the most civil of servants,
whose gift is the mist of tongues,
rising from the doom gray of council houses
and snuffed coal mines.
I love the sound of sporran and kilt in his voice,
his refusal to give in to King Street's dove gray manner.

It is some distance to have traveled to learn
to resist being comforted too soon.
Perhaps some moor-stiff night,
we will put on our fog-heavy tweeds
and make our way to old Glasgow,
curled in its water bed,
                    confident,
                    cocky,
                    still uncomforted.

8

Plainly cows normally shit,
but these have been instructed,

and so stand petulantly petered
to have their morning juices sacked.
Don Pepe makes the work a three-minute egg,
brings the bucket of foamy, toast-warm milk
to the patio, where the sugared rum waits in glasses
                                        on the leather table.
Stretched taut in leather, we sit to celebrate.
The rum tells us how bright we were to uncover
the rector's night work, to use it to free
your trunks from the docks. Emilia has the story
by halves, her insouciant narrative by the tail.
By the tale, the onyx morning dissolves
into a cream rose afternoon. The lapis lazuli
evening leans lazily on the gate.
Halapa, Chalapa, Shalapa (ever what you call it)
by now has its mist on, and its rain,
with its dew demeanor, clearing the streets.
Lluvia de tontos. Perhaps. And perhaps
two people who have come a long way,
welcome the rain screen and the way
the silent evening opens to the night voices,
rising to the terrace of our new home.

9

Nomadic hearts know there is no rose
waiting at every door, that often a threshold's
atmosphere can be worth your life.
Even so, memory must have led us here.

After Perote, the old bus gathers its wings
and swings us through the happy
undulations of fog- and cloud-bound hills,
toward Xalapa, with the cross in its name.
I expect a familiar sand, pillowed against
walls gone red and grainy with heat,
and a muezzin's bell
knitting the loose cloth of evening.

But the heart is a fraudulent voice, a wily ear,
and memory can be too staunchly evangelic.
So the bell goes, in the whisper of matins and vespers,
and the constant idiot's rain dresses the walls
                        in filmy gray.

I should be grateful that memory has left
an anteroom, where I can stock
the cobbled street that leads me to tortillas
and the nuns' diabolic chiles,
or watch the blue-serged licenciado
parade his cane along the Avenida Zamora.
Perhaps I should reserve another room
for the Pérgola's alambres,
and the surpliced children
(hand in hand through the park to school)
and the violet insistence of late afternoon
with coffee and *pan* on the terrace.
Looking forward, I see the moment
I will choose to leave this garden,
when, on a cloistered morning in April,
I stand in the post office's tiled vestibule
and unlock the rage that you
                        will understand
and a nomadic heart will carry away.

10

Here,
as we stand in the Mayan evening,
I know I should be able to say
something simple,
such as, it is the same moon,
that the triad—moon, earth
and that star in Taurus—
sounds right again.
Where is my synodic certainty?
I know less than the ancients

who were accustomed to a late moon
                    and its difficult omens.
Day by day,
from west to east,
the earth rotates on its axis
and the stars,
going against the grain,
shimmy around the one point
                    that seems fixed.
So I know a star stand
when I know where I stand,
linked by that sphere to my own earth.
But these are constant matters,
as measurable as love,
as comprehensible as the heart's ecliptic
you have followed to here.
Some stars neither rise nor set;
some hearts never open.
There is trouble here with the eye,
or the body adapting to a different
                                        latitude,
that moment when we know
a star forever invisible,
the body closed upon its own desire.
I am learning,
this deep on the continent,
to remember the Dippers
                        and Cassiopeia,
and to guess at the right linear
constellation,
and the confident moment
when the same moon arrives on time.

11

Down in the lower field,
the doe carcass lies white
on the autumn amber.

This seems to be the end
of the last star-blanched night,
wind sharp with coyotes,
when you felt the deer flow
out of the stream, going
pace by even pace
into the evergreens.
Here, the morning rises,
charged now with a weak sun.
Later, when I return
to stalk birds and darkness
in the evergreens, I
will be as reticent
and serene
as the least of these bones.

12

Oh, dark things always
        cover you in Scotland:
moor fog,
                noxious gloom,
                        bloody haggis breath.
I hear the perch in Perth are troubled,
that the jute in Dundee
        has slipped a knot
                over the city's heart.
This is no place for one who loves roses,
or remembers the absinthe spunk of honeydew melons,
        or the creamy ease of papaya.
There are moments
        when the quair strivings
                on The Castle's backstairs
                        become perfectly understandable.
But in spite of my suspicion,
        night settles and cuddles
                my cloak of the smoothest malt
                        and a curry on St. Nicholas Street
                                in Aberdeen.

13

(ERATO ↔ KHAT)

When the cold knuckles in, we come to this spot
and wait for these Salt Lake hills to walk into the garden.
Moments like these nurture the comprehensive light,
and a tangled voice upon a path in the distance
                                    speaks of still water.
That voice could perhaps tell us of games,
prizes given to bodies as fit as ours,
or as fit as that of the young man
who steps into the morning just as we arrive.
          So the he-goat, pillowed by cloud, comes
          from the locker room onto the range,
                         to sniff at myrtle.
          Ares or Anchises, stern Wasatch lover, he knows
          the honeyed cleaving the blue snow promises.
          I say he dreams,
          of the swan's slow wing and the dolphin's exhilarated
          leap and plunge when love is near,
          though, like my unbraided self,
          he no longer hears a sea or a river sound.
          I could give him a seat at Cyprus,
          with fire, flowers and incense, salt in exchange
          for the penny gift he brings the woman.

All gifts are brass to one who rises from the sea,
even if the gift recalls a dance and a divining,
                              and every divination, a betrayal.
What is the boy but a boy who waits
for his solitude to tell him who will relieve it?
There is a slight cast in this one's eye
that sits like a saddle upon his impurity.
I shall still wake him from the cold night
with maize beer and bean porridge, something
to remind him always of your presence.
Your love is turtle slow,
a sea calm, cradled by pots at Oshogbo.

You must teach this boy how the long black hair
you used to weave in the water disappeared,
and how your desire created and left him
unfinished until the white one came.

Now, the gold air tunes his brass rod body
to the stallion's bell hoof, that voice
we had heard without hearing, and the horse
shudders and begins its patient, memorizing descent.
Twins, whose faces I recognize, lead the tethered horse,
and the nude black woman upon its back flows
into the young man's awakened, dark and Apollonian
embrace.

14

(CALLIOPE ↔ SAḤU)

Night enters the Plaza, step by step, in the singular
flaring of lamps on churro carts, taco stands,
benches set with deep bowls of pozole,
on rugs embroidered with relics, crosses, bones,
pamphlets, dream books.
Around this Cathedral, there is an order never shaken;
all our eyes and postures speak of the certainty
of being forever in place.
These are the ones who always hear the veiled day fall,
the street tile's serpentine hiss under the evening's drone.
Compadre, not all have come from Reforma, along Madero.
There are those whose spotless white manta tells me
they are not from here—as now, you see, a village
wedding party come to engage the virgin's peace.

This evening, in the Zócalo, lanterns become candles,
or starlight, whatever recalls a woman,
beating her clothes on rocks in a village stream.
At her side, a man buckets the muddy water for his stove.
What does the spirit say, in its seating,

when such impurity can console,
and the slipped vowels of an unfamiliar name
                                        rise from the shallows?
Lovers meet here,
and carry consummation's black weed into dawn,
and meet again when the full moon,
                        on its flamboyant feet, surges
over the mud floor of a barrio Saturday night.
She, of the rock, has offered the water man
beans, flour tortillas, cebollas encurtidas and atole,
a hand for the bell dance that rings all night,
the surprise of knowing the name of the horse
that waits in the shadows when the dance has gone.

She knows this room, where every saint has danced,
revolves on its own foundation,
and that the noon heat ache beneath her hair
guides her through a love's lost steps.
Her love lies deeper than a heart's desire,
far beyond even her hand's intention,
when midnight at the feast sings
with the singular arrow that flies by day,
                                        a sagitta mortis.
Now, in her presence, I always return to hands,
parts of that "unwieldly flesh about our souls,"
where the life of Fridays, the year of Lent, the wilderness,
lies and invites another danger.

I sit at the mass,
and mark the quail movement of the priests' hands,
as they draw submission from us.
The long night of atonement that burrs our knees
                                          feeds those hands.
But there are other hands—our own, yet another's—
in the mortar, in the glass,
                    tight with blood and innocence.
A cathedral moment may last for centuries,
given to us as a day, and a day, and half a day,
as a baroque insistence lying over classic form,

as the womb from which the nation rises whole.
Inside there, the nation walks the Chinese rail,
arrives at the Altar of Pardon,
                                        lingers, goes on,
to the grotto where the kings stand in holy elation.

Perhaps, this reticent man and woman will find
that moment of exhilaration in marriage, born
on the mud floor when they entered each other
for the good hidden in each, in flesh that needs
                                                  no propitiation.
There must be a "*Canticle,* a love-song,
an *Epithalamion,* a marriage song of God, to our souls,
wrapped up, if we would open it, and read it."

                Adorar es dar para recibir.
How much we have given to this Cathedral's life.
How often we have heard prophecies of famine,
or war, or pestilence, advocacies of labor
and fortune that have failed to sustain.
Compadre, I wish I were clever enough to sleep
in a room of saints, and close my senses
to the gaming, the burl of grilled meat and pulque,
the sweet talk of political murders, the corrido
laughter that follows a jefe to his bed,
all these silences, all these intimations
of something still to be constructed.
But forgive me for knowing this,
                that I have been touched by fire,
and that, even in spiritual things, nothing is perfect.
And this I understand,
in the Cathedral grotto, where the kings have buckled on
their customary deeds, the darkest lady has entered.
Be still, and hear the singing, while Calliope encounters
                                                              the saints.
The wedding party,
austerely figured in this man and woman,
advances to the spot where the virgin
                                once sat to receive us.

15

(EUTERPE ↔ AB)

In Oaxaca,
women, who speak to no one, carry
boxed hearts from market to market.
Elena brings me a hardwood box,
along with that other life,
now wrapped in manta, and I hear
the river still pecking in the cloth.

Days gone by,
I knelt in the water, in the way of women,
cradling a grief that could only be named
                                        by going away.
I remember
I saw the river pull its drying legs together,
and heard some thing, or some one, cut
a dark path through the trees near the shore.
I imagined the god had gone to ground,
and that river stones would then dull
                                    and grow silent.
I, myself, was a boy in a box,
                cradle or coffin,
and the voice I heard above me
dressed me in despair.
                                      Moment to moment,
my limbs and spirit grew to fit my Iroso boat.
I had no idea that I would follow
an Indian stream to Manhattan,
and be bereft of the skill to escape from,
or to live within, my heart's box.

Life in this place has taught me to scamp love;
therefore, I find it easy to sail Manhattan's
watercourse,
                    with Elena,

though her eyes are rose gardens of injuries,
and her voice shakes the dry bean of Oaxaca
within her.
I know her heart is a double flute,
and that the blue mountain she left,
above the starched plaza,
is truly made of water,
and that the gift she brings in the hardwood box
rests, awaiting the bone flute sound
of my washed desire.

16

(Thalia ↔ ka)

It is simple to ache in the Bone, or the Rind.
Sit here with me, near this solitude.
Sweet black coffee and *pan* close the heat out.
Down below, ship lights
bubble up and bob on the water.
The chains being dropped into the water ring bells,
recalling the anklets the city wore,
when it danced both day and night.

We then dressed in the finest sunspun white clothes.
No corner in the Villa Rica de la Vera Cruz
lay without lovers, or ambition,
memory and precept of the soul's discovery
in coffee, tobacco, bananas, sugarcane
and cattle still steaming through the cool moments.
The city was a soul admitted to itself.
Blessed and spirit warm,
it flew from wall to wall, to feed upon
funeral offerings of meat, cake and beer.

Some of us had been once removed,
and had gone north of the Cuban vowel,
the dropped consonant,
to arrive

on the fortunate side of the double face,
to affirm the heart's education
                    in leaving home, to arrive
fulfilled with the same desire.

I met my twin on a mountaintop,
in an ancient theatre, in a new world,
where the black-robed turns and counterturns
involved me in a dream of a polar privacy.
I could then speak of happiness
                    a child could understand,
and rub shoulders with a grace,
               descended from a mother,
who had often given birth to despair,
and had laid it in the weed of her solitude.

Come sit here, now, with me, in this solitude,
and teach me to hear the song
I have composed,
and teach me the reason why
I avoid so narrowly
                                        my fidelity.

Double heart on a double journey,
I ache, in the bone and rind,
to enter the mask that guides my eyes
from a dead thing to a green bird,
opening its sail into a greener forest.

17

(MELPOMENE ↔ BA)

I awaken to the silver spur bells and ecstasy of a city
                                                  astride the sun.
My eye chooses a narrow path.
In the rose dark, I see a sannyāsin arise,
set his pot upon the ground and, shedding

his flayed orange skin, step into the Ganges.
Black spirits such as mine will always come
to a crossroads such as this, where the water moves
with enabling force, and the body snuggles
in the arms of a weightless mother
who will not let go.

My mother travels the night sky,
in the light of a sacred rose, and rides
a lotus blossom that shines with the "unbroken
light of heaven."
She has become the center of her own mandala,
Kāśī itself, seated upon a trident above the earth
that sustains her.
She was,
when the world began,
a heron who clutched the conical stone
as it pierced the receding water at dawn.

"Dawn is the sacred hour in the City of Light."
Now, when morning unwraps the Age of Strife, and lays it
in the crimson mud heat of the Rio Grande,
I enter the water again,
to uncover a visible heart,
to hear the mother's tale of a woman surging
out of a brass pot, over this desert.
How can I be made by John a watchful spirit,
a water boat, when the water I enter
is shell and vision of a god's body,
spring of a devotion without book?
Sun cannot save us, skull bearers,
scourged by memory and the great vow,
even when the vessel in our hands turns
on its axis from darkness into light.
Day by day,
my skull cup fills with a longing,
a desire to see that black virgin queen,
enthroned with the child in her lap,
or a woman made whole through a Śiva dance,
and the morning clarified by meditation.

This skull I carry is wet with ashes,
tea leaves I read in back rooms, in leaky
houses, at the end of dirt roads, lined with sycamores—
leaves which recall an exalted nest, with the bird voice
fading away.
Why should I carry this coffin, this pillar
from the childbearing tree, and out of the cradle
endlessly rock my sarco-phagus self?
Pandās, when they speak, remind us of the way the city
peels away, layer by layer (Kāśī,
Varānāsī
Avimukta)
until we reach the stone in its heart,
and the blossoming well of bliss.
The soul walks Kāśī,
spins its fibrous body, then plunges
into the light of a water so deep it has
disappeared.
When I walked away from the cathedral passion of slave markets,
free at last,
my bones were dressed by the wind,
my breath danced in a cavern
where I had held a universe of vision and desire,
death and its imaginative discipline,
life, with its intensive and aged compassion.

I knew my heart a flayed thing,
unable to contain the tīrtha glow that would light me
to another.

No ship on the sea of night waited.

Like the god I had many faces,
but mine were unfamiliar, singular,
rope tense and edged with poverty.
For the death of the seed within me,
I thought I would annoint myself
with ashes from a funeral pyre.

So I travel from life to life with these God thoughts,
in a time of vision, having put away all hope,
having undone my freedom in meditation,
in austerity, in sacrifice,
yet with my work-instructed hands spinning
the jeweled beads of the spirit's life.
This bead ticking calls me back to Kāśī
and the bronze gleam of water on these pilgrims' backs.
There I go, swaddled in white, strapped to a bamboo litter.
Lifted up, I arrive on the last ground,
slide into the gray water and rise to assume my pyre.
That son, invested with his age and seamless white,
transports the fire, circles me.
I flame again in his last embrace.
I will be blind to his indifference
when he bathes my gathered form with water
from a clay pot, and walks blindly away.
I will sleep on the water,
and hear no mourning, no lamentation.

But I have slept before in an invested tree,
and solicited the wine succulence of the women's
grieving voices.
I was once a scholar,
who, following the bee buzz of a Maya text,
left my Arizona orange groves for the shag cut
and tensile heat of Jalisco, and there I died.
Huichol men who had seen me pass—
morning after morning, night after night—
who had dipped their heads in coffee cups
and day-old newspapers when I greeted them,
sent their wives to exult in their common grief.
I followed that text to the cottonwoods in Mississippi.
And there I died.
I stood apart from my breath-emptied form,
while men in black and women in white
rode the waves of their grave fitted voices,
to my bier, and tossed their nickels and dimes into it,
for my burial.

Out of the cradle, into the nest,
onto the cross and into the ship of the dead,
by the light of a great lamp,
I moved by degrees toward a still center,
able to deny my rising and falling,
able to inhabit my many hearts
and to accept my soul's singular involution.

My day continues.
I must now go down to the water
to hear the phrase that binds me to the truth within me.
Who will sit with me at the water's edge
to retell the story of my devotion,
to celebrate the careful way I have stepped around
every holy moment
to fix my mind on auspicious things?
Who will understand how willows and their water roots,
Guinea hymns, guilt and fear turned me,
burdened by a sacred thread,
away from the sight of my north star,
made me unable to take even seven fraudulent
steps toward my liberation?

Here, in Banāras, my day continues.
Having entered the city,
I thought the dark one had cut my defiance
and self-mutilation away from me.
I know now I am no longer perfect.
I decide to approach only the twilight water,
and to take my ash-filled cup,
against all assurances, to offer an invitation,
and to retain the power to thread a skein
of injury from my life.
Even in Kāśī,
I cannot ask for the white depth of forgetfulness.

Follow me,
as autumn throws its crisp haze over the uncut fields.
Old wood—poplar, pine, ash, beech, some birch—

has been tumbled, and stacked in the near corner
of the nearest field.
Tonight, the slim moon leans on the hill.
So still, we can hear the bear snuffling
around the dying apple trees,
and the baying of an old man at his well.
Surely,
here is the cabbage smell of peace,
the venison taste of an earned happiness.
Kāśī, clamorous and brassy with its silks and bronze cups, lies.
I lie, when I extol a moment that shows us we are alone.

Still, I have my devotion.
And perhaps only the skull bearer knows
how devotion, the water urge that cut us
from the fire altar, binds us to a new land.
When, tonight, under a new moon,
the soul's calendar turns another page,
I will go down, ash laden, and walk
the transforming light of Banāras.

18

(POLYHYMNIA ↔ KHAIBIT)

When the light struck me,
the hostile road grew calm.
I heard my name, tintinnabulating
in the desert air,
and felt the sea spray of fear in my belly.
How could I have been blind when I saw so clearly
what the others had been denied?
And how can I explain how the enharmonic
rapture of my name left them deaf?
Perhaps, at that moment,
they shivered with their Whitsun agues,
arrogant as ever with their baskets of first fruits.
But death, the potter, had given me a new vessel,

and I shook it before their eyes
                    though they were blind.
I needed Ananias to make sense
of the blood I now carried with me,
and when he swaddled me with the white water,
my bull roarer voice released the rising song in me.

Buried, therefore,
I remember the flowering water
and how it lifted my ship,
            the *Flor de la Mar,*
out of its solitude,
and prepared me
to bring forth an obedience of faith.
How did I know then that that very boat
would become my coffin, my cross,
the shadow my name would wear
under a new dispensation?

I write these letters to people who distrust me,
and assure them I admire their evangelical successes.
I wish I could forget my own successes,
the days I spent beating the scrabbling Roman pilgrims
            away from their convictions.
No one forgives me for showing love's failures.
Yet I know that love awakens grace in the one
                        who struck me.

I remember the flat curl of the road,
the mangy dogs scurrying away from us,
the round silver tray of the sun,
        as it slipped out of a cloud's pocket.
My only defense, against the enticing cloth
of the women's voices,
was to count the steps I had taken.
But now that I lie on this Teotihuacan bed,
only the mathematics of my ascent to here
                        concern me;

only the singular obsidian urge
that obliterates the trinity in me
                    brings me any peace.
Yet when the knife's glaze surrounds my heart,
I plunge, and plunge again,
into a desert river,
      where cross and coffin and shadow
compose my mother's absence,
and raise the anchored ship of my life
from body to house to spirit,
into the recognition of a sea deep need
                         my death commands.
I glow with this necessary entry.
And every entry is "a circumcision of the heart by the Spirit."

I should have written my life on cave walls,
and shut it away from light
                           and falling breath,
held it free of the crafty penumbra
                         of my New Spain dáma.
You then would have had to sit in my cave,
and light juniper twigs
to burn ox fat in a limestone cup,
and watch Affonso play among his many disguises.
I am that Affonso who found some comfort
in the purl of rails and cactus,
the silent skid of white pine out of the Zuñi mountains,
the crisscross of Aztec lives that waited for me here
                  when my king abandoned me.

Sea-green birds, hungry after their flight,
peck at the new morning in me,
and the nine syllables of Egyptian desire
                    spell my ancient name.
I must learn the dialectic of love's form
in the call that came with the light,
and live with the three-petalled rose of my new name,
                    here, in this new world.

19

(Clio ↔ khu)

In my Biṅu shrine, the sọgọ altars pull me home.
The stone I lay upon on Teo found itself
in a dance of stones,
four sisters turning near a brown pond,
each a promise of the sea within me.
For years now, Bamako has been dry.
Millstones,
                which held Nommo's
                        and the rain gods' gifts,
fade into the bilious doors.
Nevertheless,
the bilu still whisper in spirit ears,
and my father seeds my spirit
                with the first fruits of autumn,
pots that address the dead in me.
Yet I know myself an "intangible ethereal casing,"
lucent intelligence,
heavenbound by being bound to the emblems
                                of my person.
Clio call me,
scroll of the brave,
with one foot in the bush,
                one foot in the city,
a human tongue fit for taunting
the pretensions of pure love,
and an ear for the wind sound of a woman
riding a seashell into this desert desolation.
Though I have second sight,
my creations wither and die.
The balance I found easy escapes from my gardens.
I continue to weave my checkerboard
cloth of the Word,
healing music of the head,
my soul's improvisation.

(ART TATUM)

When I sit at the piano,
I don't count the keys.
I see you looking at my eyes;
you wonder what I see.
What I see is in my touch,
and in the assurance
that the sound will be right there.
Some cats always carp.
They say the music isn't mine,
keep asking me for "an original."
So I lay two notes in the bar ahead,
diminish a major,
tunnel through the dark
of the brightest minor,
and come out on the right side of the song.
I pick the composer's pocket,
and lay the hidden jewels out there.
This wired, hammering woman
wants her fortune told.
Hammer and anvil guide the music of my house,
smithy of the ear's anticipation, forge
of the mind in what it denies
and what it fulfills.
On the terrace,
altars resonate with the water sound
of goatskin over hollow wood,
and the frog pitch of the mudbanks
within the house
answer.
I dream of the smith music within me,
and hear its cithara voice in the dyēli's craft.

20

(TERPSICHORE ↔ SEKHEM)

"The night has a tree / with amber fruit; /
the earth has an / emerald hue."

Late, by Waverley Station,
Edinburgh draws its foggy curtain.
We et our mixed grills and hotpies
in a blue forest of a room that stood
at the head of the stairs on St. Andrew.
Wilson walks me from the bus station,
to which he will return,
threading the maze of the summer's fog.
When we arrived this afternoon,
we saw St. Christopher sitting alone and stoned
on the still bus to Lanark.
We would have invited him into the puzzle
of our afternoon,
but his Kāla Bhairava eyes kept us away.
No loss. No reason to remember
the Pentland flax and tweed that warm his tongue
when he sits in the Edinburgh dock.
Furies dance for the three of us
with a Dumfries list,
and, even though I click my cowries,
I hear the Dionysiac thiasus lag
at the Castle gate.
That "changes the image /
but not the virginity of its daring."

Ramón laid his anguish in heaven,
squeezed a grieving waltz from amber earrings
and jasmine in a woman's hair.
But perhaps even here in Edinburgh,
we share that same "bruma de invierno,"
and fall out of control into a Celtic dance—
beat and counterbeat where the ambush occurs,
sleepless nights following the rhythm
of a seed in love.
I imagine St. Christopher set spinning in New Town,
and his turn and counterturn reinventing
a flaming solitude, burning a heron dream
grown truly dark.
Even such a dream has its arid corner,
an appleless neighborhood,

withered by desire and ambition.
In the Zócalo,
a red candle under a cross sits
to remind us of a stellar mask
                                        that dawn on Teo recalls.

Every dance is convivial,
just as the pipes and beers we share,
waiting here for the train to take me away.
The absent one gives our love shape,
dresses our "dreams in indigo, our joy in gold."
I know you will not accept that form alone is empty.
                    No se cumple, no se cumple,
                        my teacher sings.

"Llevo tantas penas en el alma."
What is the obstinate death without end?
What can be spoken when the bird falls away
from the fullness of its song?
What memory governs loss,
                sekhem of solitude,
                Huichol eye into bliss?
Under the amber Edinburgh night,
the singing mask arrives,
The-One-Who-Comes-in-Good-Time,
precursor of the Cool World.
"Nada puedo entender ni sentir sino a través de la mujer."

"Power made visible."

I staunch you now in faith's blackness,
a compassion that being strange revives
                                        and secures.

21

(Urania ↔ ren)

Letter by letter,
the Villa Real de Santa Fé de San Francisco
                                        fades away.

It would have been better
for the village to withhold its name,
and to lie in the arms of the Sangre de Cristo
and dream only of the healing oil in myrtle.
But the city has grown out of its rose and dove shape,
become an abiku, with bells for the war in its spirit.
Santa Fé no longer hears its dolphin voice,
or the bronze stroke of Mali emblems,
marking the road from region to village
                    to this rosewood door in my adobe wall.
Santa Fé seems always to be rising and falling,
seems always amidst a turtle walk
                                        toward its own body,
always ready to embrace the figure
that reveals its incompleteness.

We had escaped from the pagan nets
set low in the two rivers,
had struggled, and landed on the high ground
of Pueblo faith,
and there set down, where those
with drier hearts had abandoned the sun.
Yet faith requires a larger globe than this plaza,
and more water than the bishop's bronze cup
                                                                    can hold.
When the faithful plunged into the Rio Grande,
toward Guadalupe,
I dressed myself in their cloth,
burned their crops, and sat clear-eyed
in their churches, waiting
                                                  for my name to appear.
That was an informative loss,
one in which the mussel shell of devotion
would draw my groin's heat
                                                      down,
into the forgotten water of orisha love.
I lost the city again,
traded in sheep, wool, wine and pelts,
learned how an unknown apple
                                                  had been my only globe,
the formal starshine of a face I could not put on.

Now my trade is dust.
But my name has retained an immaculate dew,
drawn from waterless places.
In my stolen forest,
Odomankoma guides Urania's hand
through the formalities of a house,
where love's formal body has set its passion.

Saints' Days

22

Nuestra Señora de la Paz (January 24th)

At the upper end of this continent,
along the St. Lawrence,
one has to learn to live with winter,
a wood cat with a devouring patience
and a tempered ear for the softest harmonics
of resignation.
Some of us call it an affordable peace,
and tuck the winter in journals
that stand hip to hip with rose bibles,
and string, on midwinter rosaries,
our spring weariness.
Hour to hour,
coquettish January sits in our warm rooms,
undresses, draws near and caresses
the longing within us.
Strange to think of such a virgin,
drawing a midwinter veil over our hearts,
and trying to sound the enharmonic note
that will distinguish peace from death.

23

Nuestra Señora de Lourdes (February 11th)

Morning memories take root in me,
here, a winter away from New England.

I solve the maze of milk and papaya,
coffee and sweet bread, the new black cigar
laid on a silver dish next to my coffee cup.
Doña Ana, on her way to the cathedral
on Zaragoza, just before the Hotel Salmones,
nods.
I drop her mild satisfaction
into my own honey jar of contentment.
Black, they say, she wears black days about her;
no sun lights them.
I have seen, on certain rainy Saturday nights,
women, who speak no Spanish, emerge
from the shadowed tiles,
with limping or dazed familiars
clutched to their breasts, curtsy
and enter through her figured door.
A year in this city has given me
a thirst for the waters of that basilica,
and the courage to walk the bridge
of the silence she displays.
Peasant ears like hers, I know,
can hear the spring beneath the grotto.
Her voice glows with the rainbow of passion
that speaking to holiness must disclose.
She stands, in her bones, giving evidence
of the *bhakti* of suffering.
I know that, if I could go beyond
that figured door, I would see her walls,
figured with every victory
over such suffering.
I speak the words now,
by which I fortify myself against
the left hand of my person,
and recall that the Lady sits
on the left bank of the Gave de Pau.
Promptly, this morning, the rain begins to fall.
The spring New England promised comes
to sit at my side.
And in the stillness the rain draws from us,
I seem to hear Doña Ana begin her prayers.

24

San Juan de Dios (March 8th)

Today,
in San Juan,
winter turns a scarlet eye upon us.
Dry rain slides down a dry amber path.
I should be gone.
But I have nestled the wind in my beard,
and lifted my head to the feather voice
of a stricken bird within me.

Now the day doubles at my feet.

It is always at this hour
that I recall the exhilarated,
red Sunday moment,
when the cross lowers another bull
to the gray, exhausted Mexican earth.

25

San Anselmo (April 21st)

Who will say he saw me
when I lit the twin tapers
of those cottonwoods near the river,
or knelt, with my face in muck,
to hear the bull roar of locusts?
Those who knew me then
knew I had been given
                    the vernacular of streams.
But, though the cottonwood blaze lit
an envy in the valley for the crux in my person,
I had no wish to be holy
                    nor any need for devotion.

I had come from Tepic,
with a Huichol graininess so deep within me
it lingered on my breath.
I lied to those around me about dove-headed gulls,
rose purple water at Vera Cruz,
moons strung full and radiant
                    above sunless noon plazas.
I carried, in a goat hide pouch,
the secret day of my naming.

So prophecy, without my consent,
followed me, and took me in hand.
I grew rich under the Gaulish peat
and Celtic chamois that buffed my Roman name.

But I go too fast.
Gradually, the fermented milk of liturgy
claimed me; I read myself into stupors.
My mother ground the red corn of my absence,
and washed me away.
My father hired a wanderer,
a vagabond, a slave, if you wish,
to walk beside his oxcart in my place.
No one, in the high airs of a deserted village,
chose to remember me,
or the nasal explosion of my name.

I went further away.
I followed an Augustine, or Agustín,
through the Florida everglades.
I knew him then as one who had come
            hard tack- and callous-laden,
                out of Fort Smith, Arkansas.
He walked with a wave-like limp,
a result of the chains they bestowed upon him,
further south,
for the black Baptist challenge in his flute voice.
This, I told myself,
would be my *pandit,* arguing with a river darkness,
my dyēli, lifting the prayer from a harmattan life.

I say, those who know
know I would be ruled by faith,
but that I profess nothing,
and have no anodyne for the spasms
                                        of a speechless heart.
Why else should my heart have led me
out of Piedmont, to Bec,
where I would learn to speak
                                        of blessedness and grace?
Why should I now be sailing
the backwaters of these slave sabbaths
to dispute salvation with those who have
                                                  the book by ear?
Why should I suffer Gaunilo's tone-deaf carping,
when I sound my soul's perfect triad?

Still I go on,
past the moment in the Zócalo,
when the bitter pozole of doubt
fell into my bowl,
past the moment when I furled
my Burgundy credo, and drifted
past the dock of God's name,
past the ship's bell of Agustín's
                                              singular love.
The fool has said,
                              I desire to understand.

It is far too easy to be left alone.
I learned to speak simply,
while others raised willows
around their words, and to lead
those who would pick a simple dandelion
through the oak and hickory forest
                                              of my own words.
And so, by degrees, I packed my solitude,
my desert father's inclinations,
my hawk-headed urgencies,
my Mixteca discontent,

and brought them to the water
my faith would stir into rapture.

Standing in the gold mosaic of a forest wall,
my heart promised me an eternity.
Still, I saw a white depth,
a blank arch in my faith's house.
What but a promise could I be?
What, when I turned my soul-heated eyes
upon the forest's cross, could I see
                                        but emptiness?
I knew then,
in spite of my mind's heavy parchment,
that I could prove nothing.
That morning, surely, you remember
I reached into the brazier of my devotion
for the fire I took to the cottonwood tapers,
lit them, and lay down in the ultimate flare
                of a moment, when someone
might have seen and dressed my spirit's
                                                        naked body.

26

Corpus Christi (May 25th)

So the White Sunday,
when the real presence of love
is possible, passes,
and mud heat rises once again
in the red hours,
field hours, recalled
in the faint trembling of cowbells.
Life here is so level
a quick spray of fireflies at dusk
comes as a starburst over July.
In such an atmosphere,
some live on visions,

the blood-stained marble of an altar,
devotion to a boned body that has
a king proceed by candlelight
amidst a flag flying of trades,
                    a clamor of crafts.
            At Kāśī,
            in the Vishvanātha temple,
            a worshipper approaches darśana
            with a joyful noise,
            and you can hear the surge of that river,
            as it rises and falls
            here in the sabbath air.
But what are days but the soul's definition
                                dominicae trinitatis,
moments that arrive veiled,
a question of number and the absolute IS,
which is, in Jerusalem, a bride?
I tell you there are only three festive
moments in a life,
each a seed dancing in a wayward mistral.
Ask me for evidence.
I tell you,
in Liége, I saw
Bedouin-draped nuns circle
the festering hide of a Trinity Sunday,
and heard a kora ecstasy
                still vibrating within them.
Even in blue-stockinged Rome,
those who had tolle'd and legge'd with the saint
felt a discontent when they were belled at last
to bed, and rose, with a peasant Pope,
quarreling with serenity.
But the temple will not open its sabbath door
                              to such delight,
except on Thor's day, a jovial, perhaps,
market day, thick with omens and oaths.

I will open a temple,
where joy becomes more than a body

raised and pressed to a penitent's tongue,
though I know that love must remain
                    festum of and in the body,
and a plainchant for a rude southern evening,
when work is the name I take
                                    and most adore.
There, when the Real Presence defies me,
the blue lamp of a forest spirit leads me home.

27

San Pedro/San Pablo (June 29th)

Last of all, as to one untimely born, he appeared to me.

There are moments when I wish that my mother
had less of the book by heart,
and that the sugar bowl of her faith
                                        were sometimes dry.
Who wants her spicy saint's eye
following you into the plaza's dark and curiously
curled corners,
after you have left the dance in your neighbor's stall,
and gone currying for the love thorns on Nicolasa's body?
And who wants to hear her voice,
exalting the coverlet of a light blue morning sky,
while you, fastened in the pinafore of your petate bed,
toss in a faceless novia's arms?
It is enough that she imagines that this lake
is Bethsaida, or Galilee, and that the rock hard
sustenance she finds in you grows
from the temple bell voice you've heard,
calling you away from your exhausted nets.

But so, my name was given by my arrival
in summer's first heat,
and by my mother's understanding
that what is sown dies and comes to life,

love's seeded protestation,
the spirit's rehabilitation after it has denied itself.
And yet, when I stand and pull the radiant fish
from Ajijic, I feel the Pauline tension in my body.
I know this day holds a double blessing,
and perhaps it would have been better
for my mother to conceive,
and to bear upon this very day,
a second gifted child, too diffident to deny
                    the authority in my name.
I would have had reason then to argue
with her need to lament the withered fig tree
of her body, her desire
to extol the conversion of a rejected stone,
into a riverworn altar,
or into a sun calendar,
                turning of its own weight.
And, though this lake lies distant from every gate
my mother's heart has entered,
to prepare me to hear the divinity in my calling,
and to see at the end of sun-benumbed days
the Lazarus light of this Mexican soil,
I would have welcomed the starfall of suffering
her life had promised me.

Now, I go slowly over the rock of my name,
touching the water-smoothed edges,
listening for the cock crow in my spirit,
the threefold betrayal of my mother's grace.

"Why am I in peril every hour?"

If he has appeared to Simon,
it is by the grace of God I am what I am
and the desert light becomes lake light.
The saints have married.
And my mother will call me Peter,
and ask me again to "speak to the people
            all the words of this Life."

28

Santa Cristina (July 24th)

Even then the cypresses were dying,
and olives rarely raised their black heads at our tables.
Prophecy had given us that Dalmatian slave,
with god's mark in his name, an Imperator and a Dominus.
Maximian fixed us in the yoke,
while *he* rose golden from the cocoon,
silk-webbed in his own importance,
weaving preferments and new houses in his flight.
If he had been born to more than tolerance,
patience and strength in his own ambition,
faith's river would have flowed smoothly at Bolsena,
and the Anicii would sit fat and undisturbed.

I wish they had given you a name such as this:
    María Christina Henrietta Désirée Félicité Rénière.
Though yours is hidden there,
I can't be sure of yours—Barbara? Catherine? Ursula?
The Austrian walked, by renunciation, into Spain;
you walked, through destruction, into the silence
                around your name.
Loss and double loss.
The person gone through the house's door into death,
the body gone through marriage and, finally, death.
Passage into passage, what remains of you
shows in an intimation of loss, or in faith's intimacy.
So your head rests on the high altar of the Milan Cathedral,
and your heart in the House of the Noble Ladies of Saint Theresa.

In a saint's body, familial hegemony breaks down.
Or, in one who remembers the saint and dresses in spirit,
the body, buckled against Carlists and banners that flare
the sky with a strange trinity, decomposes.
Where could you be found apart from an enclosure?
How could you retain even the hint of your name,
                except in retreat?

Saint and regent, you move out of the world.
Father gone.
Diocletian gone.
Isabella gone.
The monarchy shapes itself again;
God's many voices fashion redemption's wheel,
but nothing saves you, for no one sees you.
Even Cranach and Veronese, lifting a hymn
from a millstone, pincers and afflicting arrows,
disguise you,
and the sharp castanets of a Catalan night
only recall your double loss and your spirits'
twin passage into a sacrifice you must return
to renounce.

29

Santa Clara (August 12th)

(crucifix)

Clara Agnèse Di Favarone Ortolana Beatrice
The knight's disposition fails; an order falls.
The first to move is light. Love's intelligence invades her,
and the silver moonlight of the Gammadion, or the tau,
draws her into cloistered space, where the family
begins to reinvent itself.
If sullen Constantine, browbeaten by a vision, knew anything,
he knew his mother's story,
how she was led by the Palestinian to dig, just at that spot,
for the crosses and the nails; how the injured woman
was stretched upon the proper boards and rose
with a dance in her body.
So the legend reinvents the form of suffering
and the exuberance of discovering what time,
or another hand, had buried,
and you, who now require light's investment

in cloistered figures,
embrace the familial strangeness that the book alone
can give.

(LILY)

After the sackcloth and alms, comes marriage.
In love's white lace, you approach Portiuncula,
through a curtain of candlelight,
there where the altar promises you excision
and its own chaste obedience to the light within you.
How full you appear, λείριον, in that invested darkness;
how, like the red lily's, your spirit toils, unappeased
by the rumor and thrust of red robes in your life.
Say that an eastern austerity shaped you from Hera's milk,
and that the spring's cuckoo has taught you the wrong passion,
or that the tense brown field you inhabit leads your heart
astray,
toward ecstasy and a devotion you disguise
as absolute penance.
I know you by another,
the name wedded to the cross,
the voice encouraged by the many gifts
acquired through suffering.
Yet such suffering never releases Aphrodite's rose,
and both the rose and the suffering you disdain.
Your tempered life leads toward a different order,
and the clarity of rule.

(BOOK)

He refuses
—through Assisi indolence or excessive love—
he refuses the book upon which your heart is set.
You have only the Form of Life and the Last Will,
pentatonic scales for which no composition calls,
black marks inadequate to devotion's choir within you.

We are talking now about need,
and every reason to recall how, out of the huts,
they wander two by two, ragamuffins
more comfortable with prayer than with the Book,
patched souls who refuse money's hard and liberating
touch,
God's jongleurs, lifting an evangelical hymn from labor.
We are talking now about initiation, and the way
a double mind looks at the red chapel of the book,
and flees, toward sacrifice,
and the dissolution of its own claims.
How could he write you out of your intuition
and into the keeping of love's hearth-seeking candle?
How could he place your name near the blue vowel of loss?
The book now rests on a lotus blossom.
Words have been changed.
You retreat.

(CIBORIUM)

Death in the deep awaits the Great Mother.
Death in the water lily.
Death in the cup suspended over the altar.
What is the domestic day to the altar?
What covered chalice can contain
life's unequivocal ascent and descent,
the spring flowing and returning
to its own enclosure?
I must tell you
that wisdom sits, circled by star silver blossoms,
on a lotus chair, under a canopy of light.
She is that canopy,
the great lamp on the sea of night,
wood of the hieros gamos,
suffering bed of the awakening
and of the going away.
He now would step down,
leave the garden's tending to Elias, leave you the rule.

How unlike the vessel to disappear,
to deny the creative wood of a heart returning
to itself.
Still your passionate lily flowers by the altar,
enraptured by its austerity, enthroned
by its own seclusion.

30

Nuestra Señora de los Remedios (September 24th)

"When they came to my house that night
the dog barked twice, and the old man got up
and went out of doors and then came back and lay down;
she flew out again, and I got up and went out of doors;
I knew the slut barked more than usual,
but I could see nothing; I went back into the house,
and just as I got into bed five men bulged right
against the door, and it fell right in the middle of the floor,
and they fell down."

They fall before James and San Ramón,
with their vows and an urge to be useful;
they move in the waters of an old text.
Such piety turns on a name change
—Pity, Mercy, Ransom—
and under the spin of a different star
becomes Remedios.

Remedios.
Time now to reconstruct salvation.

They have come to take back their losses; they fall,
and thrust their hands into the night's cowl,
a caul for the woman's devotion to her offensive husband.
What can that lunar memory tell them about their failings?
What can their white hoods conceal, except the moment
when the sheared soul chose to cover its face,

and tuned its voice to a withered heart's power?
            Hannah will testify,
      "In the red times, how many times have
      they took me and turned my clothes
      over my head and whipped me?
      I do not care what they do to me now
      if I can only save my land."
In Hannah's life,
Remedios sutures her vindication in the earth,
and the morning upon which her melon seed begins
its slow descent into life, Hannah sings.
But here in the dark,
her eye lights a disfigured tree,
and remembers the river beneath that cross.
Death rises from that supple water,
and washes over the firstborn among the dead.
What do these five men, trying to circle
their stumbling shadows in a shattered cabin,
know about that One who is the Beginning, who is
a verb change that opposes self-possession?
What can they take away,
when the woman's assurance has dispossessed them?
And so, for no reason, they wait.

Who here, even in the heart of the Vera Cruz, remembers that river?

The burnt brown edge of coffee in the air
inaugurates Wednesday near Consolapa.
The small waterfall breaks over the smooth stones
under the bridge,
where Doña Elpidia, with an eye on me,
thrashes and mauls her manta in the white water.
In the distance, a hummingbird catches a phrase
from the stream, and sends it spiralling
                              over the chestnut trees.
September has spread its peace between the woman and me.
The sun lingers.
Elpidia sets a star of stones on the bank,
and stretches her wet clothes there to dry.

Elpidia, the water, the frayed clothes
cradle me now in their chronometry.
On the old house's water-stained walls,
I still see visions.
At night, the flat leaves of the cactus
in the patio become palms upon drums.
Witches know me.
And Elpidia knows my need to embrace
the bull's horn in their voices,
or the silence when they are gone.
Late September recalls Elpidia to her saint's day,
to the feast of her own flowering in sacred water.
In New England now, the leaves are already auburn-haired,
and the Herefords have begun to huddle against the intimation
of the first snow.
I have followed the earth's spine out of the White Mountains,
and have leapt, by my own impulse, away from a familiar
body, to here, where Doña Elpidia has shown me
the left side of solitude.
In the water's froth, she wrings out her losses:
a son in the cotton near Bakersfield; a husband
scrabbling in Guatemala; a gachupín daughter in Perote;
the stranger in the holy house by the stream,
who hides his eyes until she looks away.
A mile away, she keeps her hectored cattle
moping in the stringy grass,
and waits for her silence to invite me home.
I wake, sweat-cold, in midnight's brightest light,
shawl myself in gray, and take my first step
toward her adobe house.
I breathe with the stream's breath,
as I go up and against it.
Darkness lays its red crown on her land.
I continue,
up, where I will fall, and be unable
to promise more than my own vindication.

Rhythm rules, even when the darkness covers us.
Spirit's clock measures the self's repossession.

Five men, intent only upon a killing, ease themselves
into Hannah's dark.
                                        They will not be comforted.
They will not understand how the cradle breaks,
and how the ship she keeps on the sea of night
                                                    sails away from them.
Death here is the ultimate refusal,
the search for redemption's new name, the verb
that only Hannah hears and will learn to spell.

                    Mendicant, I flow as the river flows,
                    seeking the pledge of fulfillment.
                    I hear the hidden tone in Elpidia's name,
                    and see, for a moment, the act
                                                    that name elicits.
                    Green water under a green tree responds
                    when I call into her house.

31

San Rafael Arcángelo (October 24th)

Enoch, I walk about the earth the *angels* have defiled.
Strange, that, in this high valley, summer rain
at four in the afternoon clears the Alameda air.
                    Perpetuamente Osanna sverna,
as now out of my cave I climb,
an educated bear, marshing through solitude's mud springiness.

I see him turn out of Dolores, and come toward me.
I recognize him as one who keeps the nickel dances,
down along San Juan, alive by day.
But early evening sweeps him, a twisting leaf,
along Juárez and into the park, where he fastens himself
                                            to an old bench or a trouser leg.
My turn to read his book—
the tattered bracero breviary passed from Empalme,
through Tepic and Atotonilco, to here.

I know the story as a water legend,
made miraculous and difficult by being true.
We take the city's slowly kindling streets,
                    smoking, spitting the sour fish taste
of words we will not say into the gutters.
                    God heals, he tells me.
Why should this limping peon believe in a book
he knows, if at all, only by ear or by hearsay?

In Bernalillo, above Albuquerque,
a curandero has his own disguise, a hobbled shepherd,
folding his sheep along a dust-veiled road.
Down by the thinned river,
someone's pain addresses us, but only he
dares to raise his eyes or to tumble his hands
                              in the foaming water.
His knowledge lies blood black and sun red
in spider lines, etched in his goat's hide folio,
where every morph of injury submits to his healing's syntax.
In my tomb, I hear his voice.
Now here, with one who follows me, I wallop
the cabaret-lit dimness of Luis Moya,
and step into the second water, rising perhaps
out of a deer's lair, hare's seat, bird's nest, or the grave.
I recall my curandero's virtue,
and the way he arranges his materia medica—
herb-laden, with creosote and Mormon tea,
lavender-starred white horse nettle, the sego lily bulb—
                                        before our eyes,
a cloud of flowers, from which the lily bursts,
and the echo of a blessing welcomes one
who has been embraced by Remedios.

Having no destination, we know we will arrive,
leaves blown down the back streets of night town,
pages from a scattered book
                              not even the night can read.
And yet,
          Within its depths I saw ingathered, bound by
          love in one volume,

the tobaquillo dance of my curandero,
and heard, at once, the hummingbird, whispering
                                        in this bracero's voice,
felt prophetic notions in the hands filled with lilies.
This patron of travelers knows I will not perish
through secret things, and that my spirit
has walked out of a racially shattered house,
to find comfort in his likeness, challenge
                                in the book of his difference.
This saint's day opens a book I thought I had closed.
"And I, who never burned for my own vision more
than I do for his,"
find love the perfect vessel to trouble the waters.

32

San Diego (November 13th)

At home, at this hour, the fog would just be braiding
the willows, and there would be time and light enough
to slip into the lake with gum boots and a light pole,
looking for breakfast.
                                Here, when the morning foghorn groans,
he can only dream of sea bass, or admire the tuna boats
                                scudding home with the catch.
Though his water life has gone, Jake always wakes
in a starched room, kicks off the night's heaviness,
                                                and prays.
I call him son of Zebedee,
and reach for the thunder in his laugh.
His black sons search his blue eyes,
and call him Yacub, the wrong Jack of the common folk,
the quivering seajockey out of Lake Charles,
too dumb to know his uselessness, or his use.
They would have him beheaded, or have him wait
in the desert for some ghost's descent,
and, if I should confess how I, like him, wait
in my buffed room for a call in the night,

or for the ascent of veiled women,
poking with their staffs in the swamp ground around me,
I would be rewarded with their cold kiss of peace.

Jake walks his gum boots on Ford's car lot out on Pacific;
I flit my jitney around Todd's shipyards.
Pillars, perhaps, to those who depend upon us,
we return, in the evenings, to cold melons and silence,
and plot a slow escape down to Tijuana, in an old car
with wintry breath.
Our sons will not sit stiff in their beers, and listen
to two old men reconstruct the geography of sainthood.
Let them sleep.
I would turn left at San Diego, toward Imperial County,
and follow Mountain Spring rocks, with the Toltec and Maya
faces now reconceived in the rock face,
and the desert sky lit by Yucca elata, God's candles.
Back there, in San Pedro, something rides us
—memory of a white horse in a field, or of the ring
of a Spanish coin with the twin's face stamped upon it.
Only a crippled king—a lord lion, whose name threatens
to decompose and reappear, figured as the name of this city—
can save us.
I reach for the sweet seat of Pico, the Mountain Star,
or clutch at the Aztec urn and cross in San Diego's yard.
Surely, continents revolve on my brother's name,
and I invest him with the power to sit in judgment
on my shallow faith and the patience to wait
until compassion rises out of the many deaths
he left in the valley at Lake Charles.
Time now to compose love's epistle.
And for that I have waited, in my faith's confusion,
if only to be the scribe of the darkness by which we live.

The car moves slowly on.
Jakes sits beside me,
his smile a radiance about him,
his silence a hant's song near the altar
from which a god has fled.

33

Santa Bárbara (December 4th)

Who now takes an oath on the peacock, Hera's bird?
And who could depict that feast on Barbara's table?
The day the saint's father struck her, Ọya stripped and shivered
him in the earth, Hera's lightning sheared him,
and he became another exposed to sudden death,
subject to his daughter's care.

Jarena Lee feels the lightning in a psalm,
and thinks of dying,
returns to herself under the thunderclap of another text
that shows her her troubled heart,
and in that instant,
"as if a garment, which had entirely enveloped
my whole person . . . split at the crown of my head,"
and I could forgive *every* creature, and "tell of the wonders
and of the goodness of him who had clothed me with his
salvation."
I exhort you, even though I ride
only the broken buggy of my own conversion,
and even though I think that no one will
believe power's promise in my voice.
Must I, like incorruptible Hera,
cinch my husband's failings?
or be the faithful wife
and follow my man out of Ọyọ,
become a river goddess only when he
knows himself as a god?

Where does the crown sit,
being neither royal nor liturgical?
Why does it shine only in conquest and games?
I adorn my own with Graces and the Seasons,
and the cuckoo sits upon my sceptre to remind me
of spring, and of love.
Every celebration now speaks of the power in love's form,

and the way a flowered diadem recalls my tubular beads
and the conviviality in plantains and beans and mashed corn.

Even so,
        "At a certain time, I was beset with the idea,
        that soon or late I should fall from grace,
        and lose my soul at last. . . ."
But I know that I shall never return from the cross,
or that I shall return only when I have fashioned,
out of my own creative wood, the ship upon which
                I will write my real name.

This will be the hour of my redemption, a second blessing.
For death holds no promise.
And men who preach with my voice can only sanction my gift.
My gift is in the ceaseless journey from moment to moment,
from place to place, places given in dreams and clothed by the Spirit.
"But let it be remarked that [I] have never found that Spirit
to lead me contrary to the Scriptures of Truth."
Coco de mer, I lie with him, nourished by my vision,
set free by sailing away, and into,
                gold, silver, ivory and peacocks.

New England Days

34

THE WHITE DEER

The sun says she is there,
a dawn moon in a green field.

I imagine she came down,
riding the wooden horse ark;
or perhaps she was coiled within it,
and leapt from its serpent's embrace
when it lightly touched the earth.
But these are matters for a winter evening,
after the snow has been cleared,
and the thick docks of maple and birch
have been split and put away.
No need to resolve them now,
or to imagine that they are resolvable
without the enhanced water of the neighbors'
                    contemplation and resolve.
Before spring fully arrives,
we will all be thoroughly adept in her roots,
and able to hear her wet foot ripple the grass,
as she paddles from under the evergreens
                              into the clearing.

Night hunters seek her out.
I turn in the close air of my nightmares
because I hear their goose-voiced pickups

splash through the field's jade waves.
Those voices only serve to veil her.
                                        And the light
the hunters cast in darkening circles
never seems to fix her white coat.

Deerjackers have the tail of things.
It would be better if they came,
                disarmed and in awe,
when she feeds on withering apples
                                        and fallen buds,
when the only sound in a crowd of seekers
is a common breathing,
or the hushed tale of a memory like prayer.

I have grown,
day by day, in my own regard,
and in the distinction her tranquility
                                brings to the field.
I have grown, even though it is she
who has taken the field I say I own.

Each day I mark her pilgrim's satisfaction
and the way she satisfies these other pilgrims.

I would be taken into the depths of her crossed bones,
to encounter the seed that gave her such an exact light,
and to spiral under that clairvoyance that taught her to bear
                                                her body with such grace.

Danger lies in that grace.
Danger lies in the moment when the others have come
to understand the seed's white presence, in a body
that could father us without a hint of solace,
and induce us to dance out of the first dream,
into betrayal, and the word that takes its first step
                                                        into death.
Life here, I know, is a middle term,
breath arising from the arc and dimension

of a soul in wood, and the wood within a sheltered wood,
being a desert design, winding
toward a new moon in a green field.

Night must fall upon your rosary of explanation.

Now, a man,
who has made himself intimate with the night,
sits, camouflaged, in a tree, and aims
his silent magnum at the white deer.

35

Indian Pond

All through a bitter April,
spring has refused our invitation.
Still, the inner seasons turn,
and, when the ice breaks
and the blue water furs white
over the rocks in small streams,
the silence that had blanketed itself
in the crippled apple tree
walks away.

I hear that silence in the water
when I stand on the pond's edge,
and watch my father brace himself
in the stocks of his fish house
out on the ice, a silence
that seems a loon weariness,
a burden of lost bear,
lately moaning coyotes cutting
through the sheep's straw fur,
for the kill.

Over the ridge now, I see morning
rise in white smoke over white houses,

and know the cows have awakened
to their milky certainties.
I awaken to the depth charge of my own
stove's fire, having dreamed all night
of the smoky weeds lying deep in the pond
and the past certainties of mid-May,
when a blaze of dandelions lit my path
                                        to the water.

Spring's reasons come hard through the trunk of winter.
A father like mine can spend too long in a mind's ditch,
filled with paper potatoes, curdled cabbage, squash
and zucchini blooming in floods;
                                        can huddle too long
with death's gazette, chimney fires, a son's leaving,
a barn gone down under heavy snow.
I would awaken the water's flow in winter,
and have him uncoil in his boat,
with the peppery summer wind tugging at his laziness.
That would be more than the sap of April's promise,
less than April's refusal.

Mid-May.
I grow impatient with the lazy sting of blackflies,
with the patient way my neighbors snuffle
in their gardens and gauze them for the cold nights,
with the loggers' bourbon legends, and with the clouds
down from Canada spreadeagled over treetops.
"Something the heart here misses."
But wise old Indian Pond erupts on the left hand of spring.
In the sand at its feet,
someone, borrowing the incense and fire of another life,
has cut a crescent moon, to mark the place
where tethered April broke
                                        and disappeared.

36

The poplars have grown their winter cotton,
snow that winds a shaggy warmth around the branches.

At night now, even when the moon has tucked itself
into its patchy quilt,
you can go from this house in the hollow
to the house at the point of the stone wall,
following the trees' light and silence
through fog that inexplicably rises
                                        and suddenly disappears.
White seams in the lapis lazuli skirt of a New
Hampshire night remind us of the first time
we saw the aluminum shimmy of northern lights,
the hants' tree houses,
from which, through the fluttering doors,
we expected to hear an *hechicera* voice
and the *montuno* of a home we had swiftly
                                                    abandoned.

There is another voice,
high in the White Mountains,
one we carried in your father's urn
from appleless Jersey and scattered
in the moss shadow of a singular apple tree.
In spring,
it comes in the white-throated sparrow's song,
a melisma of misery tempered by the thrill of survival.

Soon, the mauve summer sky
will strike its evening tympanum,
and move you through the deep waters of wonder
                                            into a forgiving sleep.

Sources and Roots

37

Ayer me habló el corazón,
y su pena me contó,
llorando; so I lie doggó
in the skirts of a cantina known
for the quality of hearts bled
on its Moorish tiles; style, my man,
undoes the grandest among us.
But listen, whatever the fuss,
the story will be taken in hand
by the keeper of my cups and read
by charros polishing the mine-
cut diamonds of a grief so
fertile that water lilies flow
on desert sands, greenly wind-blown
by love's fortunate demise. Crone-
wily skill might give me a bow
to sling and round couplets to sow
under cherry trees, though I have flown
with mynah birds, and they have shown
the arc of your love's flight, the low
trajectory of escape. No,
cosas de Catalonia son,
paschal lacerations. ¡Merced!,
peacocks toward an open hand
swim, swerve, ride their calamitous
mother love—hope that sustains us
through dawn's late tumult and command

of pearlish fevers which have led
hearts astray, seen them overthrown
when they were ready to bestow
themselves upon one's grace. I know
what this spent heart has left alone.

38

Un siglo de ausencia might,
when the axe bites the ceiba tree,
matter; two fast-moving rats, three
kolanuts, an Iroko light—
business for the domestic bird—
a blessing, one by one—I live
on flowering water and give
you penny songs, by which the surd
of a fallen flower raises
hope in me. Such penny phrases
have lit a Oaxaca morning,
love's very rim-fire adorning
the *humillación* of falling
away from flowers, the galling
remembrance of a hill bereft
of turtledoves. If only deft
Tlacahuepan would offer me
his skimpy sun to enchant, free
of his dolens nature, his crest-
ed heart might sing us to our rest.
Un siglo de ausencia, night
fails to find you here and I see
my loss has now become the lee
side of my heart, mask of delight,
encumbrance upon the one word
Náhuatl songs do not forgive,
or speak, when they serve a deliv-
erance the tempered heart has heard.

39

Dime en donde encontrar-
te, disposable heart, red star
by which I set my course and flow,
a vessel marked by the dim glow
of pride. I am a song that cleaves
to its Guinea way, stops, deceives
itself, falls through a lowered tone
and returns, enhanced by its own
failure, to the key it sustains.
Not one word in this song constrains
my delight in you, or tells me
why, that without you, I am free
from pain, bereft of clemency,
or how the domestic bird, sea-
wise and durable, can inspire
the yellow feather of desire.
A plumed Huasteca feather bed
kept my floating spirit dry, wed
me to lilies that would soon wither
in Xochimilco, the slither-
ing sound of the dead in my ear.
I have come upon my own bier,
deep in the soft spur of your eyes,
though I know your ransom denies
me passion's hobbyhorse, the same
voice that ancianas use to flame
the wine bowl, in which my name
blossoms, floats, furls and dies. They shame
me with the easy way they ride
love's sepulchre, the way they hide
compassion in a mother's sleeve.
No one has taught me how to weave
the green threads of the sparrow's song;
in motion, my voice takes the wrong
turn, becomes a syllogismus,
contradance of an ambitus,
embodied and redeemed. Now all
the versions of love's death enthrall
and enable me to recall
light that shrouds us in its slow fall.

Coda I

Esta tierra da de todo.
Oh, perhaps, you will see no sloe
plum, or no white-tailed, ginger doe,
break-dancing at sunset when snow
shows us its blackberry wine skin.
But you will never see a thin-
ly dressed table, or be distressed
by a forged love. Here, you are blessed.

Coda II

Council houses turn gray faces
south, Andalucian traces
being perhaps on someone's mind.
Your mind is on the color blind-
ness that led you to draw this moor
heat about your shoulders, a poor
shawl against the withering kiss
of absence, timeless, returning bliss.

Coda III

Without your dead, faith dies, and one
learns how the extensible sun
of belief and aspiration
serve such an exhilaration
that only faith in love allows.
So even that pine can arouse
your suman heart, call spirit's rain
into the heat of your domain.
Químbara cosongo,
Químbara cosongo,
Químbara cosongo. . . .

Transformations

The Navigation of Absences: An Ode on Method

(CONSISTENCY)

This is the year of my birth. I recall
the blue, water-driven urge that robed me,
and set the boat of my name on the sprawl
of turbulent waters, the legacy
of souls I had been given to install
me in faith. I had the river's name,
incised on a ring so small it would fit
a snakeweed stem. I knew I would cross it,
and come again, and extinguish its flame.

The sun has lit the limestone on the plain,
and yet I think of lava, the domain
of adobe, the way the tobacco
red river turns south by west through sacred
mountains, changes color and turns to flow
over Cambrian rock. These cottonwoods bed
me into peace; I hear my body burn
the sugar-sap of despair, though the frayed
cloth—called death—stands ready, competent, stern.

(INDEPENDENCE)

Where will I find the message, if not there,
inscribed in a forest grown dense and strange?
or in the density and interchange
of heat and force that mark the fairy stone,
the carbon trace that whispers of frail bone?
or in a ring of cloud, where I prepare,
a protostar, for the creative thrust
of the stellar wind? I have found that rare
incision that sutures me to the spare
powers I call my own, sufficient, just.

My laughter is palm-kernel oil, palm wine,
a distillation of dangers and dreams.

I dance among love's numbers, the extremes
of solitude, cactus I will assign
to my adampa and hold in the fine
air of Jemez. I know now to align
myself with my going-away, the earth-
invested desire by which I sustain
my being; I must now approve the plain
words that design and call my sunsum's birth.

(COMPLETENESS)

Capullo de cempaxúchitl, flower
that speaks of the dead. You will remember
the sound of bells and the perfect hour
that embraced us in early December,
our patient ascent past rivers gone dead.
I was learning then to follow the thread
of stories that spoke of grace, with no hint
of holiness, and to face down the flint
in salvation. Floripondio, a shade
that recalls a craft I cannot evade.

Should I call this thorny bud redemption,
this perfect aquifer, grace? How shall I
figure the ground of being in the wry
granitic face etched on these valley walls?
Can I now deny the oak of spirit,
and shape the unseizable wind to fit
a fractured temple? This false confection
of souls pursues and endangers me, calls
me to contradiction. I now address
the logic of loss, find myself artless.

(DECIDABILITY)

An old star, I will flow from state to state,
full of myself, an impeccable guide

to hesitant streams and to the ornate
exigencies of death, to justified
disappearances that substantiate
the slow birth of the earth's crust and sanction
the eruption of a flawed stone, the ascent
of another to its own element,
the soul's return to its own election.

A saint's name fills the bay, but my river
has disappeared, become the lawgiver
no one knows, a categorial flaw,
voiceless, except when it calls my other name.
I have heard the distant, embracing caw
of an absent bird, a resilient claim
against my own erasure. I resume
at that darkest point where knowledge took flight,
the scene of our invention, love's anteroom.

The Emerald Sound in Kagamé's Kairós

All being enters here, by force,
an adjunct hemisphere, fragile
center of a self less agile
with the arc and docking source
of the bronze ark, variable star,
a spirit's descent and bright scar.

Each element argues its sun,
phonemic heir to its own world
and, though it finds itself unfurled
before an emptiness, undone
by its morphemic destiny,
it will tune its reality.

The emerald sound in the shell
secures the turtle in its dance
upon our altar and will enhance
the limestone in this sacred well.

Lao-Tzu had a passion for ice,
shading into a love of stone;
he heard perhaps that green alone
measures a critical time twice
endured, twice denied, and under
every grave he heard the thunder.

On winter nights, when the ice lies,
spun cotton in the evergreens,
a man embraces his book, leans
into the forest of his eyes
to see a gold light bend and flame
the darkness of his other name.

Again I say,
the emerald sound in the shell
secures the turtle in its dance
upon our altar and will enhance
the limestone in this sacred well.

These consonants are not the source
of God, a figure so fragile
that a being on an agile
systo- and diastolic course
could stand openly on the bar
of desire, its own avatar.

I believe my kinku self spun
from a longing for a lost world
of feathers and hides, a soul curled
upon itself and half begun.
What power will strengthen the lee
of my longing, and set me free?

Still I say,
the emerald sound in the shell
secures the turtle in its dance
upon our altar and will enhance
the limestone in this sacred well.

If Lao-Tzu had come and been twice
denied, and Don José had known
the emerald as a herringbone
design, then love would be the dice
of compassion, and no sunder-
ing wish could take the world under.

The open sound of love defies
its force, even as the day weans
us from itself, and itself cleans
its voice of what the day denies.
Kairós here has a middle name,
difficult, jealous of acclaim.

I go on to say,
the emerald sound in the shell
secures the turtle in its dance
upon our altar and will enhance
the limestone in this sacred well.

We are not consumed by force,
but lifted by a star's facile
flow into a new and fertile
atmosphere. Over time's watercourse
love comes down in a burnished car,
and the soul lights on passion's bar.

There is a moment when the one
you have become questions your pearled
desire, and leaves your heart unfurled
in a closed room, bereft of sun.
There is a moment when the sea
voice within you alone is free.

And the voice repeats,
the emerald sound in the shell
secures the turtle in its dance
upon our altar and will enhance
the limestone in this sacred well.

Being in that voice
the dead make the choice
will allows; the voice,
aged by intuition, sails, an arrow sent
searching for that other well of love's intent.

Seguidilla with a Double Heart

May wants a mandarin heart,
commitment, a writ
of raven's art, touch of ice,
a fugitive spin.

I call my balsa
choir and there ride my desire
to be enthralled, fall.

Spring, in Esmeraldas, cleaves
to itself, admits
to stars turned cold with music,
is lit by spirit.

Spring's psalter hauls me
away from desolation;
all love befalls me.

I would engage devotion,
sit, tacit, displaced,
under flange and splice of love,
submit to moonlit bones.

A footfall recalls me
to April and the dance
that stalls me and galls.

Spring is Esmeraldas' faith,
spit and withering

breath that solaces the body,
knits the culprit heart.

All my tall hopes rest
with the jackal in the bush,
small, and called by wrath.

Naming the Asturian Bird

Me casó mi madre
con un pícaro pastor. . . .

I would be carried away
by my name, adrift
in a sound that only wind
could secure and draft.
I know that I have sprung head-
first, bereft of signs,
glabrous, mute and spiky hard.

I stand apart from the law
of graves and thrifty
sacrifices, the dew
of devotion—my deftness.
Once I thought death alone held
secrets so feigned
I need not stand to be healed.

Nomen, cognomen, the straw
of a faith so scruffy,
so fallen, so swiftly wed
to a loss uplifted.
Why should I, unfrocked, now hide,
and then be impugned
by the death they apprehend?

Why should I see the flaw
in my mother's craft,

the torn seam in her blue shawl,
the rage gone spendthrift?
There must be a bead hidden,
a link that designs
the soul's unbidden heraldry.

I must find faith in the swell
of vowel, the deft
plowing of consonant, awe
dampened angels, love's crafters.
Faith seeds me in custom, holds
me to the slogans
of my house, and binds my hands.

I know my mother has strewn
her skill in my croft
and set me all softly down,
my soul's own grafter.
Seated now, I am haunted
by the magnitude
of the earth I have harrowed.

I turn, ready to bestow
my nomadic gifts
upon a pícaro, wi-
ly, and derelict.
I must accept these hurried
tokens and the reign
of another's holiday.

My name will be a weaver's
cloth, adorned with grief
and pressed beside my dowry,
to serve as my shrift.
I now turn to the haunted
page and signature
of a free song I have heard,

and awake to a wedding
song, the blessèd script

of testament and sorrow,
light in the soul's cleft,
and recall all the hunted
—the significant
other, wearing a bird's hood.

The Bullring at the Quinta Real, Zacatecas

So the old bullring died and was reborn,
a haven for hummingbirds and silence,
a bed and brimming table to adorn
with the rose lace of another presence.

As you descend, a bull's breath rises blue
against the terra-cotta and sandy hue
of the cave, and you think you hear death's call
in a bull's threshing of dung in a stall.

Someone has turned this center to a star,
and has drawn a light from the silvery stone
to a darkened flower bed that has grown
radiant and weightless, death's avatar.

Shall I here search a flightless bird to hear
it sing, and singing, turn and disappear?

Leaving the Buenos Aires Cemetery

The evening folds the sun in its blue skirt.
Time to think of fire and the marbled face
that makes an old man come to assert
the flesh of his sign, his singular grace.

I heard, in my cradle, the song that flamed
the year's new mountain and heard myself named

by gourds and wooden horns under the tree,
and in that shade I set my spirit free.

In Buenos Aires, José Paz sleeps
under five angels; while one uncovers
a mortal woman's eyes, one discovers
death's form and, standing above the cross, weeps.

This fire blue evening has become my cross
and the capped candle of my every loss.

Rewriting the Light

Night is the color of the sunbird's eyes.
Some have seen the lightest blue turn to jade
and a blood red moment flow into green.

I have been busy with a nightingale,
a pheasant of redemption, a blind bird,
perhaps, that flutters and sits on the third
rail of desire, an only and wagtail.

Should the bridge from love to love be undone
and the sharp night cast out and sent where none

can see the movement of spirit in shade?
Montesino felt shame at being wise
to his own absence, strength in being seen.

Pájaro lindo, night's dawn is the one
dolorous light by which I set my sun.

The Buried Barn's Own Nocturn

Who am I to contradict what the wind
says when it sings near the barn's absent side?
And how am I to know what the deer hear

when, in shadow, the mountain lion moves
to the edge of stagnant water and waits
for the moon to withdraw? My ear vibrates
alone to a music my heart approves.

If I could hear a grieving fox return
to the barn's abandoned stalls, and concern

myself with the star-ride these nights provide,
I would be able myself to descend
to a music that has escaped the sheer

ecstasy of silence, the ever stern
prompting of wind, rising from the barn's urn.

Another Hymn to Trees: Juniper and Pine

All those hymns to trees. We sing what lies
greenly flaming, deep in the woods, beyond
the perishable reach of jackers, drunks
and sullied others heir to their urges.
The evergreens turn blue white with solace,
and now I imagine the qui tollis
of Arcturus, as the wind here surges.
That morning in Santa Fé, oh, we stood
before the juniper's blunt leaves, the hood
of its redberry making us so fond
of late summer, or a spring in disguise,
of the obscure presumption in tree trunks.
Gin, sandals, prayer sticks, anklets and wood,
gifts of a dry source our love understood.

Compassion's Bird

I have been taught by dreams and fantasies. . . .
—Edwin Muir

I know the incapacity of dream,
the failing copper light that falls upon

night's froggy skin, rises and flies, supreme,
above dawn's carapace, pale blue icon
of sleep and death, love's only eidolon.
Am I awakened by this firing pin,
a memory, bedizened by my twin?

I sleep again and know it false, a scheme
against the grain, the flashing circuit gone
awry; in that domain, I hear the scream
of elm, the pulsing hearts of angels on
a tear, the bold advance of bush, a wan-
ton thrust of force against my second skin,
and there in dream I lie, and lie therein.

We count the alphabet of fact extreme.
When all our measure sounds the carillon
of love's determined sphere, coordinates seem
to form the bone of myth, to lead head on
to one intent of form, a going-on.
Now thát is góing, knowledge all akin
to grace, objective, sure, a Jacobin.

A braided water furs the bank. Midstream
I see a floating gold, the paragon
of loss, savannah twilight with its teem-
ing darkness still intact, my myrmidon.
I know there is that white phenomenon;
and up above the snowy shackles din
me home to this, the bliss of origin.

The book of sleep now opens to redeem
another valley, lost, and thereupon
abandoned, urging me through a gulf-stream
more apparent than fact, something quite spun
from that other memory not quite sun
enough to buckle me fast to the yin
and yang of love, not quite ecstasy's gin.

Oh, I should never think to blaspheme
against that mortality, be egged-on

into an inclining silence, cold-stream
given once and back to the Babylon
I abandoned for the sense of a gryphon,
inconsolable as death, not quite all in,
or all there, or sure of which way to spin.

And spin I do, tipped by cold self-esteem.
If I could write the tetragrammaton
of desire above my name, I would seem
to be free of hope, prolegomenon
to love's first betrayal, faith's hanger-on,
and set my own destruction. Within
love's discontent I recognize my twin.

Compassion's bird recedes; that is my theme
—resonant exile, a tempered agon.
No elastic universe can redeem
the pain of my heart's red shift, the python
embrace of madroños. I have gone
into the dense light of dream, origin
of love's structured star, love's own mandarin.

Restaurant Bonaparte, Rue St. François Xavier, on a Rainy Day

Old Montreal can only dream
of pine, the star cradler, a green
presence as heavy as the sheen
of daybreak on walls. The rose cream
hand of evening alone must seem
a purfling absence, an *X* seen

on a street sign, just at the seam
of street and bay, where swallows, keen
to indulge us, wave and careen
from early shadow, the blue stream

of a day caught in the extreme
act of gleaning this rain-trimmed scene.

Mid-Spring, Coming into Buenos Aires

Out of the north, we follow spring
down the jacaranda river
in Buenos Aires, wherever
the yellow ombú leaf, palling,

recalls the old city stealing
slowly through its ombú cover
to come upon itself, reaver,
reawakened by the sprawling

design at our feet, by the strong
current of delight that hovers
near the Colón and discovers
a strange, dark and bitter streaming.

By November, mid-spring has sprung
us above despair, survivors,
clamoring for pardon, shivered
by purple on the river's string.

The Anti-Fabliau of Saturnino Orestes "Minnie" Miñoso

The day the bobcat reigned in the near wood
the moon had turned milky white and stood
in anger over my cavernous roof,
delirious, I thought, with the liquor
of my stove. I then sat with the wicker
of my discontent, content with the proof
of that consolation, "broody all night
over the bones of a deadman," the slight
prefiguration of hamhocks and beans,

the wasteful hours burry with the sound
of the turn from fall to a winter bound
by its need for solace by any means.

Often, an obsidian sun will lift
itself above this rose green bed, the gift
of the sea's folding, configuration
of absent water, or conjuration
of liquid rock, a life so soon disclosed
in this, the one I feel now so disposed
to reveal as festival song, the torch
of a life gone dry. I sit on my porch,
and recall summer's spent temper and claims,
the devious intimation of games
bunched and bound by the yucca twine of grief
and ecstasy, spirits who teach time's thief.

I do recall a Sonora summer
and the vague burnt potato smell of earth
flaking in the heat, the red chile sheen
of the evening star and the stark, pristine
invitation of night plowing the firth
of an ancient and revealed midsummer.
I can speak of the moon in Miñoso,
with the enchantment of a boy immersed
in sophistry of ball games and bus rides,
in the lemon stench and doloroso
companionship of old hotels, the tides
of cut-price cafés and all the rehearsed,
ill-fitting deceit my timoroso
nature led me to explore, in my pride's
spent fortune, bled by my spirit, coerced
into a celebration that subsides
into an agile failing, the disbursed
relation of the moon in Miñoso.

I will never submit to his humor.
I despise the flagellant expertise,
abhor the sweet stroking way he can tease

a salutary scandal from rumor.
Oh, he still bothers me about the night
he strung the ball on a line to the moon,
and a cluster of hot, young stars took flight
and danced in his patio, out of tune
with the season, happy in the cocoon
spun by the master's needling skills, the light
fantastic of his evasions, the soon
emptied ecstasy following the right
guess on the wrong pitch. Think yourself immune?
I did, until I met that watertight
assurance with tales of his constant sleight
of hand that makes the skeptic a buffoon.
But I was spelling ecstasy, shag-strewn
graces, being carded into delight.

Ted tells us hitting is a simple thing,
a digital spin in the hips, the spring
in the wrist, the cool vise grip of the eyes.
No need for witchery or the lutestring
of emotion that might paralyze or blind.
The mind becomes, you might say, the bowstring
prepared for the luster and wary wing
of the curve, and anticipates the ring
of the wood's sharpest note, counts itself wise
before the fact. Whatever can you bring
against an ens that will happily bind
you to the discipline of chance, the sting
and starch of prohibitions, the hamstring
of facilitating designs that wring
success from nature's every compromise?
—I mean, the way you step over lines, cling
to the fiction of bobby pins, the rind
decaying in the left pocket, and swing
away from graveyards and black cats, offspring
of disaster at the plate, the wellspring
of wrong turns that force you to exorcise
the benefits in darkness. The lapwing
of failure flies where an astringent mind
has emptied all the signs and will not sing.

Ah, but I was caressing that old Ming vase
of Miñoso's deeds, now the mainspring
of my intent to shrive and catechize
you, even as I catch your breath and fling
it into space, and then, but never mind.
Here comes Miñoso, full-scale. Let him sing.

Friend, I know you know the chivalrous horse:
    Mi caballo es caballero
    no sabe comer cebada.
    Mi caballo se mantiene
    con el zumito del agua.
Some think of him as god, some as the source
of envy and spite and degradation,
and will say that riding the watercourse
of years turned him secretive, cunning, sly.
Qualities you will observe, in due course.
Perhaps there is only one, and, of course,
you have met him, and called him to endorse
some wily dream or a celebration,
told him of your wish to acquire the force
necessary to escape the purblind
bird of necessity without remorse.
You laugh, because you think I will enforce
a village claim, by which I will divorce
you from yourself, mug the constellation
you take for your own, leave you no recourse.
But forgive me. You see, I am resigned
to this moment's sweet chivalrous discourse.

Friend, imagine my ball club's fashion plate,
the horse we nightly sent to demonstrate
our power—cuarto bat, an architect
of easy wins, the scrappy magistrate
of exhilaration, who all alone
could draw wind from fire and put boots on fate.
I remember the town, where the Vulgate
of slow hours and voices would overstate
the nostalgia for what was circumspect.

In that air, we dallied over a plate
of neckbones and greens, drank the overblown
lightning, waiting for dark and the tollgate
of the diamond, our very own estate.
Oh, demons would follow us, and dictate
rules we never followed, try to direct
our attention to failures and abate
the flow of good juice, or steal the shinbone
that hung on the door, still bloody, ornate.
You laugh, and wince perhaps, when I relate
how love trailed us from port to port, sedate,
but far from tongueless, by no means abject.
Ah, the look in your eye cries expurgate
this book of ambling joy, this graph and clone
of ecstasy I try to annotate.
    Dios mio, mi escanciador
    mi muerte ávido desea.
    Me incitó al vino
    y se instaló en su corazón asustado,
    disparando agudos proyectiles.
The song disturbs. You want me to placate
you with watery hymns, leave the mandate
of failure and fretless pain in effect.
My authority comes through power, late,
as it seems, that sits upon a hearthstone
in Sweetwater, dry well of a dry state,
and inexplicably flows to create
my cupbearer, clamorous, an innate
catechumen, one of the black elect
who have coursed with love's despair and cognate
wisdom, and found themselves suddenly shown
the repetitive shame of love, love's bait.
    Pero . . .
    Una noche llamamos a la puerta de un convento en que
        servían vino
    y nos encontramos entre guardianes y trasnochadores.
We stopped the bus and planned to desecrate
the temple, and I meant to orchestrate
the Rubaiyat of the gifted, infect

each one with an urgency and frustrate
every inclination to silence. Stone
business, Jim, I know how to aggravate.
The night passed, with moments to celebrate.
I found the crew to my liking, first-rate,
innocent, feisty enough, in effect,
a ball club. Do I have to illustrate
the dips we took around the gramophone?
I sing, yet I know my silence can grate
upon the curious who deprecate
the thought of a thorny bush near the gate
of curiosity, and will deflect
letrillas and lies I accommodate.
But I think it time to return the tone
of a tale I want you to meditate.
After the convent, the horse would stagnate,
stop hitting, talking, even vacillate
at the table, courting his own neglect.
We thought hard, trying to abbreviate
his fall, but some rubbed the emerald stone
of envy and bad faith, would titillate
him with noxious cures and leave him prostrate
with fictions and psalms all so out-of-date.
Nothing we said or did could resurrect
his bat, or him. How could that night deflate
the lion of lines, erect his headstone,
how can slump's fortune so appreciate?
Those guys had him going. All billingsgate,
decir bagualadas to compensate
for the hole in the spirit, the defect
in prissy vision that forces you to skate
around open doors, avoid the curbstone.
Indecent. Such tales must intimidate
and curry favor with all the fifth-rate
hackers who bail out and never create
a situation. It takes self-respect
to keep swinging, and pride will let you wait
until the stars turn and you can atone
for the ponches and pebbles, the clean slate

you have brought home at night. Why inflate
the dangers of success, why insulate
yourself against a cold that might detect
the nerve and bone heat that would designate
the spirit's home? No, I could not condone
this chacabuco or affiliate
myself with such huevada, separate
the fool from the fool's waltz, negotiate
the whitewater of self-pity, and expect
to be myself. I let him confiscate
my sense, the rookie, homie, my millstone.
I slept less, lost weight, tried to abdicate
my responsibilities, dedicate
myself again to the tensile template
of rules and good sense, though, in retrospect,
how willing I was to associate
with the unspoken, the whirling field moan
of discontent, power to ventilate.

But you can imagine how suspicious
our man became, living the atrocious
clarity of his decline, the nitwit
of a court in decline, a shade bilious,
almost ready, I said, to copyright
his injuries. Now call me pernicious,
but I found his ache too fastidious,
and soon began my own insidious
squirreling in the archives and lamplit
chapels that offered us some auspicious
turning, or counterturn, or a blue light
into the red-seamed and invidious
profession we had found so propitious,
until the horse lay in injudicious
agony. Speak of the horse, that culprit,
but, no, not yet, only the capricious
way we fled from one Areopagite
to another, from one imperious
claim to another just as malicious,
thrashing for that one ceremonious

end our man would accept, the Holy Writ
he could not turn aside. Meretricious
me, you see how deep that singular bite
of ambition had gone, how infectious
the thrill of control. Ollie, too cautious,
had no chance against our delirious
desire to see him bound with bells that fit.
Bueno, cochinada, sacrilegious,
but I had by then become a cenobite,
shamelessly bound to the adventitious.
You wonder, I know, how he could abide
such virulent concoctions, each bromide
as sulphurous and indigestible
as the one we had empurpled and plied
him with before. Why should I now rehearse
the tuntunes that kept our man slug-eyed
and exhausted? Events you would deride.
I remember, for example, the ride
to Venegas to find the impossible,
a curly-haired brown pig from whose hide
we would gather the lightning and coerce
the curves to hang and put our man in stride,
his horse, and the green water from the side
of a bald mountain that had to reside
on his dresser and be as visible
at midnight as noon, an eternal guide
to vision, a salutary and terse
reminder of blindness often denied.
I had my turn with güijes. I complied
with country wisdom, would often confide
in a bilonguero, the irascible
tenant in spirit's house, a deicide.
Such a past made me true to the perverse
exchange we tempered, attuned to the bride
of misfortune we courted, gratified.
Even so, I too often had to glide
around my doubt, the irresistible
urge to smoke the butt of this stupefied

changeling, happily driving his own hearse.
Better to linger with saints, ride the tide.

I hear you say I should be crucified
for abandoning him to the rawhide
stroke of his own and incorruptible
doubt. But pity me, trussed and mortified
by my part as the compromised wet nurse
of a fledgeling buckled and certified
to be senseless and damned and petrified
by one night in the convent, a hayride
we all take. I am not responsible.
No bateaba, and only magnified
his faults by mooning over the commerce
with experience. Ah, leave that aside.

I had heard reports of a sanctified
woman in the town, one who could provide
hope in a dry season, a flexible
mind still green enough to be fortified
by spirits ill-at-ease with the curse
placed upon the fire-stricken, the ox-eyed.
I needed a season near the seaside
of belief, the quick descent that would guide
me through the mischievous, corruptible
labyrinth I made for this stupefied
cousin, oily with his own and perverse
derangement, innocent, too satisfied.
But how could I bring myself to confide
in one who would bathe me in a flood tide
of improprieties, the frangible
schemes she would erect only to deride
my faith in her, leave me only the tense
contentment of my ego's frenzied slide?
Who was slumping? Who needed the bromide
of forgetfulness, the intensified
other made suddenly accessible?
I knew the sullen innocent relied
upon me, courting my need to reverse

his fortunes, too engaged by fear to chide
my hesitation, in spirit allied
with the choricera I now denied.
I stood at my Monday door, sensible
of the treacherous timbre, amplified
by faith, in my voice, ready to rehearse
my petition to a woman of pride.

Walking beside the water, I could hear
the morning taking shape in the austere
chanting of fogbound gulls, the sibilant
praise of comales and the cavalier
clemency of church bells all out of phase,
so early, I walked in an atmosphere
of lingering celebration, the sere
fantasies that circle and rise and veer
toward self-delusion, the aspirant
blindness that creates an unruly sphere
where love never comes undone and displays
a reticence that can never appear
too sure of its command, or too severe.
Oh, but I must take you back to the drear
approximation of a youth buoyant
with the charm of others' silks, the veneer
of skills that always seemed the metaphrase
of my failings, demanding, much too dear.
The rose cream dawn embraced me as I stood near
the stream. I felt, beneath me, the career
of a horse on the loose, sensed the blatant
insouciance of its pace, and knew no mere
petition could set Ollie's heart ablaze,
or provoke the woman to interfere.
I knew my sullied kra would have to veer
toward the solitude a charioteer,
bereft of his horses, too flamboyant
in his misery, would take for the sere
anatomy of love, the flowered maze
of astonishment too bright to appear
a danger to his cloth, and knew my ear

would accommodate itself to the queer
semiquavers my own and aberrant
nature could compose to help me endear
myself to the woman, provoke her praise,
and see beyond the image of my bier.

There is a body that will not submit
to being bound in custom's cloth, the kit
that makes of desire an unruly cloak.
I sensed the scandal of hers, the bones knit
as though abandoned; the dark, grainy skin
with its intimation of fire; the fit
fierceness of eye that could read the Sanskrit
of turmoil and aspiration, the writ
of unease set to another, invoke
the ram's horn of ecstasy, and acquit
us of despair. Oh, how could I begin
to speak to her? I? Culprit, soul's bandit.

But speak I must, and I had to recall
the old songs of that first step, that first fall
into the soft and disfigured allure
of being in flight. Courting the windfall
of fear I could feel rising to consume
me, I thought I'd fly with that mother shawl,
concocted of cojones and blue gall,
and stand finally at ease in the stall
of my flagellated self, too cocksure
of sacrifice and of the Peter Paul-
ish confusion no self-respecting broom
would touch—a choricera, the tall
order of arranging the awful haul
of crows into a harmony of small
delights, into (we say) a sinecure
of disfigured treasures, and the woman, all
transfigured by distance, became the loom
desired, carted from bush to village wall.

We lay on the wrong side of the river;
I would have to cross it to deliver

Ollie's soul to the one who would assume
its education. I walked, aquiver
with the night, through bee balm and horsetail
milkweed, wild rose and bear grass, a sliver
of welcome intimacy. The river
would rise and fall; light would shiver
at a hillcrest, tumble, rise to resume
its stately desert ride, a lawgiver,
a chancellor of dreams, jealous of detail,
the assessor of what I would give her.

So I crossed the bridge, a seamless ascent
through a labyrinth of mudhuts, the scent
of danger and decay around my skin.
I came to a post, and followed the print
of a feather-light creature that would lead
me further into the incandescent
dark; birds chattered, seemed to know my intent.
I awakened from the astonishment
of being attended to the khamsin
flare of a horse, unbound, some atonement
for the silence so suddenly decreed
upon my person, a benevolent
intrusion of order true to my bent.
I lingered a moment in the crescent
cut by the cholla and in the virgin
descent in the valley, my cerement
perhaps, or perhaps the angelic seed
house of forgiveness for a penitent.

A la izquierda y a la derecha,
¿qué desea su corazón?

I thought of angelic Miñoso, sent
to disturb me, sent to effect some rent
in my macho rags and in the doeskin
fabric of my self-regard, bring judgment
against our ball nine failings, make us plead
for his apostle's presence, the adornment

of his bat. But stop that. This indictment.
I have sacrificed to this astringent
calm I suffer now, to this mandarin
urge to be of service and competent.
This story ought to be enough to feed
the saint in me—go, laugh, you decadent.

Imagine Althea in the blue lace
of dust around her door, the blue embrace
of a night receding into shadow.
Imagine, if you will, the steeplechase
of urgency and despair that would keep
me tethered to her breath and to her face.
It was late, and difficult to retrace
my steps, too late to attempt to erase
my presence; I could feel the undertow
of morning's insistence, the commonplace
awakening that I could hear set deep
in the river valley, yet could not place.
Was it night, or dawn, rising in a brace
of cock's voices, redolent with grace,
still burdened with the solace of sorrow?
What could I do to help me to efface
the valley's power, the unbridled sweep
of spirits I would have soon to displace?

She knew me, or so it seems to me now.
It would have been easy to disavow
my purpose, to slip my cocoon, pretend
a different urgency, and allow
myself only the intoxication
of the river night and the silent tau
of her presence. I ride the shapely prow
of my imperfect innocence, and bow
to my encompassing deceit, and end
where I began, clutching a barren bough
that swings me to false exhilaration.
She called me, or so it seems to me now.

It is true that at a certain hour—no,
I have heard that song, a delicate flow
constricted by the honey on the page,
and have been so engaged with the scarce eau-
de-vie that assaults the air around it
that I have determined to admit no
soft measure to Althea's song, no show
of amber on a night when the shallow
waters of salvation danced in a rage
familiar to few in a valley so
far removed from cypress, so strangely lit
by traces of corn and mi caballo.
Stand-in for a vagrant. How could I throw
myself upon the woman and burrow
into her well of pity to assuage
a boy with no guts for this sump below-
stairs business, this no-hit, brooding, half-wit?
How could I discombobulate that crow?

You see my temper had turned. The crusade
I had knocked up, and led, seemed a parade
in a bottle; there was a joke in my
advocacy I could ignore, or shade,
with a touch of scorn, until the moment
I found myself riding a barricade
of cholla, thinking of winter, arrayed
in its seams, thinking of the masquerade
of motives that could never satisfy
one as adept in escape, the brocade
of evasion—but why should I comment
upon the way my scarfish body laid
itself before Althea? The nightshade
temper that gripped me seemed enough to trade
for the gruff therapy, the dragonfly
net of her laughter, enough to persuade
her that we were two of a kind, ardent
amateurs of subversion, retrograde
pastophors, ready for a cavalcade
of pleasures, any succulent charade

we could, by chance or design, misapply.
I had, I suppose, come, a renegade,
home, or to its disguise, a transparent
act of psychic piracy still unpaid.

Tu madre era un rejoneador,
Tu padre una ama de casa.

¿Qué chistoso, eh? The woman was pregnant
with insult. She sang an extravagant
litany of failures, a prodigal
conjunction of fevers and repugnant
secretions, a maul of misconstruction,
deformity that tuned her malignant
eye. Believe me—she loved the ululant
fascination of her voice, the celebrant
tone she used to litigate the scandal
of my body. I, far less arrogant
than she, overlooked her sly invention,
a rehearsal of my faults too blatant
to be true, though I admit the fragrant
exhilaration in the gray, stagnant
stream she whipped and stirred under my royal
bark. She had broken our covenant.
I had to count upon circumspection;
I had to be a proper postulant.

"Have you seen my horse?" I thought of the blue
slant of light grazing the hills, the sinew
and bone mimicry of a horse I had
seen, if at all, raised in the skirling flue
of Miñoso's swift imagination.
Yet I was not about to misconstrue
the command in Althea's voice, the bayou
timbre that set my heart slightly askew.
I had crossed the river under sail, clad
in the chutzpah of guilt, a false dryad
without a tree, or the exaltation
of a wood waiting for a retinue

of ancestral spirits. The marabout
I had called in the past, the overdue
spirit, trolled other waters, perhaps mad
with my insouciance, weary of the clue-
less scrambling in virtue, the flirtation
with redemption's daughter, with temps perdu.
The horse was becoming an albatross,
a trace of misconception, a pathos
too dear for the cliff rose and coral bean
around us. I knew, of course, how to gloss
Althea's question; how to contradict
her insistence upon the thanatos
glow around my body, the witching moss
of doubt and the unfamiliar crisscross
of motive that beggared my Nazarene
benevolence; how to slip the bathos
she would sleeve about my soul to convict
me of inattention and the willing loss
of my own figures of faith. Such chaos,
occasioned by a horse not there, Southern Cross
bereft of its hemisphere, the serene
dramaturg of faith's goat song, who would toss
us from fever to fever like bulls picked
into holy rage, the flaring logos.

I faced a bird's nest of hair, carious
teeth, a wen near her nose, a serious
burn that ran from her forehead to her throat.
She put me off with her felonious
manner, holding a mirror before me.
The river had made me fastidious.
I cringed in the cycling, insidious
bravado of her voice, that spurious
structural intent that set her afloat
on a wave of her own harmonious
incapacities. She offered me tea.
Out of a strikingly commodious
tobacco can, she drew an odious
draft of wet leaves, a ceremonious

thrust into a circle she would devote
herself to construct with laborious
calm. Such, as I sat, was the jubilee
that threatened to drive me delirious.

Summer in the south. I had to beware
of herbs and teas and of the rocking-chair
comfort I would find in finding substance
in Althea's gifts. She brewed me the dry hair
of cota, Navajo tea, a roadside
indulgence with its piney scent and flair.
On the other side, I would chase the rare
explosions of light into woods, to scare
up the herbs that bloomed in such abundance;
here, on this side, I could see no dispar-
ity in the rogue's game, the Whitsuntide
urge that had me dicing with noxious air.

Los aretes que le faltan a la luna
yo tengo guardado en el fondo del mar.
Los aretes que le faltan a la luna
yo tengo guardado para hacerte un collar.

Was it she who sang to me, or was I
tuned to my own nostalgia, the magpie
scolding that would shift the stones in my craw?
I accepted the tea to fortify
myself against her evocatory
design, for I knew she could crucify
me with river saints and transmogrify
the meaning of my visit. I damn nigh
had forgotten that it was not mý flaw
but Ollie's I had come to justify;
his ass belonged in this purgatory.
Ah, sunflower, how can I gratify
such longing? the flitting verse with its sly
inversions? the trumpet to clarify
the singer's space? Ask me now to withdraw
that image of Miñoso on the fly,

steps ahead of Maddern's dilatory
shot, and to forget how to magnify
the café serenade to ratify
such grace, moments set to identify
the ganglion of need, the rustic law
of the soul's arrangement, to occupy
the blue-tinged and stark conservatory
where love's fudged markings often go awry.

Arroz amarillo
habichuelas negras
plátanos maduros
lechón
ron

A celebration of the soul's intent.
Althea had me thinking of a rent
party, a room of angels on display.
Faltar solo los—bells to orient
us, a harrowing hymn and fuguing tune.
I heard the music of a star's descent.
The time had come to open my parchment
of desires, to unfold my testament
to my chacabuco and not betray
my trust. I speak of the astonishment
of bells, their rough sanctity often hewn
from despair, their virtues often misspent.
Althea had heard the just amendment
of Ollie's pain in coral bells, fluent
roots for a belly gone badly astray.
She lay before me her incandescent
confection of coral bean, a cartoon
of healing only a percipient
spirit could sustain, an embodiment
of shag hills and rock, the lineament
of hummingbirds. I knew that she would play
with me; I knew that my bewilderment
would feed her scorn and close her picayune
purse of compassion. I would not relent.

Esconder la leche; I tried in vain
to call her back home, to break the membrane
of her self-regard. She bound me in her
sacred datura, the legerdemain
of her leafless milkweed, the sugar sap
of leafless trees. I could see her domain
expanding, watch her light against the grain
of darkness she had conjured to constrain
me, though I was certain she could inter
the sorrow that had me mining the vein
of her displeasure, daring the flytrap
of her disregard. I had to campaign
for a cure she refused to entertain.
She began an elaborate cross-grain
story, one meant, I suppose, to deter
me on my hard ride over her terrain.
Such an ill-fitting coat, such a foolscap
of evasions and lies in her refrain.
Oh, I knew I could not expect some plain
chant or paean or threnody, some strain
of civility, something to refer
to my crossing the river, the inane
border between us. Yet, what would I tap
by interrupting her in her insane
account of breaking free of the mundane
perils of solitude? She had to drain
me of my faith in her slightly demure
existence. I sensed her open disdain
for my fraudulent faith in the red burr
of her voice. Nothing I said could restrain
her; she lifted me in a hurricane
of song, and engaged me in the urbane
entangling of impulse she thought would spur
me to challenge her, to force her profane
delights to surface. Ah, life is a knap
of distemper, aerie of hidden pain.

See-see rider

Did I dream of the rider or the horse?

See what you have done

I could see light below in the village,
and could imagine the crisp sacrilege
of birdsong on the river, the agon
of river and sun, and the pilgrimage
to sheltered places forbidden to me.
My sleepless night had scaled my vassalage
to Althea. I wanted to salvage
Ollie's bones, but could see no advantage
in going on, sounding the antiphon
of need. I might confess to a vintage
skill in corrupt petition, and agree
that there was more than a taint of spoilage
in my benevolent basket, leakage
in my wine cup of grace. This short voyage
across the river, prolegomenon
to a deeper journey, a tutelage
I could not escape, uncovered the lea
and cast of a mind waiting to ravage
itself. I had come to my orphanage,
a sacred grove too lush and too savage
to be of use to the sacred moron
who had sent me to scoop up the spillage
from Althea's horn. What more could I see,
if I allowed myself the patronage
denied to her? I denied her suffrage.
I had come, pfrancing with the green plumage
of a horse I had barely seen, a con
man without a mark, almost in bondage
to his soft necromancer's pedigree.
I lay, cushioned in the gold foliage
of light, preparing a grudging homage
to Althea's domain and to forage
among her words' green skirts to come upon
my green and naked self, a new coinage
in desperation and debility.
The woman would not admit the damage
to her reputation, or encourage

me to interpret her cure, or manage
the movement from failing to grace, put on
the white garments and unsullied visage
of her art. I felt myself falling free,
out of the sun's chariot, a wreckage
my dreams had built for me. My lineage
seemed plucked from rivers and to disparage
my shining body, a crude electron
out of its track that moves to discourage
light. All that I saw now referred to me.
Althea had become my soul's image.

Quien engaña
o abandona a su amigo
¿cómo puede consolar?

Had Ollie ever been with me on this
journey, or was it my anabasis,
the river crossed, the woman overcome,
my rueful rooting in the orifice
of shame that kept me buckled to my yoke?
Althea had refused my Serapis
invitation, and every artifice
I could inspire to invest a Memphis
river clay with the power to become
poultice for a spirit's scars, genesis
of a spirit that could only provoke
the shine of the dark and that Anubis
error that would adorn a precipice.
I had hardly understood the axis
of her body, or grasped the mettlesome
indignation she felt for my Apis
posturing. She had indulged my baroque
recall, my commitment to a fey bliss.

¿Quién me dará la gacela esclava . . . ?

I had come, looking for an accomplice.
I had become a hopeless apprentice,

or so, seated in the palladium
of Althea's regard, I thought—remiss,
perhaps, in fidelity, a scrub oak
out of my sphere. I had let cowardice
claim me and braid me with a nemesis.
The river no longer seemed that hospice
the night had promised. The uncanny hum
of midnight had been a Nunc Dimittis
I had obscured. I waited for the stroke
of dawn and some peculiar armistice.
What would Miñoso, with a leaf amiss,
have to say about the necropolis
that I had taken for an asylum?
What would make him suffer the oxalis
the river folk dipped in my bowl, a joke
of origins, a rude parenthesis?

La gacela no tiene par
en la hermosura casta;
es una beldad que no existe
más que en la imaginación.

I moved now in a new constellation
of urgencies, a configuration
of variable stars I nurtured for
a changing light, the exhilaration
in near obscurity. What atmosphere
of sanctions could dampen the pulsation
of my bones? I had my confirmation.
Althea's air was a dispensation
I could evade. My pícaro pastor
nature saw me through the modulation
of a text and song so strict and severe
that a saint would question her vocation.

The river's blue light had begun to fade.
I heard Althea's voice open the shade
of another grove. She called Miñoso
and, with him, the horse; set a masquerade

of pleasure at her door—a scurrilous
act the initiate could then parade
as vision and design, and the renegade
heart could deplore as the small, retrograde
tremblings of featherless, virtuoso
spirits in love with the harlequinade
of spirit. I had found the blasphemous
rapture lifting me from the everglade
of austerity and into the jade
investment of another self, waylaid
by redemption and my amoroso
intent. I found, then, every barricade
had fallen, and Althea's mischievous
song had ceased. She turned from my escapade.

Friend, I know you will remember
my chivalrous horse.

A Cowry Rispetto

Sauced, the garrulous gastropod has tucked folds,
fled the sea and the urchin, floating, numb, bled
of its innocence, dealer deft in old molds,
water bed of desire. Below us, oúr dead
economic of love has made a left turn,
and the mollusk must pay for light, a green urn
and the right to exchange the body's spent shell
for a feeling so lately struck when love fell.

Popper's Dilemma

Se yerguen nuestras flores en el tiempo de lluvia.
—*Poesía Náhuatl,* 3, III

Amada vieja, your old sleight
of hand marries me to the rain,
a shroud that sits over the rune
of my retablo altar, slough

engendered. Your white rose seems caught
on love's rise and fall; you retain
such coherence in the rowen
squared by love's transcendence; the slight

trace that I recall as love's slant
in God's eye stands here as God's rain
in a logical fall, ruin
of all correspondence. I slouch

toward truth, a voice or echo, stint-
ed evidence. Can love be the grain
of event, plainchant of roiling
fact, goal of a lonely and skeigh

eye, the pragmatic and sluggish
moment that coheres in reason?
Or must we forever remain
where love only mimics the light?

I turn my eye now to the right,
and to the red flower, reflection
of an artful rose, reaction
to my passion, and though I might

awaken into dream, be fraught
with fury for my own region
of peace, and know myself raven-
hearted and wise, clearly the thought

of love's solace comes with a slight
resistance and the heart's grainy
door seems to close upon the ring
of fire in the rose. A jade weight

upon the heart sets the heart straight,
compels its flower to retain
what substance needs, gives reason
to rain's incensing of our light.

Noche amiga, your name lights
the limit of all relation.
A red flower standing in rain
knows only the curve of time's weight.

Ntu and Emerald: The Day Divine

"Day makes itself divine,"
so I begin and turn
to the red urn
on the altar, a sign
that the spring and holiest stone
flourishes here, misplaced, strengthened and alone.

What strength I have may wait
deep in a turtle shell,
the only bell
my spirit, with its strait-
ened life finds to give it voice;
I call the wrong festival; I have no other choice.

On this festival day,
my goddess will hammer
me and clamor
for the hour when I say
what quality, what passion
I need to endure the weight of her compassion.

Emeralds and blue water
restore me, rubies fight
under the slight
tear, search for the tauter
fabric of my heart; I feel
the surging water brace itself against my keel.

Yet these fragile letters
of my being, a three
in one, the free

fall of force in fetters
bind me in your whitest cloth.
I am with you, at your flame, ontology's moth.

If death is without end
and the garrulous grave,
its architrave
incensed, serves as the wind
to my heron wings, I lie
in wait for the moment love moves on its lace of sky.

And I hear, above
all else, the spinning verb
tack and disturb
that atmosphere where love
goes, with the sound of three dark
bells upon the air, and know the air to trace love's arc.

The spring stone will help me
to recover the dance,
to look askance
at my loss, at the plea
I feel compelled to savor
when the morning's sea rises and runs for my favor.

Indeed, there will be time
for that perfect presence
to influence
this moment's orbit, the rhyme
of existence on the rise
and fall of love within us, the body fulfilled, wise.

(ESTRIBILLO)

Why should this holy day
commit me to obey
the long breath of desire,
and seat me in a choir

that will endlessly sing
its own transcendence, bring
sustenance to its own heart?
Why should the holiest stone submit to being's art?

The Metaphysics of Sorrow

Fix, in the morning's true measure, the spray of old light in the aspens.
Line upon line of a gold so ensnaring might lead her soul astray.
She must imagine the flighty intent of a river, a curled green
poised on the crest of a cloud, and be able to see, as the day ends,
night ride the silvery edge of a red, an intense and sublime blaze.
Darkness will ripen, the arché of evening will surface and be spent.
What does it mean to embrace at the crux of the moon and to haunt fens
festive with promised regret, and why dance in the juniper, display
thirst for disguise, an extensive resilience for grace? But my thought mends
nothing of value, proposes no arrow of time, nor the consent
given to bodies affected by force and a singular escape.
Why do I turn from the sight of a woman secure in her descent?
Shades of the cliff rose at dusk now recall the achievement of piñón.
Clusters of cottonwoods teach me their stances. I linger in that gray
dowry of desert the night has uncovered again, where I listen,
clutching my ears, to the sound of the scurrying birds and to that thin
voice of the satisfied soul, the persuasive intent of the jaguar
pelt, the rhetorical flare of the clay, the authority that bends.
How can we measure the light in a name that will fit, or go breath deep
into the substance of rivers that run undisturbed by the light's shape?
How can we measure the limits of virtue, the cognitive mask set
whirling in space, unresponsive to virtue or limits, an aspen
sorrow that none can describe, the extrinsic distress of a fixed star?
What you have heard is the language of herons asleep on a salt lake.

Love's Augustine or, What's Done Is Donne

Dawn will see you leaving her, a fury
at her own burial, a shaded widow
attuned to a double shadow,

the Manichaean conjury
by which you navigate
a narrow stream of passion, and dilate
upon the silent footfall, the innate
obscurity of craving and desire,
or tell how death, callando, enters the choir.

This is the history of a quarrel,
a refusal to acknowledge disparity
in rooted love, the clarity
of self-love, to see the aural
beneficence of need
in a cleansing at twilight, though I will read
the fire in a bird mask, peck at the seed
of love's imperfection set within me,
and set myself inescapably free.

Intransigent as macaw on a clay
riverbank, I fly to snap at the fruit
of words, scornful of the acute
Carthaginian on display
in Roman words: amor,
dilectio, caritas. How they soar
toward salvation and grace. How they roar
with the inexhaustible fire of faith
in the other soul, the exalted they bathe.

Imagine now the mother on the white
water of a son's charged inconstancy,
how she would deal with his frenzy,
temper his belief in the slight
imperfections of being, the design
of honeyed grace, and consider the wine
of isolation just that anodyne
flare of fulfillment his spirit allows.
This is the spirit the spirit disavows.

Amor amoris Dei, love's riddle changes.
Death's sleeping figure awakens a healing,

a certainty of congealing
light; implacable, it exchanges
its grief for the serene,
pulsing danger in the perfect and obscene
solidity of kinship, that pristine
reading of solitude, that open page,
the dialectic of recall, our age.

The Economy of Power

La bellísima luna
se ha alzado. . . .

The song is forever false,
though the words are true,
and a lover with a faith
obscured by trust

feels the power in a flash
of limestone. The tramp
festivity of night flees,
and the soul construes

its own deception, falls,
on its way, to treat
a flowered heart and to flaunt
the gemlike turtle

shell of a nomadic faith.
I await the terse
exchange my heart, fearless
after its triumph,

matches with that instant flare
that sustains, travels
the weave love's figure fledges,
the soul's swift trouvaille.

When every shadow that falls
is desire's own trope,

arché that moves and might fleece
the raven and tropic

promise of night, lift the fault
of a betrothal
to power out of the flesh,
death sets its trifling

indifference in our flawed
forest of rapture,
there to engage the twin's lais
and to reconstruct

an allusive hymn to flint.
So we must destroy
your rose shawl and all those fables
of the blue treasure

your name hides, the mayflower
by which you suture
your presence to the faltering
flare of a lost tree.

I am now bereft of face,
and the tremulous
consent you give my failings
can only betray

a legacy that will fail
to hold and transcend
the thrifty soul that follows
and cries its tribute.

Dreaming: Rhythm I: [Monday]

Mi coraçon se fue perder
amando a quien no pudo aver.

A horned moon hangs in my hair.
What awakens me is despair.

I know that, soon,
power I tune
to birds, immune
though I be, will be hard to bear.
The heart, pivoting, goes elsewhere,
and devotion finds me unfair.

I cannot have this blue flare
of birds near me, and yet I dare.
Love's my cartoon
of air, cocoon
come opportune-
ly to enweb my centaur and mare,
I say, and saying so, declare
none of my power gone, threadbare.

An emerald moment, clair-
voyant egg, enters with its flair.
Now dread Oshún
comes in her moon-
fed boat, a loon
of my desire, a golden lair
that calls me home, there to ensnare
me in the one domain we share.

There is a silence we tear
in the unbroken depth of prayer.
I importune
your left and lun-
ar side, commune
with the slight run-
ish figure you have turned to spare
my heart its loss, and now repair
my power, become my own heir.

How can I enlist the rare
blue light of faith, come home, prepare?
Shall I attune
myself to moon-

dazed light gone dune-
dark and dangerous, and beware
of darkness I will not forswear?
Mi coraçon se fue perder.

The Fall into Love's Atmosphere

Winter will leave those apples near
the withered tree, untouched, and snow
on the wing from Québec will shear
the branches of that root life, so
scrupulously sheltered, the flow
of a spring ambivalent, dear.

Say, if, under the pine, you hear
still my lost voice speak with the slow
music of cattle, those that show
themselves in fog's wool blanket, here
where the seed in my gourd might veer
from radiance through dark to death's glow.

After the fall, when love's austere
and weightless other sings below
the water, will the spirit know
which voice to assume, or the ear
attentive to an urge set low
in the soul's house? My heart, dawn's deer,

lifts its head to the wind and clear
promise of winter's sly and sloe-
eyed return, though wind is a mere
occasion for night's undertow,
or a chance for the dead to row
from pool to pool, into this blear

forest of desire and to steer
passion's unruly bark as though

compassion for our dead could grow
with the turning from year to year.
I say this moment may cohere
in dream and lie on the rainbow

untouched in its singular sphere.
One can see a withered moment sow
spring in a dash of moon, and throw
a rising light over the sheer
darkness in earth, ready to bestow
the pain of a fall without peer.

The moon has a shadow in tow,
and, in that light, I come and go,
a deceptive bird, all aglow
with the night and the hemisphere
of spirit's deep water. I gear
myself to ride love's atmosphere.

Ecstasy, Bird and Oak

And the bird knew me by sunrise,
and had my spirit dicing to chastise
itself. I arise
and light the oak.

Now in that light I recover
my dream's white sheen, entry I discover
when I uncover
what yóu invoke.

Someone has me in his night eye.
I have come to a temple stone to lie
near the sharpest cry
love can evoke.

You hear and interrupt my flight,
foretell my healing, measure my delight

in the brief twilight
that you provoke.

I must enter my dream, devise
its downfall, and then learn to improvise
my death, realize
my spirit's yoke.

Death, say, is the dance the lover
becomes, ecstatic reason to cover
the body, hover
near a white oak.

I have slept in beds to deny
the womb that seats me, though I justify
the thing I defy
and try to cloak.

The bird, at sunrise, sees starlight
as white as the song by which I invite
the first acolyte
home to the oak.

Don José Gorostiza Encounters el Cordobés

Victurosque dei celant ut vivere durent / Felix esse mori.
(From those who are to live the gods conceal / The bliss of death; so they endure life.)
—Lucan, *Pharsalia*, IV, 519–20,
tr. J. Wight Duff

You wake in a Córdoba
disguised, bereft of its gold shoes and green
sash bound to its middle, yet you call it home,
or call it quaint, deceiving,
portent, prophecy, matron and, finally, Rome.
Here you can play with death, become a go-between,
a talent given to its own decay, sea-foam.

The heavy mango blooms and falls
greenly to rose
earth, where burrowing dogs come lately upon its
sweetness. Such wealth of intrusive calm befalls
us that night and coffee-fragrant air astound.
Would it be better to compose
the burning sugarcane, and water its sound?

José Gorostiza recalls
the lace repose
of a provincial Sunday, and hears in its rain
the slow course of a gypsy song that enthralls
him still, with the stillness of a page he found
in Lucan, ready to disclose
his own betrayal, senseless, himself spellbound.

I remember going up
the Callejón Diamante, feeling unclean,
savoring the adobo and the palindrome
talk at the tables, the eyes
that seemed to promise adoration or the chrome
steel grip of the grave, nothing soft or as obscene
as envy, nothing set to the soul's metronome.

I will tell you what I hear.
Córdoba has a beggar's way with a song, a mean
gift for self-conscious display, a monochrome
alacrity for effect
—call it a clever youth, like you, Benedictine.
Still there is some virtue in its speech and, on the gnome-
like exactitude of its silence, a worthy sheen.

Such elegance stuns and appalls.
Time will expose
it for the crude burden it has become, a shield
against self-examination that forestalls
the same dispassionate crossing, the musclebound
spirit the spirit should oppose,
the shadow that rises, falls, goes underground.

A singer can adorn death's shawls,
and decompose
doubt's entangling fiber for the light in the cloth.
I hear they pay Annaeus to build Chinese Walls
of sentiment, and raise from scratch a stamping ground,
erect a Yanga to impose
upon our troubled dead and keep us safely bound.

I grudge thee thy death, José,
the stoic heart that faith allows me to demean.
How can I, gracefully, open the closed tome
of your suffering?   This voice
you hear is your own, spinning and turning the dome
of desire above us, set to endure, serene.
Annaeus remembers death without end, rich loam.

The Cradle Logic of Autumn

En mi país el Otoño nace de una flor seca,
de algunos pájaros; . . .
o del vaho penetrante de ciertos ríos de la llanura.
—Molinari, "Oda a una larga tristeza"

Each instant comes with a price, the blue-edged bill
on the draft of a bird almost incarnadine,
the shanked ochre of an inn that sits as still
as the beavertail cactus it guards (the fine
rose of that flower gone as bronze as sand),
the river's chalky white insistence as it
moves past the gray afternoon toward sunset.
Autumn feels the chill of a late summer lit
only by goldenrod and a misplaced strand
of blackberries; deplores all such sleight of hand;
turns sullen, selfish, envious, full of regret.

Someone more adept would mute its voice. The spill
of its truncated experience would shine
less bravely and, out of the dust and dunghill
of this existence (call it hope, in decline),

as here the blue light of autumn falls, command
what is left of exhilaration and fit
this season's unfolding to the alphabet
of turn and counterturn, all that implicit
arc of a heart searching for a place to stand.
Yet even that diminished voice can withstand
the currying of its spirit. Here lies—not yet.

If, and only if, the leafless rose he sees,
or thinks he sees, flowered a moment ago,
this endangered heart flows with the river that flees
the plain, and listens with eye raised to the slow
revelation of cloud, hoping to approve
himself, or to admonish the rose for slight
transgressions of the past, this the ecstatic
ethos, a logic that seems set to reprove
his facility with unsettling delight.
Autumn might be only desire, a Twelfth Night
gone awry, a gift almost too emphatic.

Logic in a faithful light somehow appeases
the rose, and stirs the hummingbird's vibrato.
By moving, I can stand where the light eases
me into the river's feathered arms, and, so,
with the heat of my devotion, again prove
devotion, if not this moment, pure, finite.
Autumn cradles me with idiomatic
certainty, leaves me nothing to disapprove.
I now acknowledge this red moon, to requite
the heart alone given power to recite
its faith, what a cradled life finds emblematic.

Braving the Fork in the Road

Light opens the seed of distance.
A neutered light calls its name to the awakened
—Weinberg Glashow Salam—and names them,
and moves, I say, in the way of that

sarcophagus light above my breathless sister.

Some urgency at twilight on these triple roads
flames a figure eight cast on its side,
becomes a dicey desire perhaps refused
by one bereft of faith.
But what is faith?
The white track on a figured ground
in a bubble chamber, so old, so out-of-date?
This morning my wife heard the knocking
of an atom in a corner, as it spiraled
through its own desire.
No, that is an old frame, one that can no longer
dress the tirtha glow at twilight,
and one must be charitable to consider
the coruscating disgust of a scholar
confronted by these bearded and bloodied triple roads.
Who would submit to voices under the polluted earth?
Who would attend to the cleansing of an Oedipus
stopping at a "road of many branches"?

I am now crossing over from danger to understanding,
guided by that figure given in the wood,
an iron bird upon a staff,
the elemented passion of healing.
I remember that I had set down in an opening of oak,
and there found the flower that inspired belief,
antelope horns arising from Asklepios;
these I could shelter in my cloth of black and white and red,
these I would bundle on my forked tree as I tracked the sun.

Light again spells its name for the awakened.
In that chamber, a particle flowers under tension,
and the dark reveals a mapped insistence of movement,
the forked transfiguration of movement,
the debility and uncertainty gathered in light.

Oedipal, perhaps, I, like a loggerhead sea turtle,
swim toward magnetic east,

in search of the true inhabitant of mountain and bush,
the crossroad repository of assumptions no one can bear.
I recall that the swollen-footed one returned
to the liminal urgency of his being, and there
sat down to be purified and given entrance to himself.
Who could allow such redemptive contradictions?
Who could see in a particle's swerve
a claim upon the darkness of engendered space?
Bummõ rises with light in the womb,
and in that memory I hold the image
of a Theban exile caught in the exigencies of light,
and uphold the figure of an iron bird,
lifting its singular wings in a forest that melts,
molecule by molecule,
into an embracing absence, or a design
of rivers lying under the triple roads,
full of the magnetic impulse of self-discovery.
Glã arises from the void.
I awaken to a dry riverbed in Oaxaca,
where a heron, lifting a leg, responds to the pull
of sacred water.
In Xalapa, the feathering pulse of a hummingbird
opens me to the morning. I turn the laser of my
disrupted concern upon the triple roads and upon
that seedlike pulsing in a bubble chamber,
the intimation of a signature of aesthetic design.
I recognize my twins in the multiplicity of their being,
in tomb light, or creative light,
in the transfigured intimacy of light's danger.
This is morning's first song,
first unsettling dark.

The Healing Improvisation of Hair

If you undo your do you wóuld
be strange. Hair has been on my mind.
I used to lean in the doorway
and watch my stony woman wind

the copper through the black, and play
with my understanding, show me she cóuld
take a cup of river water,
and watch it shimmy, watch it change,
turn around and become ash bone.
Wind in the cottonwoods wakes me
to a day so thin its breastbone
shows, so paid out it shakes me free
of its blue dust. I will arrange
that river water, bottom juice.
I conjure my head in the stream
and ride with the silk feel of it
as my woman bathes me, and shaves
away the scorn, sponges the grit
of solitude from my skin, laves
the salt water of self-esteem
over my feathering body.
How like joy to come upon me
in remembering a head of hair
and the way water would caress
it, and stress beauty in the flair
and cut of the only witness
to my dance under sorrow's tree.
This swift darkness is spring's first hour.

I carried my life, like a stone,
in a ragged pocket, but I
had a true weaving song, a sly
way with rhythm, a healing tone.

Intuition: Figure and Act

In the oldest book, no word can name
an ibis on a perch, the space that shades
a dense but finite home, or set the frame
of holiness, the absolute that fades
and withers as the river and persuades
us of a perfect star, its heat intact.

We know by feel the measure that evades
the lunar barque, the spectral shift of fact.
Light has become an ibis-headed god, exact

and comprehensible, a mark of flame
and closure, set against the masquerades
of law, the passing, fraudulent and tame
insistent symmetry, the escapades
equivalent to death; in death, charades
of innocence, the parity abstract
enough for theory to uphold, light trades
its innocence for words that will enact
the fit uncertainties of nature's life, transact

the memories of spirit. Why now claim
the corn seed in clay, image that abrades
the spirit it sustains? or is that the same
disordered form that sustains and pervades
the field set spinning by death, all those shades,
trophic, brief and small, that serve to attract
and to recall the darkness that invades
the history of time? A critical tact
inscribes and measures doubt, a wholly scripted pact

that sets the light apart. Call it a game.
There is a moment when those renegades
of spells and charms, restless, contest the fame
of self-restraint, and a galaxy parades
its bright, insistent deaths, the astral braids
of time living and time past, the inexact
transcription of voice, and those short-lived shades
begin their dance only to counteract
the intuitive grasp: death's figure, figure's act.

January, Love, and the Galician

Ambition is that amber heron stretching its legs
    above a lentil lake.

Words enter my body's house, nod, and retreat.
I am in debt to the clarity of assuagement,
        to a shallow lagoon on a turquoise island
        and the powder blue surgeonfish that stir
                                        me to silence.
I hear that the air before my face has been armored
with fragments of dead stars, a Jovian moon, fungal spores,
the marriage of electric and magnetic fields.
I hear that my spirit has taken its ancient form
and flows with the ease of rivers.
January breaks, near Durango, on the Animas,
crosses the border in the arms of warm water,
a nostalgic privilege given to ambivalent presbyters,
such memory tracing an imaginal event,
        a wasting of mountains under the sea.
I had escaped Okup'in, the turtle mountain,
                                        or so I thought,
had developed a feeling for bead water,
a thirst for the black mountain,
                                K'usem'ing
                                        or P'i'anuge.
Even now I sit with a desire to go downcountry.
I realize that I have been at war with grace,
and that my isolation has been a blessing.
I insist that, as the earth solidifies,
my soul begins to spell its age,
to number the forms of its transfiguring intent.
I take comfort in the unbridgeable mathematics of spirit,
                in the knowledge of being known.
The Augustinian has told me that love never fails,
and enables me to possess what is most my own.
January settles in.
I hunker down with my mind fixed on devastation,
the village life of a downcountry place,
the urgency of a moment that seizes me
                and presents me with another name.
Here, I confront my quantum world,
the reality of force,
the necessity to speak the proper word.

Lichens and Oranges

What would the apteryx say,
observing lakes
of your flagellant display,
the grain that makes
a flexible home of bay
rock, signs, cars, cakes?
Call it will,
there is still
an algebraic absence,
a landfill
of edge, spill
of matter, lack of sense.

Imagine the winter play
of witch's hair,
the cantankerous shrub gray
that fed a rare
purple, sovereign forms that pay
trust in the air.
Pigments fill
their civil
function at the dance, a dense,
sacred skill.
Toxins chill
the earth, restructure defense.

Patience defines you. You weigh
each breath that takes
a life to compose, the clay
earth mask that flakes
imperceptibly. Midway,
the wolf's voice breaks.
Now no knell,
a due spell
of desert dewfall begins
the slow swell
and eggshell
memory of origins.

The Hieroglyph of Irrational Space

(INSTRUMENTAL)

Coral bells teach me discretion,
a self-restraint in the deed.
How do we measure perfection,
the bright, introspective seed
that rises and falls
incessantly, calls
its name,
turns along the wall's
exactness and sprawls,
the frame
of an imagined event,
the unmarked, figured ascent?

(FUNCTIONAL)

We speak of a resurrection,
or the light by which we read
the small, coherent intention
of light, that structuring reed
of intention that shawls
us in faith, recalls
the game
of design, enthralls
with echoes, footfalls,
the flame
of all the magnificent
absence structured by consent.

(AXIOMATIC)

You will tax me with my limits,
and ignore the calabash
closed upon the bird, the digits
that compose that singular, rash,
ambiguous state

of order, the eight
clear beads
that inaugurate
design's space, the gate
that leads
perhaps to incertitude,
faith's inventive solitude.

(JUDICATIVE)

Who now sits on primeval ground,
defined by benevolent
waters, the fundamental sound
of stellar wind, the insistent
aptitude of stars?
The distant one scars
the dead.
Say that nothing bars
those swift avatars
who bed
their contingency, that bleak
law by which the just speak.

(NORMATIVE)

I would be fed on the fifth day,
and become an active force,
a first logic of disarray,
a flawed executive source
of exchange, a staff
radiant, yet half
buried.
Leave this epigraph
that once tarnished gaff,
curried
from desire and discretion
intact, the measure of passion.

Coda IV

Hummingbird of hummingbird
wing of air no one has heard.
Now the wing contains a flaw,
red lines on a box of straw,
threaded veil, bone root or shale,
bred of a corrupted tail.
All bereft, you are death's tree.
Nothing here remembers me.
How I marvel that your bill
has incensed my tongue and will.

Coda V

Blessèd be bright brood birches
bred blithely beyond bridges
clustered clutched crustily close
cunningly composed cover
demure dire docents doubtless
December's decent double
endogenous eloquence
enchiridion essence
ferns' ferrous ferocious friends
fit fetish freighted forged found.

Coda VI

Starlight is my measure,
that one clairvoyant texture
set upon the plane
                    of the tau.
Dark light is my nature,
the spirit's own erasure,
creative domain
                    of the tao;
creative domain—
                    ask me now.